CHILDREN OF A TROUBLED TIME

CHILDREN OF A TROUBLED TIME

Growing Up with Racism in Trump's America

MARGARET A. HAGERMAN

NEW YORK UNIVERSITY PRESS *New York*

NEW YORK UNIVERSITY PRESS
New York
www.nyupress.org

© 2024 by New York University
All rights reserved

Please contact the Library of Congress for Cataloging-in-Publication data.
ISBN: 9781479815111 (hardback)
ISBN: 9781479815166 (library ebook)
ISBN: 9781479815135 (consumer ebook)

Manufactured in the United States of America

10 9 8 7 6 5 4 3 2 1

Also available as an ebook

For Eric

I felt race even before I knew what race was.

—EDUARDO BONILLA-SILVA

CONTENTS

Introduction: The Kids Are Not All Right   1

1 The "Trump Effect": Growing Up in the Post-Obama Era   9

2 "Feeling Race": Waking Up after the 2016 Election   26

3 "I Had No Idea the Country Was So Racist!":
Racial Discomfort and Disgust   43

4 "He Likes the People with the Lighter Skin Better . . .
and That's Not Me": Racial Fear and Solidarity   76

5 "Racism Is Fine": Racial Dominance and Apathy   104

6 "Hurry Up and Build That Wall!": The Future of
Dominant White Racial Ideology   137

Conclusion: What Can We Do?   149

Acknowledgments   173

Appendix A: Tables of Participants   179

Appendix B: Methodological Considerations   181

Notes   191

References   203

Index   219

About the Author   229

Introduction

The Kids Are Not All Right

I am worried Trump is going to make racism worse.
—KENNY, AGE TEN, MISSISSIPPI

Trump is racist and sexist and should not be president!
—ZENA, AGE TWELVE, MISSISSIPPI

Trump is racist, but I don't really care.
—CAMMIE, AGE ELEVEN, MASSACHUSETTS

A few days after Donald Trump won the November 2016 presidential election, seventh-grade students at a middle school in Royal Oak, Michigan, were recorded chanting "Build the wall! Build the wall!" in the cafeteria during their lunch period. After school that day, their chanting started up again in the school gymnasium. When school officials became aware of these students' behavior, a statement was issued in response. The school principal told his community that this "incident" had made some students at the school "feel alienated and unwelcomed" and "unsafe."[1] Although the principal referred to the behavior as a "mistake" and assured his community that all students were indeed welcome at the school, at no point during his message did he draw any attention to where the phrase "Build the wall" originated, why kids might be using these words (and doing so gleefully), or the racist implications of this chant.

The principal in Michigan was not the only school administrator forced to navigate racism and political divides on a regular basis during the 2016 campaign season, during Trump's presidency, and during the Biden presidency. Over the past few years, I have been invited to communities around the country to share my findings from my book *White Kids* on how white children learn about race, racism, inequality, and privilege. Adults at almost every place I have visited have told me stories about the impact that politics has had on their local community. I have listened as school principals and teachers have shared concerns with me about white students sending racist images via Snapchat during school assemblies or showing up in blackface to school events or repeating language used by President Trump in class discussions about "shithole countries" or "Mexican rapists" without any regard for the consequences of their words or how what they said made their peers of color feel. These school officials have also talked passionately with me about their struggle to navigate tensions in their school community between different groups of parents—groups defined by race and/or by partisan affiliation. I have heard stories about schools and communities that had long viewed themselves as politically progressive and opposed to racism suddenly confronted with explicitly racist acts happening in their towns and cities. Adults I met told me that for a long time, and especially after President Obama was elected, they truly believed US society was beyond racism—or that, at the very least, members of their own families and communities were. For these adults, the election of Trump disrupted this idea entirely, and they expressed uncertainty and uneasiness in this moment.

Parents I met also agonized over how to talk about the trauma of President Trump's immigration policies—such as the Muslim ban or the practice of separating kids from their parents—with their own children in ways that their kids could understand but that would not be overwhelming to them. Parents told me about their struggle to help their young kids make sense of racist tweets written by Trump insulting their children's country of origin or people who looked like them. They told me stories about their efforts to encourage Black joy and build racial pride in their Black kids despite the regular anti-Black words and actions of the Trump White House. I also heard stories about blowout fights at family gatherings such as Thanksgiving and how parents did not want their white children to spend time with their white grandparents anymore because of political differences tied to ideas about race. I was asked repeatedly for advice about how to talk to white kids about racist actions of white supremacists that Trump refused to condemn.

Listening to these stories and having these conversations made it very clear that school administrators, teachers, and parents from across the US and across different racial and class-based groups were struggling. They were struggling to help their kids make sense of a racially and politically polarized nation and an explosive political moment. But while I learned a great deal from listening to these adults, I was also curious about how kids themselves were processing racism in a post-Obama America. What were kids thinking about all of this, especially since they had spent their entire lives to date with the first Black president in office and persistent, popular "colorblind" claims that race no longer mattered in the United States? How would experiencing this portion of their one and only childhood during the era of Trump shape their ideas about racism, their country, and democracy altogether? How did the political landscape—both at the national level and also in their states and communities—impact their ideas about racism?

This book is based on sociological research I conducted with young people growing up in the Trump era. In the pages that follow, I focus on what I found from conducting interviews between 2017 and 2019 with forty-five children across race and class groupings between the ages of ten and thirteen. Interviews were conducted with kids growing up in places with drastically different state-level political landscapes: Mississippi and Massachusetts. As you might expect, the local political climates of these two places vary in major ways, as Massachusetts is one of the most politically liberal states in the nation, while Mississippi is one of the most politically conservative. But I interviewed kids who thought of themselves as conservative and kids who thought of themselves as liberal in both places, and they expressed remarkably similar ideas across regions. Racism, this research documents and as many others have previously found, is not just a local phenomenon; it is a broadly American project.

In each state, I chose one town from which I recruited kids to participate. These two towns were similarly divided along political lines, with a relatively even split in each place between registered Republicans and Democrats, and these towns had similar population sizes. These towns were also similar with regard to the proportion of white families living in each place compared to families of color, though the specific racial and ethnic identities of the families of color in each location varied due to regional demographic differences. As such, the kids in this book come from families with different political leanings, different class backgrounds, and different racial identities.

Throughout this book, when talking about specific children, I use the racial or ethnic identity terminology the kids used to describe themselves. This is because I believe it is important for children to have the right to choose their own language of self-identification. However, when referring to kids as a group of children who experience racial marginalization given their nonwhite racial identity in a racialized society, I use the purposefully ambiguous and encompassing term "kids of color."

I also had the assistance of two outstanding research assistants who helped me collect data, particularly in the Mississippi context. One of my research assistants, Courtney Heath, helped conduct some of the interviews with white children from conservative backgrounds. As a white woman who grew up in Mississippi and who is familiar with experiencing childhood in a politically conservative community, Courtney had the interpersonal skills necessary to build trust and establish rapport with the children (and their parents) as opposed to me, a perceived outsider to the Deep South. My second research assistant, Kimberly Mason, helped conduct some of the interviews with Black children in Mississippi. As a Black woman from Mississippi, Kimberly was also able to build trust and rapport more effectively with Black children who might not feel comfortable talking about racism with a white stranger like me. Without the help of these two research assistants, and their own social positions and experiences, I am confident that the data produced through these interviews would not be as rich or truthful.

This book focuses on offering answers to three interrelated sociological questions. First, how did white children make sense of racism in the Trump era? In other words, what racial ideologies did kids express? What can we learn about whether and how dominant racial ideology shifts by exploring kids' perspectives as they interpreted this particular political moment in history?

Racial ideologies are the taken-for-granted explanations that people use to "tell particular kinds of stories about the way the world works," including stories about how race works in US society.2 Colorblind ideology has been well documented to be the dominant racial ideological framework used by Americans over the past few decades, including by kids.3 Colorblind thinking argues that people no longer "see" race, that racial equality has been achieved, that any inequality that can be seen is the fault of an individual, and that since racism is no longer a problem, "there is no need for institutional remedies to redress racial inequalities and that any attempts to raise questions about race are problematic."4 Given the increase in explicit expressions of white nationalism and white supremacy in the post-Obama era, this book considers whether colorblind racism continues to be an accurate depiction of dominant racial ideology, especially with the youngest and newest members of society. As the sociologist Eduardo Bonilla-Silva argues, "addressing the complexity of the dominant racial ideology means recognizing that, like all ideologies, color-blindness is a political tool or 'meaning in the service of power.' This means that color-blindness is flexible and must accommodate new racial developments."5 Perhaps colorblind ideology remains dominant, or perhaps it remains dominant but has shifted. Or maybe colorblindness is no longer the dominant way kids understand race, and we need to describe what has taken its place. This book explores these concerns.

Second, how do the political times in which kids experience their childhoods shape how they develop ideas about race and racism? How do aspects of the macro-level political landscape of a child's life—that is, the national political rhetoric of the day, new policies that are put into place by the nation's leaders, and controversial current events—shape how kids form racial ideas at the individual and interactional levels? Using a sociological framework to study how kids learn about race rather than the psychological and developmental frameworks that are typically relied on in this area of scholarship and that tend to focus on the micro level of analysis, I explore how structural arrangements and social hierarchies shape children's ideas and experiences.6 I explore how thinking sociologically about racial learning, or using one's sociological imagination, can help expand existing theories of children's racial socialization processes that too often focus solely on individual children in the context of their individual families without any consideration of larger social forces or broader historical realities. Although I value and put into conversation the intellectual thinking about racial socialization and racial learning processes of scholars from a range of disciplines like Black studies, child development, education, family studies, and political science, this book is fundamentally rooted in a sociological approach to understanding how kids learn race.

Third, what role do racialized, group-level emotions play in racial learning processes? As I interviewed children, I noticed how often they expressed their emotional responses to various things Trump did or said. I started paying closer attention to the full range of racialized emotional experience these kids described. I began seeing patterns across groups of the kids with regard to what brought them feelings of fear, anxiety, delight, pleasure, a sense of group solidarity, and especially anger. As I did this work, I realized that within existing scholarship on racial socialization processes, or how kids learn race, there is very little discussion of the emotional component to this process.

Much has been written about emotions and children—for example, psychological theories of emotion regulation, literary accounts of affect theory, biological studies of the physiology of emotion. But this book takes a different approach. I build on the theoretical work outlined by the leading race scholar and sociologist Eduardo Bonilla-Silva in his 2018 presidential address to the American Sociological Association on racialized emotions.[7] In a society organized by the placement of people into socially constructed racial groups that are organized hierarchically with respect to power (i.e., a racialized society), racialized emotions are "emotions related to race that people experience when they engage in interracial interaction."[8] Racialized emotions are "'not substances' in the interior of individuals, but are transacted between actors who are already shaped by social relationships and history."[9] In the following pages, I focus squarely on this sociological theory of group-level, relational *racialized emotions* in the context of childhood racial socialization. What do racialized emotions do in the context of racial learning? I argue that racialized emotions are *foundational* to the racial learning process and guide kids into different racial ideological and political positions. Racialized emotions, thus, drive the racial learning process.

Overall, we can learn a lot more about how kids develop understandings of racism by listening to their reflections on race *and* politics, as well as taking seriously their expressions of racialized emotions. In the following pages, I explore how young people feel race and how these racialized emotions guide them as they try to make sense of conflicting, contradictory, and inconsistent messages about race in the Trump era. Considering how the macro-level political realm contributes to "racial contexts of childhood," this book expands our knowledge of how the newest members of society learn, experience, reproduce, rework, and challenge racism and considers what this might mean for the future of racism.

1

The "Trump Effect"

Growing Up in the Post-Obama Era

One day after school in Mississippi, ten-year-old Crystal, who is "African American and mixed," recalled what she remembered from the night of the 2016 election and what happened at school the following day:

> My family was very scared the night before. . . . When I was sleeping, I did have a bad dream, so I think I could kinda tell that it wasn't going to end up as I expected. I asked my mom and dad first when they came in to get me from my bed and like woke me up [in the morning]. I didn't think they were in their usual happy mood, so I could kinda tell [that Trump had won]. But then I asked anyway, and they said, "We lost."

Crystal and I talked for a bit about how she felt that morning, which led to her telling me what happened later that day when she went to school. For context, her school was made up of about 70 percent Black or multiracial students and 30 percent white students.

> A lot of people were talking about it, but I didn't really talk much about it. . . . I stayed quiet. But some Black boys and girls were saying that, like, they really didn't want Trump to win or that he had won

and [that they] didn't really like him and were mad. And then some people who did vote for Trump were like, "I'm so happy!" and they told their friends who also voted for Trump, and they were all jumping around . . . [makes a facial expression conveying disgust]. It was like allll day [frustrated tone].

I asked her if the kids who supported Trump were Black. Crystal immediately responded, "Definitely no! They were all white."

* * *

As soon as Donald Trump took office, experts predicted that his presidency would negatively impact kids in the United States.1 They were right. Trump's rhetoric and policy decisions, informed by members of his administration with ties to far-right white supremacist and white nationalist groups, proved to have devastating effects on kids.2 These negative effects were especially seen among undocumented children, immigrant children, Muslim children, Black children, Indigenous children, Chinese American children, and/or children growing up in poverty.3 I begin here with a focus on what we know from existing research about the effect of the Trump era on children. But I also point out what we do *not* yet know about how this political moment impacted kids.

The Trump Effect: What We Know

In 2016, the Southern Poverty Law Center (SPLC) published findings from a report on racism and violence in schools across the country during the lead-up to and within the early days of the Trump presidency. This report was called *The Trump Effect*. This report found that 90 percent of teachers surveyed indicated that their school climate had been negatively affected by the political campaign and presidential election of Trump. The report also found that eight in ten teachers noted increased anxiety on the behalf of students of color, immigrant students, Muslim students, and LGBTQ+ students.

Instances were reported of white youth engaging in forms of racial violence and other forms of harassment, such as chanting "Build the wall!" at athletic competitions against school sports teams that were predominantly Latinx, bringing Confederate flags into classrooms to taunt their Black peers, sexual assault in the form of nonconsensual "grabbing" or groping girls, putting racist images on Snapchat or TikTok, inflicting physical violence such as pulling hijabs off Muslim students, and on and on.4 Clearly, this political moment caused "political trauma" for many marginalized groups of children—trauma related to Trump's actual words and actions but also trauma resulting from the hateful interactions kids had with their white Trump-inspired peers at school.5

One area in which the Trump administration's policies harmed children was that of children's health. The Trump administration left out five million children from receiving emergency Supplemental Nutrition Assistance Program benefits during the COVID-19 pandemic and proposed further cuts to this program in the future.6 At the end of the Trump years, there were 726,000 more children without health insurance compared to when Trump first took office, reflecting the largest jump in uninsured children in a decade.7 Access to health care is essential for children's health and well-being in childhood, with implications for the rest of their lives. And certainly, the COVID-19 pandemic illustrated the long-standing racial and socioeconomic inequities in health care in the US impacting children and adults alike.8

In the context of the COVID-19 pandemic, Trump's anti-Asian comments related to China had a negative impact on the mental health of Chinese American kids. According to one study, "one in four parents and youth reported vicarious racial discrimination almost every day, and most respondents reported directly experiencing or witnessing racial discrimination against other Chinese or Asian American individuals due to COVID-19 at least once."9 Chinese American children were found to have higher than average risks of clinically significant mental health problems as a result of experiencing this form of discrimination in everyday life—discrimination that was unequivocally informed by Trump's choice of words and framing of the COVID-19 pandemic.10

Quality, affordable, and stable housing is also key to children's physical and mental health, as the home is ideally a place of retreat and security. Research shows how poor-quality housing, lack of space, lack of safety, and negative environmental factors like mold and dampness significantly increase children's likelihood of negative physical and mental health outcomes.11 During the Trump years, housing assistance was insufficiently funded. Similarly, child care, another key aspect of healthy child development, was not funded adequately. In fact, "due to inadequate funding, just one in six children eligible for child care assistance—and one in five families with children eligible for housing assistance—receive[d] it."12

The Trump administration also cut funding to essential programs that benefited Indigenous communities—and especially Indigenous kids—across the country.13 He exhibited disregard for environmental protections and sovereign tribal land and expedited controversial pipeline projects.14 When the COVID-19 pandemic hit, the first COVID relief package did not even include tribal nations; once funding was allocated, it was slow to arrive to the communities in need—communities hit disproportionately hard by the pandemic.15 As one historian put it, "From the time Trump announced his intention to run for president, racism directed towards Native Americans has become an increasingly visible part of cultural and political life in the United States."16 Perhaps Trump's attack on Indigenous communities is what inspired a group of white boys from a private Catholic school to openly mock Indigenous elders on the Washington Mall, wearing red Make America Great Again hats while doing so.17

Trump's Anti-Black Racism

Despite Trump's claims that he cared about African Americans, evidence demonstrates that his words and actions increased "racism-related stress" and trauma, as well as racial discrimination, for Black people, including Black kids.18 When Trump used racist, derogatory language to refer to entire nations in Africa and the Caribbean, he dehumanized kids with connections to these countries, challenging these children's sense of confidence, identity, and pride.19 He disrespected a long list of Black celebrities, politicians, and athletes—heroes in the eyes of many Black kids—especially famous Black people publicly protesting racist police violence in the United States. The Trump administration also rolled back provisions designed to address racial inequality in school discipline practices, enacted stricter drug enforcement laws shown to target Black communities, and encouraged the use of brutal police tactics, which are disproportionally used on Black youth.20

Trump refused to consider Black Lives Matter a legitimate social movement, even as people across the country marched in the streets in protest of the police murders of George Floyd, Breonna Taylor, and many more Black people.21 Trump also refused to denounce white supremacists defending a statue of a Confederate general who enslaved people in Charlottesville, Virginia, much like he told the Proud Boys, an extremist white supremacist terrorist group, to "stand back and stand by" during a presidential debate in 2020. The leader of this group burned a Black Lives Matter banner belonging to a historic Black church in 2021.22 In 2020, Trump had Black Lives Matter protesters teargassed in front of the White House. Many members of this activist group nationally are Black youth and young adults.23

The SPLC reports that many teachers across the nation saw an "increase in use of the n-word as a slur, even among very young children." Black children expressed concerns about being "deported to Africa" or that "slavery would be reinstated." And as one teacher explained, her Black students wondered if they were "being let in on what all white people truly think and feel" when they heard Trump's racist words. Many Black kids said they questioned whether they are welcome in their own country.24 Overall, Trump's rhetoric and policy decisions negatively impacted Black children in a variety of ways.

Impact of Trump's Anti-Latinx and Anti-Immigrant Rhetoric and Policies

In 2019, on the first day of the new school year in central Mississippi, 680 undocumented immigrants were detained after seven chicken-processing plants were raided by Immigration and Customs Enforcement (ICE) officials.25 When young children returned home from school that day, their parents were gone. Images of children with their faces in their hands, sobbing and crying out for their parents, made painfully obvious the emotional distress and fear that immigrant kids experienced as a result of Trump's immigration policies.26 In 2018, similar distress was observed on the faces of migrant children separated from their parents at the Texas border with Teflon blankets wrapped around them.27 Clara Long, associate director of the Human Rights Watch organization, submitted to Congress a firsthand account of what she observed at these facilities, detailing how these children suffered with fevers and unsanitary conditions, had little adult supervision, and did not know where their parents were—all of which she deemed was evidence of inhumane treatment.28 Indeed, research shows that family separation, a practice that the US government has far too often drawn on historically, is one of the greatest risks to the health and well-being of children and can have long-term effects on development.29 As experts explain, "there may be no greater threat to children's emotional security than the fear of being separated from a parent."30

It was not only the actual experience of arrests, raids, and deportation that caused this high level of distress among kids, though of course living through these experiences firsthand was incredibly traumatic—but this was true during the Obama years as well. It was also the persistent threatening anti-immigrant rhetoric and the subsequent uncertainty of losing one's parents that also contributed in devastating ways to the well-being of young people.31 For example, a young boy in an elementary school in North Carolina was observed by his teacher making a list of what he knew he could cook, including peanut butter sandwiches and cheese sandwiches. He was doing so to reassure his little sister that they could survive if their parents were deported.32 As a result of living with this looming threat of family separation, and the dehumanizing rhetoric propagated by national leaders, young people across all age groups were negatively affected, including very young kids. Preschool children experienced separation anxiety, withdrew from their school environments, expressed sadness and fear, and were observed biting their fingers or eating lunch quickly while refusing to talk.33 These behaviors were exhibited in response to the tremendously high level of stress and fear that they would return home from school and find their undocumented parents missing. Even kids who were not growing up with an undocumented parent experienced this fear, according to the SPLC report: "Because young children can't understand the details of immigration policy—and may not even know their parent's immigration status . . . children feared the worst based on what they heard around them. A Head Start teacher in Pennsylvania [reported] that a four-year-old girl in her class said that President Trump wanted to send her mom back to Mexico. 'Her mother is not even from Mexico,' the teacher told [the SPLC]."34 Simply growing up as a Latinx kid during this political climate in the United States was traumatic for many children regardless of immigration status or ethnicity as a result of the persistent rhetorical attacks against this group by the president and his administration.

Alongside the psychological and physical consequences of what experts refer to as "toxic stress," families also opted out of enrolling in nutrition programs or accessing health care for fear that they would be deported.35 This led to fewer routine visits to the doctor (including prenatal appointments), parents hesitating before bringing children to the emergency room in some cases, and reduced access to healthy food, all of which increase the risk of young people having health problems. When a family member is deported, this can put families in deep economic peril, as sudden loss of income to a family that is already economically insecure can be devastating and lead to housing instability, food insecurity, and increased parental stress.36 And of course, when parents opt not to send children to school for fear that they will be taken away from them, children's ability to be academically successful is challenged.37 Further, older adolescents with Deferred Action for Childhood Arrivals (DACA) status experienced fear, stress, and anxiety as well as a loss of hope about future possibilities for which they had otherwise planned— and younger siblings also feared being separated from them too.38

The racist rhetoric that accompanied these policies deeply impacted children during the Trump era. Certainly, children with families from Mexico were deeply hurt when the president stated, "When Mexico sends its people, they're not sending the best. They're sending people that have lots of problems and they're bringing those problems. They're bringing drugs, they're bringing crime. They're rapists."39 Studies showed that at this time, Latinx youth reported feeling targeted and threatened by the political climate, the policies, and the rhetoric of the Trump administration.40

But it is not just that Trump said these words and that Latinx kids heard them. White kids who supported Trump were also listening. Trump's statements about Mexicans were what inspired white kids to shout "Build the wall!" at their Latinx peers. And it was what led children in a 2020 study of Latinx high school students to report that not only were they more skeptical of the other kids at their school in this political moment but that their teachers did not do enough to protect them.41 These kids reported that teachers remained silent when white peers made racist comments or that their teachers made "space and time to comments supporting whiteness and white supremacy for the sake of debate." As Jaqueline, a high school student in Colorado, explained, "In the classroom, [the teacher] had to listen to both sides. Students were saying really racist stuff, and we had to listen to it."42 Her observations are also supported by ethnographic research in middle schools that found that white teachers expressed "racial disgust" toward Mexican American children and used racist historical tropes about Mexican Americans in their teaching.43 In yet another study, about teasing and bullying in high school after the 2016 election, research found that kids living in communities favoring Trump reported higher racist "bullying" at school compared to kids living in communities favoring Hillary Clinton.44 Clearly, the political context of the Trump era impacted young people across racial and political groupings, especially with respect to policies and rhetoric tied to immigration.

The Impact of the "Muslim Ban"

In early 2017, a five-year-old US citizen who was traveling with a family member from Iran was taken into custody at the Washington-Dulles International Airport. He was detained for over four hours by government authorities in response to a recent executive order, commonly referred to as the "Muslim ban," in which Trump banned travel to the US by people from seven Muslim-majority countries. When the boy was finally released from custody at the airport, people around the country watched his emotional embrace with his mother.45 Certainly, another group of children who were negatively impacted by the Trump administration's words and actions were kids who had connections to the Muslim-majority countries that Trump listed in the executive order—as well as Muslim kids in general.

In the months following the September 11, 2001, attacks, research found that Muslim American youths' "religious commitments as Muslims were often framed as fundamentally incompatible with the 'American' identity."46 Likewise, in the days leading up to and following Trump's election, Muslim kids in the US, as well as Arab American kids, faced similar forms of exclusion and violence. The SPLC reported instances of Muslim girls being physically assaulted by kids at their school, and research in classrooms across the country found similar patterns. In fact, "research among Muslim students suggests that political trauma related to identity and belonging is pervasive."[47] While little research has considered the perspectives of Muslim and Arab American kids as told by them during this time, a handful of key studies offer insight into their experiences. According to one study, not only were Muslim kids asked to serve as "experts" on Islam in the classroom, but they also reported frequently being stigmatized for their identities and often incorrectly perceived.[48] Findings from another study illustrate how Muslim middle school students drew on history lessons in their school curriculum related to how other social groups in history resisted political trauma and drew parallels to their own experiences in Trump's America.[49]

Much like the fear generated in Latinx children by Trump's anti-immigrant rhetoric and policies, immigrant children from countries included in the ban experienced heightened fear and anxiety too. One middle school administrator in New York reported her observations following the ban: "Crying is a regular thing. . . . Kids were sobbing, especially immigrant children, saying they were going to get sent back to Guinea, Senegal, Yemen. They were totally distraught. And then one kid would try to explain to another kid about deportation and it would turn into an argument about, 'You're going to get deported.' 'No, you are.'"[50] In 2017, the Kaiser Family Foundation conducted focus groups with one hundred parents from fifteen countries, including those from countries impacted by Trump's Muslim ban, as well as thirteen interviews with pediatricians serving immigrant and refugee communities from across the world. This study was designed in order "to gain insight into how the current environment is affecting the daily lives, well-being, and health of immigrant families, including their children."[51] According to this report, immigrant families from Afghanistan, Iraq, Egypt, Brazil, Syria, Korea, Mexico, and other countries felt a high level of fear under the Trump administration. Many were scared to leave their home and felt uncertain about the future, and many reported that their children experienced racism and discrimination at school (regardless of immigration status). As one parent put it, "we feel that in any moment a new rule could be issued leading to expelling us and sending us back." Pediatric experts predict that these kids are likely to face "increased challenges across a range of social and environmental factors that influence health" now and into their future as a result of this traumatic childhood experience.52

Mainstreaming of Far-Right Ideology

Being a child during the Trump era also meant being a child during a period of heightened far-right extremist violence in the United States. Research shows that in 2018, the midpoint of Trump's presidency, white supremacist extremist groups in the United States grew by 50 percent, and hate groups overall reached an all-time high.53 In 2019, the United States saw the highest level of white supremacist propaganda distributed, according to the Anti-Defamation League.54 Perhaps most alarming, "white supremacist extremism is currently the most lethal form of extremism in the United States," and 81 percent of extremist-related murders in 2019 were committed by white supremacist extremists.55 Although little research has explored the effect that this resurgence of white supremacist hate has had on children, it was absolutely a defining feature of their childhoods.

Specifically, in 2017, a "Unite the Right" white supremacist rally was held in Charlottesville, Virginia. The rally was held in response to government efforts to remove a Confederate statue of Robert E. Lee as part of a move to confront white supremacy following the mass shooting of nine Black people at the Emanuel African Methodist Episcopal Church in Charleston, Virginia, in 2015.

Members of various far-right groups joined together near the campus of the University of Virginia wielding Nazi flags, Confederate battle flags, and other symbols of hate, along with weapons and tiki torches. They marched and chanted, "Jews will not replace us" and "white lives matter." Nineteen counterprotesters ended up injured, and one woman, Heather Heyer, was murdered when a white supremacist accelerated his car into a crowd of people.56

The following year at a Pittsburgh synagogue, thirteen people were murdered by another white supremacist terrorist, who believed in far-right global "white genocide" conspiracies that claimed that "Jews were orchestrating the resettlement of refugees in order to create a multicultural society that would eventually eradicate whites."57 In 2019, at a Walmart in El Paso, Texas, twenty-two people were murdered by a terrorist claiming that he was concerned about a "Hispanic invasion of Texas."58 In a message he posted online prior to the attack, he also referenced the recent terrorist attack on two mosques in Christchurch, New Zealand. And in 2021, as the US Congress gathered to vote on the certification of election results, Trump gave a speech to a group of his supporters wearing Trump paraphernalia and some carrying symbols of white supremacy. Members of this group then stormed the Capitol building. Multiple people were killed, and congresspeople had to be quickly escorted out of the building and to a safe location.59 Following the storming of the Capitol, investigations found that some of these people were members of various white supremacist hate groups, right-wing militias, and antigovernment groups who came together to disrupt democracy.60

In addition to these acts of violence that took place during the Trump presidency, what is also of concern is the fact that these far-right ideologies are becoming more mainstream and therefore increasingly normalized.61 As Cynthia Miller-Idriss, a leading expert on extremism and nationalism, finds, messages of racist hate and white nationalism are finding their way purposefully to the mainstream. She finds that attempts to cultivate far-right hate are found on college campuses, at music festivals, at youth summer camps, through clothing and other commercial products, and in a range of virtual spaces, from gaming to social media to YouTube. This means that *young people* are increasingly exposed to extremist ideas in everyday physical and virtual spaces, sometimes leading to their own engagement with these ideas and groups themselves.62

Even if kids do not become involved with far-right groups, they are still coming of age in a moment during which these ideas have grown more popular and widespread. Kids encounter these ideas in everyday life, including as they use internet tools. For example, one very popular virtual space where young people encounter far-right white supremacist messaging is TikTok.63 Kids are required to negotiate iterations of these extremist ideas when other kids at their school play make-believe games at recess involving "the wall" or when youth chant "Trump! Trump! Trump!" at them and tell them that this country is not for them. Growing up in the era of Trump, then, also meant growing up during a moment in which far-right hate and violence became more explicit, more popular, and increasingly part of everyday, mainstream American life—including American childhood.

Overall, existing research documents the profoundly negative impact the Trump era had on children and child well-being in the US. This account of the "Trump effect" is certainly not intended to be exhaustive. For instance, Trump's words and actions also negatively impacted LGBTQ+ youth, inspired gender-based violence, and harmed women and girls, which other scholars have researched extensively.64 But for the purposes of the questions posed in this book, this summary illustrates powerfully how kids encountered Trump's racist rhetoric and policies and how these encounters contributed to high levels of childhood racial stress and trauma, fear of separation from family, and experiences of discrimination and dehumanization for children of color.

The Trump Effect: What We Do Not Know

In January 2016, three young white girls known as the "USA Freedom Kids" performed at a Trump rally in Florida. Wearing dresses with blue tops decorated with gold stars and red-and-white-striped skirts, the young girls danced around onstage and enthusiastically sang song lyrics like, "President Donald Trump knows how to make America great: Deal from strength or get crushed every time!" Rows of white adults sat behind them clapping their hands along to the beat and moving their bodies to the music.65 Although existing research accounts for many aspects of the negative impact that the Trump administration had on children, there is still much we do not know about how this moment shaped children's racial learning processes, including those of kids like these "USA Freedom Kids" or other white children who admired Trump.

First, we do not know very much about the white kids perpetrating acts of racist violence. The SPLC identified an increase in racist bullying on the behalf of white kids, as well as an observed link between Trump's campaign vocabulary and bullying insults used by white kids, such as an increase in the word "loser" as well as racial slurs. But why did these white kids act this way? What motivated this widespread racist behavior? How did they feel when Trump said explicitly racist things? Were they surprised? Did they even care? And can their behavior really be understood solely as a form of bullying? Finally, what racial learning processes are under way for these children in this moment, and what might this mean for the future?

As a sociologist, I am really interested in these questions because all the kids in this book—including the white children who support Trump and engage in racist behavior—grew up in a so-called colorblind world prior to the election of Trump.66 For instance, as one eleven-year-old white girl told me when I interviewed her during the Obama years in a previous study, "racism is not a problem anymore."67 But colorblind ideology still holds that everyone *should* be equal. In fact, every single white child I have ever interviewed about racism prior to this study told me that racism is "bad," and they went to great lengths to distance themselves from accusations of being called a racist. In other words, these kids believed racism was a problem, even if they did not think it was still a problem in the US.

Given the dominance of colorblindness in understanding racism prior to Trump, did these kids in my new Trump-era study suddenly reject this dominant racial ideology and embrace instead a more explicitly racist perspective on how race and racism operate in US society? And what about white kids who did not support Trump? What were they making of their white peers' behaviors, as well as the broadly political climate defining at least part of their young lives? Finally, how did kids of color make sense of racism in the US during this era? Overall, we have much to learn from kids in the Trump era about how dominant racial ideologies (like colorblind racism) can shift to fit new circumstances and the role that young people play in this interpretive learning process.

Second, we do not know much about the role that the broader political landscape of a child's life plays in how they interpret ideas about racism. The question of how people develop their political ideas specifically has been of great interest to social scientists, philosophers, and political analysts, given the connection between political socialization and participatory democracy and specifically how people vote. In fact, political sociologists and political scientists have long studied how political party identification, political attitudes, and a sense of civic responsibility develop in young people within the context of their families.68 Much of this research traditionally suggested that political ideas are "directly transmitted" by parents to children in an uninterrupted fashion.69 Like the development of new socialization theories in sociology, models of political socialization have also undergone a transformation from dominant assumptions about how parents instill or "inculcate" political ideas in children to theories that recognize children's agency in this process or kids' own active participation in their own socialization process.70 As one groundbreaking study illustrates, "One of the core assumptions in political sociology, that children typically adopt their parents' political values, is not valid. Rather, once measures of child perceptions are included, we find parent-child concordance of political identification is far lower than previously believed."71 These scholars consider how kids interpret their parents' political values, illustrating that "parents create the information environment in which children are embedded" but that kids then must interpret that information on their own to develop their own ideas.72 Certainly, this is a departure from the way many adults commonly assume that kids form political ideas.

Although this political science scholarship brings new and important insights to the study of political socialization, there is much more to know about how the political landscape shapes racial socialization. Zooming out from the level of family conversations about racism or racial patterns that kids notice in their schools and communities, this book explores how the macro-level *political* landscape of children's lives informs racial learning processes and outcomes at the individual and group levels.

Third, little attention has been paid to *racialized emotions* within racial learning processes. As the following chapters explore, "the emotions specific to racialized societies . . . are central to the racial edifice of societies," or the complex set of racial beliefs within a society.73 As Eduardo Bonilla-Silva writes, "Much like class and gender, race cannot come to life without being infused with emotions, thus, racialized actors feel the emotional weight of the categorical location. . . . [Indeed], racial actors, both dominant and subordinate simply cannot transact their lives without racialized emotions."74 As the political scientist Jonathan Mercer writes, emotions connected to experiences of race operate at the group level, wherein, "group members share, validate, and police each other's feelings; and these feelings structure relations within and between groups."75 That is, racialized emotions are not about individual psychological dispositions separated from the material realities of structural racism. Rather, these emotions are group based and inform how people see and understand the racial hierarchy of which they are a part. And racialized emotions are important to study because, as Bonilla-Silva argues, "to dismantle racism, an analysis of the emotions at play in racial transactions is essential."76 I agree, and I argue that this analysis must include a close look at racialized emotions in childhood and their connection to racial learning overall.

Finally, with a few important exceptions, much of the research about the Trump effect has drawn on interviews and surveys with teachers and parents. While much can be learned from the perspectives of adults about how kids encountered Trump, it is also important to hear the voices of children themselves. As the education scholar Paul J. Yoder makes clear, "While the dearth of student voices is not a new phenomenon, the evidence that the 2016 US elections . . . led to political trauma for students heightens the need to investigate student experiences" and bring the voices of young people to bear.77

Studying the perspectives of kids is imperative because we know that the ideas they form in childhood are important for the rest of their lives. As the social welfare expert Laura Wray-Lake and her colleagues write, "Trump's election as President of the United States may be a historical moment that has lasting impacts on today's youth," including a long-lasting impact on how they think about racism and democracy.78 This is especially true for young people who experienced Trump during developmental periods of early to late adolescence, during which kids develop their worldviews, explore who they want to be, and form ideological and political views on race that evidence suggests are difficult to disrupt later in the life course. We know from research with white teenagers and young adults, racial views and ideological positions formed in childhood, as well as partisan attitudes, solidify once youth reach adulthood.79 For this reason, understanding the impact of the "generational imprint" of Trump on kids' racial learning is key for developing interventions to challenge the powerful forces of white supremacy that have flourished openly in recent years, as well as ones that have been percolating in US society all along.80

2

"Feeling Race"

Waking Up after the 2016 Election

When I woke up and my mom told me Trump was elected, I wanted to go back to sleep because I thought it was a dream. I thought it was a nightmare. I was like, "Can I go back to sleep then?" My mom, like, she poured water on me and was like, "Hey! What is the matter with you! Get up!" And I was like, "Trump is president!! What do you think the matter is with me?!" Then I went and I started freaking out. . . . I felt like the world just turned upside down. . . . Sometimes I forget about it, and sometimes I want Mrs. Obama to come and like be elected for president. And it is not just me! When [Trump] won the election, we went to school, and everybody was screaming, running around, and some started crying, "I want Obama to come back!"

—JULIANA, AGE TEN

The day after the 2016 election represented the culmination of a long, divisive political campaign season brimming with public debates about racism that deeply impacted the children in this study. The election season shaped dynamics in their families, their relationships with other kids, and the climate of their classrooms, playgrounds, and bus rides to school. During the months leading up to the election, as well as in the months that followed, these kids told me that they noticed stark divisions between their own ideas about the social world and the ideas of people they loved, like their teachers, soccer teammates, and sometimes even close friends. The kids talked with me about what they thought about Donald Trump, what they thought about the explicitly racist things he said and did, and what it was like to share these reactions in private family spaces compared to more public contexts like the bus ride to school. Almost every child agreed that Trump said and did racist things, though some of the children said he was only "sorta kinda racist," which they believed was "not a big problem."

It quickly became clear to me, though, that these kids not only wanted to talk about what they thought when Trump was elected—they wanted me to know how they felt. Kids recalled experiencing a wide spectrum of emotions in response to the election of Trump. Some kids felt really scared. They told me they were especially fearful of racist violence perpetrated by their classmates who appeared to feel emboldened by Trump and were "meaner" than they had been before he was elected. Some kids felt really sad. They told me stories about not being able to visit their grandparents due to heightened political division in their families and explicit expressions of racism by Trump-supporting relatives. Some kids were thrilled. They shared their delight with me about the election of President Trump to the White House and how they believed he would keep them safe from bad people. Some were anxious about what the future might bring, while others were outright devastated about Trump being president. Still others were apathetic about it all and told me that they thought things would be fine and that they did not see what the big deal was. But all these kids had a lot to say about how they felt.

One way of making sense of these variations in how kids felt is to view these differences as reflections of individual kids having their own unique, "interior," psychological reactions to political news and thinking about their emotions as "individual" and personal.[1] Of course, we would expect kids to have a range of different emotional responses to political events like an election—kids disagree with each other and with adults all the time about all kinds of things. And we would expect different kids to have different reactions to current events. However, the emotional responses of these kids were not just individually expressed: there were meaningful patterns, even across a substantial geographical divide. How can we explain these patterns if we view emotions as exclusively about the individual?

Another way of understanding these differences in emotional responses is to think about them from a sociological perspective. This means viewing the kids' emotions as "socially acquired and socially structured" and informed by sociocultural factors.2 Thinking sociologically about these children's emotions means moving away from an individual, micro level of analysis and considering macro-level dynamics as well. Doing so allows us to account for the way historical processes as well as the sociopolitical context in which children come of age shapes how they *feel* about the social world, which in turn has a profound impact on how they *think* about the social world.

Further, a sociological lens allows us to see that these kids' emotions were linked to how they experienced the social world as members of social groups rather than as individuals alone. When I examined patterns in the emotional responses that the children exhibited, I found that distinct groups of kids emerged—and these groups were defined not by whether they lived in the Northeast or the Deep South and not by their gender identity or their grade at school. Rather, these groups emerged based on their racial group identity.3 These kids' emotions were connected to how these kids understood themselves as members of a particular racial group. Overall, I found patterns in the children's emotions that fit with how these children experienced the world as racial subjects—how these kids "felt race" in light of the election results.4

The term I use in this book to refer to these emotions is "racialized emotions." Racialized emotions are "emotions specific to racialized societies," or societies organized by the placement of people into socially constructed racial groups that are organized hierarchically with respect to power.5 These "emotions related to race" form through interactions and relations with others but also emerge as people do everyday things, like move to particular neighborhoods or read the news or play with peers on the playground at recess.6 In this chapter, I explore this concept in detail and illustrate the importance of thinking more carefully about the role that these group-level, relational emotions play in the racial learning processes of children. This is a useful endeavor because, as Bonilla-Silva states, if we do not understand the significance of racialized emotions, "the struggle against racism will always be incomplete. Eradicating racism will require a radical process to uproot its visible, 'objective' components as well as demolish its emotional skeleton."7

In the pages that follow, I introduce three groups of kids, and I explore in general terms how they "felt race" in light of the election of Trump. Rather than theorizing their emotions as private individual experiences in response to an election outcome, I argue instead that these children's emotions have a "group-based nature" and "reflect the different positions of actors in racialized societies."8 These children express racialized emotions—and these racialized emotions drive their understandings of race and racism in the United States. Because "race cannot come to life without being infused with emotions," I argue that racialized emotions are foundational to how kids form ideas about race and racism.

"I Felt, like, Sick to My Stomach": White Anti-Trump Kids

Because the 2016 presidential election results were not announced until very late on election night, most of the kids either fell asleep before the results were finalized or were made to go to bed by their parents before the results were in. As a result, these children all learned the news that Trump would be the next president of the United States when they woke up the next morning.

In Mississippi, Paige, a twelve-year-old girl who identified as white, shared her experience with me about waking up to the news that Trump won the election. Her dread was expressed both through what she said and also how she said it:

I felt, like, sick to my stomach. Like, I woke up and, like, checked my phone, and I was—and I just, like—it was, like, the world broke. And my friends felt the same way. Like, literally, like, it was, like, I went to bed thinking, "There's no way he can win! There's no way, and, like, people are going to wake up and see, like, he can't win." You know? And then I wake up, and it just it *blew* [slapping table angrily] *my* [slapping table angrily] *mind* [slapping table angrily] how incredibly, like, *blind* [slapping table angrily] people were to his antics. . . . He is racist and sexist and should not be president!

As Paige remembered this moment, she sat on the edge of her seat. Her voice shook as she spoke, and I could sense by her body language that despite the election being a few months prior, she still felt furious about the results.

In Massachusetts, twelve-year-old Nora, who identified as "white and Portuguese," told me that when she found out that Trump had won, she immediately felt a sense of discomfort about what it would be like to go to her grandparents' house for dinner that coming weekend: "Um, with my family, . . . like, my grandparents were, like, for Trump, so when, like, we go over to their house, we would, like, argue about it a lot. Like, they would eventually, like, stop, especially, like, when we were eating dinner and stuff, and they would, like, not continue that conversation afterwards." I asked Nora how family dinners went following the election, and she told me there were a lot of arguments about immigration: "Not a lot of people are coming in [to the United States] to do bad stuff. Most people are, like, coming from places that are bad. They're not bad people. They're trying to escape the bad stuff. . . . Not letting immigrants in, I feel like that is kind of racist. . . . My family argues about that a lot." Immigration was a topic that was especially important to Nora as her father was a first-generation immigrant from Portugal, and she went to school with many kids who were themselves immigrants. Nora told me she was frustrated and angry with her grandparents and that their support for Trump made her not want to go to the weekly family dinners she otherwise loved. This kind of intergenerational family conflict about race and politics was certainly a theme in the data from this study (as well as my previous research), as many white kids reported in both studies that their grandparents were explicitly and unapologetically racist and that this caused family fights.

Zena, who was twelve years old and white and from Mississippi, remembered the moment she found out that Trump had won the election. "I'm pretty sure I cried," she told me with a sad look on her face. "I'm pretty sure my parents woke me up and said, 'Hey, I have something you would have never guessed would have happened.'" Zena went on to tell me how devastated she felt when she learned the news and how as the day went on and she spent time with other kids, she grew angrier and angrier about the election results and about the political and racial viewpoints of other people, especially those around her in Mississippi:

> I mean, Mississippi is racist. It's a racist state. If you say, like, something about Mississippi [to someone], one of the first things that comes into their mind about Mississippi is racism. . . . You can kind of see the look in people's eyes when you're like, "Oh yeah, I'm from Mississippi." They're just kind of like, "Oh, how's that working out for you?" . . . And for Trump, it's all about him wanting a certain group of Americans to be Americans and not other people. And that is why a lot of people in Mississippi like him. . . . I think Mississippi is—I wouldn't say stuck in their ways but kind of. I don't know the word I'm looking for. I guess they're a little slower to change and kind of, like, slower to, like, accepting people. . . . I've actually come up with a slogan [for the state]: "Mississippi: Racism and Unforgiving Religious Views."

Zena explained to me how angry she was with other white people in Mississippi—anger she felt at the individual level but also anger that was socially and relationally produced as a result of Zena's interactions with other white people in Mississippi. This anger also came from her interactions with the racial and religious power structure of Mississippi historically and today. Zena's anger, then, can be seen as a racialized emotion, and one that has deeply shaped her ideas about race as well as her political position. Zena also talked to me about how much she wanted to leave Mississippi to get away from people like this, her perception being that elsewhere in the country, there might be less racism. This is one example of how the national *and* state-level political landscape, in addition to Zena's own social position and interactions with others, informed her feelings and thoughts about race and politics. This example also shows how Zena's feelings of disgust, not just in this moment but as a young person growing up in Mississippi for years, have shaped her broader ideas about race and politics.

Some of the white kids in this study, like Paige, Nora, and Zena, were shocked that their country elected Trump and were horrified that so many Americans—including their family members and neighbors—would approve of Trump's racism. For kids like Paige, Nora, and Zena, there were many reasons to be disgusted with the election of Trump to office and to feel angry that so many white people voted for him. These girls, as well as two-thirds of the other kids in the study, including kids living in both Mississippi and Massachusetts, told me in great detail all of the reasons that they did not think Trump was a good person to be elected president. And across this group, these kids identified Trump's racism as one of the main reasons they believed he was unfit to be the president. Undeniably, how this election made them feel encouraged them to think differently about racism in the US and called into question some previously taken-for-granted assumptions about how "color-blind" and "postracial" the US actually is.

In sum, this group of white kids illustrated that children have agency, or free will, and can and do rework or even at times reject dominant ways of thinking as well as normative racialized emotions. This fits theoretically with the notion that any individual can engage in "racial deviance" and reject the "emotional repertoire" of the dominant group.9 As I show in chapter 3, some white kids in this group rejected the racial norms related to ideologies and emotions of their white parents, teachers, and even peers and wanted to act differently in the world as a result. Some of these white kids challenged normative racialized emotions expressed by their parents, at least from time to time. But, in a racialized society, emotional norms are "constantly reinforced by the practices, beliefs, and mutual monitoring of a collective" and are thus a "collective product expressed and felt by most members of a racial group."10 Chapter 3, which focuses on this group of children, explores the fluid nature of racialized emotions and the role they might play in how kids rework racial ideologies into something new. Chapter 3 also explores why it is hard for these kids to maintain these new ideological positions as they think ahead to times without Trump and how reverting back to colorblind thinking serves to protect these children from their racialized emotions related to feeling white discomfort.

"I Felt like the World Just Turned Upside Down": Kids of Color

As ten-year-old Juliana, quoted in the epigraph to this chapter, explained, she was scared and anxious when she found out Trump would be in office. "He lies a lot. People feel like he's going to get us bombed because he keeps, like, doing something to Russia and stuff. He'll do stuff to other countries that he shouldn't be doing, . . . and [when he] gets on the news, he'll deny it." Juliana told me that she did not think Trump liked people from other countries and that this dislike of other nations was heightened when the people from other countries were not white. "He is racist," she told me confidently. "He tried to get rid of Obamacare 'cause people of his color didn't like it," she went on angrily. She explained that denying people health care is wrong and that Trump and his white supporters do not want people like her family to have health insurance. "They only want it for themselves," she said.

Clearly, Juliana saw Trump's actions as deeply tied to racial group relations. She viewed Trump as advocating for "people of his color" while lying to and ignoring the needs of everyone else. Juliana also told me that the main reason she liked President Obama was because "he understood people" and that even though "people were surprised that a person of his race was, like, the perfect president of the United States," she thought he was a very good president nonetheless—and this was primarily because he was able to appreciate the experiences, needs, and perspectives of all people, and especially Black people.

Juliana understood Trump as not just an individual whom she did not like but as a member of a racial group ("people like them") that seeks to hold power over people in her group ("people like me"). Juliana viewed herself and Trump as a members of different racial groups with different interests. This illustrated her awareness of her own racial subjectivity as well as how the racial hierarchy works. When Juliana expressed her anger about Trump's racism, she also told me that she talked with her other Black friends about Trump and her mom and other family members, and those connections made her feel better. She did not talk about how white kids at her school made her feel better—instead she told me she avoided those kids, especially in light of the election results.

In Massachusetts, thirteen-year-old Alexis, who identified as "biracial or mixed," also shared what she remembered from that day. "I found out in the morning from my parents when I woke up. And I was like, 'Oh man. Oh my gosh.' I was *so* upset. Like, 'We're doomed.'" Alexis told me that she felt depressed, hopeless, and scared when she heard the news. "I am like, 'When is the world going to end?'" she told me with a serious tone and with a scared look on her face. She told me that because her mom is Black, she worries what might happen to her because of Trump's racism. Like Juliana, Alexis was fearful about Trump's presidential win because of her own identification with a racial group that Trump explicitly mocked and dehumanized. Alexis told me that she continuously found herself looking at Twitter on her phone, compulsively checking to see if anything bad had happened politically that would affect her family. The political scientists Bethany Albertson and Shana Kushner Gadarian find that when adults experience anxiety about political issues, this often leads them to become more engaged politically and seek out as much information as they can as a coping mechanism.[11] While this was true for Alexis initially, her constant engagement with political news took a toll on her, and after a while, she decided to delete Twitter from her phone: it caused too much anxiety for her, and she wanted complete disengagement. Though she said that she did not have any interactions on Twitter that upset her, reading the racist language of other people including Trump himself, reading stories about the Trump administration's latest decisions, and witnessing arguments between strangers on Twitter led her to feel race in ways that threatened her sense of well-being. In this way, her racialized emotions surfaced despite not engaging in any interracial interaction herself. Though racialized emotions often come from interracial interactions, they can also "surface from looking at a picture, reading a newspaper, watching a movie, or walking into—or even thinking about—a location (i.e., a neighborhood)."[12] Although researchers have found evidence that Black adults can find social media to be a site of expression and a place to build community and a coping strategy in the face of online and offline experiences of racism, for Alexis, this online space became too overwhelming and heightened her sense of being "doomed." It brought out intensely felt racialized emotions in her.[13]

A number of kids used the word "doomed" when talking with me, and some of their parents told me in our own informal conversations that they found it difficult to witness their children's anxiety, cynicism, and at times, outlook on life that "things will only get worse." As the data show, though, these individual kids were not alone in how they felt. Kids like Juliana and Alexis and many other kids of color in this study experienced collective, racialized emotions. One of those emotions experienced was that of helplessness and anxiety.

Suzanna, a ten-year-old girl from Massachusetts who identified as "a mix of Cape Verdean and Italian," was also worried about violence increasing with the election of Trump. "I felt bad when he was elected. 'Cause he's starting a little bit of trouble. Like, a *lot* of people want to fight our country now." Suzanna and many of the kids interviewed talked about their fear of increasing violence not just in their neighborhoods or schools but also on a mass scale. Children talked about their fears of war, bombings, military takeovers, and international conflict. Again, this was in addition to their fear and anxiety of increasing violence within the country as a result of racism. This fear and anxiety was felt by most of the kids in this study who identified as people of color, demonstrating how these emotions are group-based and relational. These kids also demonstrated their understanding that dynamics at the macro sociopolitical level of society impacted micro-level behaviors and emotions, even between kids in their everyday lives.

Devion, an eleven-year-old boy in Massachusetts who identified as Black, told me that he felt similar to Alexis. "We stayed up and watched it for a long time. I felt just sad for America 'cause, like, I mean, [Trump] could definitely change things around if he wants—but probably not. But he could change it around, if he does the right stuff. I just don't think he will, and that's scary." I asked Devion what kind of "stuff" Trump does that Devion does not like. He explained, "Like, he's done some stuff that other presidents haven't, and he's the president, and he should know better about what to do and what not to do. He has said racist things. He has abused women. I don't think that's right for anybody to do, especially not the president!" Devion told me that he wanted to be hopeful that Trump would change his behavior and make different choices moving forward and stop doing "disrespectful things" but that he was doubtful and pessimistic that this would happen—and that as Trump continues to act disrespectfully, this would only encourage other people, including white boys at Devion's school, to mimic Trump and bring his disrespectful behavior directly into Devion's life. He explained his emotions not only as a response to events on the macro political level but also as a response to events at the micro level, informed by the political moment. And most of these concerns were about white children at his school or in his community feeing emboldened by the election of Trump and subsequently directing explicit racial violence at kids of color—kids like him.

Although empirical sociological studies of children's racialized emotions are limited, the emotions that come with learning race have certainly been experienced and written about widely. Bonilla-Silva reminds us that Black writers have long referenced childhood as a time during which they learned racialized emotions. In his words, "I felt race even before I knew what race was and long before I recognized myself as a Black Puerto Rican."[14] He also points to the actor, director, writer, and activist Ossie Davis's description of a humiliating encounter with white police officers, during which they entertained themselves by pouring syrup on his head. Davis reflected, "Something very wrong had been done to me; something I would never forget. This was happening to me at the age of six or seven. The culture had already told me what this was and what my reaction to this should be: not to be surprised, to expect it to accommodate it; to live with it. I didn't know how deeply I was scarred or affected by that, but it was still a part of who I was."[15] As both of these reflections from childhood illustrate, growing up in a racialized society means that children develop a sense of racial identity and a sense of racial subjectivity—that is, they learn that they are a racial actor in a society where race often determines outcomes. "Emotion goes with identity," and "group-level emotion can be stronger than, and different from, emotion experienced as an individual" as "group members share, validate, and police each other's feelings"; importantly, "these feelings structure relations within and between groups."[16] Learning one's "racial self," then, not only is part of racial learning more broadly but is importantly a result of historically specific dynamics, including where and when kids grow up, their lived experiences related to the political moment of their childhoods, and what kind of group-level emotions kids produce as a result.17 Without a doubt, the day after Trump was elected, the kids of color in this research explained how they felt race and recognized their own racial subjectivity in ways that intensified and, for many, were overwhelming. How this group of children felt race, then, produced new ideas about the racialized world in which they live.

"We Were Really Excited!": White Pro-Trump Kids

Not all of the children in this study were anxious, sad, or fearful the day after Trump was elected. Some were delighted and celebratory. For example, twelve-year-old Elsa, a white child from Mississippi, shared her memories from Election Day:

> [On Election Day,] well, my dad picked me up from school, and I was like, "Who did you vote for?" and he—and he tricked me! He said the opposite of what I was thinking. And it got me really upset [laughs]. Then, he was like, "Oh, I'm just playing." And then, he was like, "I voted for Trump," and I was like, "Yay!!" . . . [Later my siblings and I] were like, "I want Trump!" We were like, "I—I really hope he wins!" [laughs]. I was like, "It's so close! I really hope we get Florida and blah blah blah!" And then, my friend, she stayed up all night watching it, and I fell asleep. I couldn't watch it. . . . And then [the next day], when we all got to school, we all started talking about it. . . . We were really excited that he won!

Joking around with her father about whom he voted for, watching the election results with siblings, and then celebrating Trump's victory with friends were all part of how Elsa reacted to the news that Trump won. And Elsa was not alone. One-third of the kids interviewed, including kids in both Mississippi and Massachusetts, supported Trump and told me that they were happy and relieved that he won the election. If they were angry about anything, it was that Hillary Clinton's supporters were complaining so much about the election results or "making such a big deal" about racism and sexism.

As Simon, a thirteen-year-old white boy in Massachusetts, explained, "I woke up, and my stepmom told me Donald Trump won. And I'm like, 'Okay, that's pretty good. I wasn't going to be like everyone else is if he lost, like, 'Oh my gosh! I'm moving to another country because a certain person got elected!'" I asked him if that is what other kids said the day after the election. Simon replied, "I mean, a *lot* of people said that. Yeah. I mean, yeah, I didn't—like, I wouldn't be the happiest person in the world if Hillary Clinton got elected because she wasn't the one that I really wanted to get elected, but I wouldn't be like 'Boo-hoo! Oh no! The end of the world!'" Simon made a facial expression that conveyed that he thought kids who were really upset about the election were being dramatic and ridiculous. To emphasize his point, he added, "I mean, there was some girl in my class who said if Hillary Clinton didn't win, she was moving to New Zealand. . . . Like, there's no point in doing that. Like, four years go by, and you vote again for another person. Like, four years is not that long!" Later, Simon told me that he believed Trump did some racist things sometimes but that was not a good enough reason to dislike him.

Grace, a twelve-year-old white girl from Mississippi, said that she felt very happy when Trump won. She explained why she was so happy: "Well, I didn't really want Hillary to win because she was a Democrat. And, um, we were excited about Trump winning! I didn't feel good that night, and I stayed up and watched it with my parents, and we, um, and we wanted Trump to win, and—and my mom voted for him, and like I said, we didn't really want Hillary to win. So [when Trump won] I felt really happy! . . . I was happy that Trump won because I think he knows how to handle, like, people who threaten us and stuff." Many of the children who shared Grace's excitement and happiness also shared her perspective that Trump would "handle people" who "threaten us." As another child told me,

"I am happy because Trump will look out for people like us." This statement certainly reflected a sense of group position and was produced by this child as she thought of herself as a member of a group in relation to others. In these examples, it is clear that these children are expressing racialized emotions.

Much of the research on racialized emotions has focused on fear, sadness, and anger; but only considering these "negative" emotions overlooks the positive racialized emotions that emerge when groups resist racist oppression. Furthermore, focusing only on negative racialized emotions fails to take into account the expressions of pleasure by lynching parties or the laughter of Trump supporters as they shout dehumanizing things about entire groups of people. In simple terms, it does not account for the joy and satisfaction of domination. As Bonilla-Silva explains, "Although racial domination is partly based on falsehoods (i.e., whites' contemporary pains are not caused by Blacks, Muslims, or undocumented workers), domination itself produces both material and emotional well-being among members of the dominant race."18 When white kids in this research expressed pleasure and delight at the notion of building a wall to keep Mexican people out of "their" country, for example, they expressed an "affective logic" that is rational to them, even if it is based on a distorted view of the world. And this logic made them feel good about themselves—it produced emotional well-being and even a sense of "fun" and joy. As I explore in chapter 5, these positive emotions coexisted with these same children's negative racialized emotions, particularly that of fear of one's group losing status and privilege in the broader society, or forms of racial resentment I observe kids developing in childhood. Again, much like with the other groups of children, the racialized emotions of these white children were foundational to how these kids made sense of race.

Conclusion

The children interviewed for this book said that they were confronted regularly with messages about politics and racism during the Trump era, through their families, their peers, and their teachers, as well as through the media's coverage of current events. These kids participated in their own interpretation of these messages, and often these interpretations were guided by how they "felt race." Despite many adults often assuming that kids are politically disengaged or unaffected by politics, my research shows that this is simply not the case, at least not for the kids in this study. Rather, these kids experienced racialized emotions in response to Trump being elected—and the racialized emotions they experienced shaped their racial ideological perspectives as well as their political positions.

Based on striking patterns in the research, three groups emerged: (1) white kids like Paige and Nora who were shocked that Trump won and angry that their country had more racist individuals than they previously thought; (2) children like Juliana, Suzanna, and Devion who identified as kids of color and who felt fearful, anxious, and mad that Americans would vote for Trump; and (3) white kids like Elsa, Simon, and Grace who were happy that Trump won and who were angry that other people would not support Trump, especially other white kids—and who expressed a more general anger toward "people who threaten us." Notably, these groups of kids all expressed anger, though that anger was directed at different targets.

The emotional responses that the children expressed in this study about racism in the era of Trump *cannot* simply be understood to be individual-level feelings. If these were individual feelings exclusively, we would not see such remarkable patterns across the data. Reducing differences in kids' perspectives to variations in children's individual dispositions or personalities—or to their parents' political party affiliations—is far too simplistic of an interpretation. This approach fails to appreciate how emotions are "socially acquired and socially structured."19 Instead, these emotions fit with the sociological framework of "racialized emotions."

The emotional responses of these kids, and the beliefs that are connected to them, varied in patterned ways. These patterns make clear that part of how these kids produced ideas about race included how they felt race as a result of their racial group identification. Further, how they thought and felt about racism was influenced by the interactions these kids had not just with each other but also with the political landscape that defines their childhoods. Certainly, then, feeling race is part of kids' racial learning processes.

3

"I Had No Idea the Country Was So Racist!"

Racial Discomfort and Disgust

"Our teacher made us draw a picture of what we think the future is going to look like under our new government," twelve-year-old Paige explained to me one Saturday morning. "It was kinda funny, though, because the teacher actually made half the class redo it because she was unhappy with the results because she got a lot of walls and cities in flames or like evil-looking politicians." Paige smirked.

"What did you draw?" I asked. Paige replied confidently. "I personally drew Trump behind a wall of fire. I just felt like we were making so much progress with Obama—like, on everything, like women's rights, gay rights, racism, like, things like global warming. Then, like, now that we have the new president—it's, like, a million steps backwards. It's, like, he will just burn it all down. So I drew the wall of fire." She shrugged and then continued, "I think that him being elected has made some people think, 'Oh, well since our president has these beliefs, it's okay.' . . . Like, him being disrespectful to women, some people are like, 'Oh, [if] the president did that in his past, it's okay for me to do that,' . . . and that's not okay."

We talked a bit more, and then I asked Paige what she drew the second time, after her teacher made all the kids redo the assignment. "Well, she gave us new instructions and said we were supposed to draw our hope for the future or something." Paige rolled her eyes. "So I drew just like hearts and peace signs and like peace words like 'love' and 'peace' and 'happiness.' Sooo yeaaaah. I ended up getting a good grade on that. But I mean . . ." She gave an exasperated sigh.

Just then, Paige's mom entered the room to bring us a snack. "Is that not your hope for the future, Paige?" her mom asked. "Yes, Mom, of course it is my hope for the future that we do have, like, world peace and stuff. But I know it's probably not going to happen now. I just think Trump being president will matter for a long time into the future."

* * *

Children like Paige are members of a generation that has grown up with a loud and popular narrative of racial progress and "colorblind" thinking. These kids spent almost their entire childhoods living in the "postracial" era of President Obama, the nation's first Black president.1 During this time, kids and adults alike widely believed that President Obama's victory was evidence that the nation had finally reached a point in history where race no longer shaped opportunities, experiences, policies, or outcomes. "Anyone can be president, no matter what race they are. Just look at Obama!" was the popular narrative during the Obama years. In my previous research with kids while President Obama was in office, many (though not all) of the young white people I interviewed told me that "racism is not a problem anymore" or that despite the fact that there were some racist people in the South or even some policies that were not fair to people of color, their midwestern community was generally free of racism. And the fact that President Obama won two presidential elections offered support for this colorblind racial logic. These narratives of racial progress were common across the political spectrum of kids who shared their perspectives with me: even the children who told me they did not support Obama politically pointed to his election as an example that invalidated claims of racism in the US.

Despite growing up in a society hierarchically organized by a socially invented idea of "race," perhaps it is not surprising that so many kids articulated the central frames of colorblind ideology, especially during the Obama era. Classroom lessons focused on racial progress of the civil rights era and paid little attention to the continued significance of racial power, oppression, and violence in present-day US society.2 Children's television programs often presented diverse characters who appeared to live happily in a racially progressive world where racial differences did not matter.3 Certainly, sociologists documented extensively the prevalence of "colorblind" understandings of race in the post-civil-rights-era US, not just among kids but also their parents.4 For example, research showed that many white parents did not talk to their white kids about race. Some parents did "not believe their children even [thought] about race."5 Even when white parents did talk to their kids about this subject, research shows that often power and inequality were left out of the conversation and parents instead engaged in what scholars call "diversity discourse" or "shallow multiculturalism," which often celebrates human difference but ignores the realities of power or racial hierarchy and reinforces notions of who is "ethnic" and who is "normal."6 In addition, if these conversations took place, often they were in response to an act of racist violence that had garnered a lot of national, public attention. During the Obama era, many white kids embraced these colorblind messages, even if they reworked colorblind ideology in their own creative ways.7

The election of Trump, however, interrupted this popular narrative of colorblindness and racial progress. Many people were stunned on election night.8 Despite President Trump's repeated claims that he was the "least racist person there is in the entire world," he entered public office with a long history of racist words and actions.9 His racism was at least part of why some people were so shocked when he won the election. Long before 2016, Trump's corporation was sued in the 1970s for housing discrimination when it refused to rent to Black families.10 In the following years, Trump's racism continued.11 President Trump's political career began with his advocacy of a racist conspiracy against President Obama. The "Birther movement" was led by Trump, and it capitalized on white fears of a Black man in a position of power. This conspiracy was accompanied by dreams of a white ethnostate as a remedy for those fears, a feature of far-right ideology.12 This movement appealed to white supremacist fears and fantasies and was a precursor to what was to come.13

Trump's election felt like a slap in the face to many kids, especially to those like Paige who had believed the nation was making progress on issues like racial and gender inequality. If the US was "beyond racism," how could an explicitly racist person be elected to the highest office—and what would result from his victory? In this chapter, I explore the perspectives of white kids who believed racism was over in the US but then had to make sense of a new president who often used explicitly racist words and who had a history of racist actions. What did these kids feel following this election? Did they change their ideological viewpoints and come to view their country as a nation that is actually racist? Or did they use dominant ideology in flexible ways to interpret the situation around them such that they could maintain their commitment to colorblind racial logic while also resolving inconsistencies they observed? And what does this mean about the contours of dominant racial ideology in the United States: Is colorblind logic still a common way of making sense of race for kids, even after Trump?

When Trump was elected, the kids in this book, and in the entire country, found themselves suddenly bombarded with conflicting, contradictory, and inconsistent ideological messages about racism in the US. Through listening to this group of children, theoretically, we can understand more clearly the impact of the political landscape on how kids understand racial dynamics in the US. In so doing, we can expand the notion of one's "racial context of childhood," or "the social environment surrounding a child that shapes how that child make sense of race," to include macro-level racial and political dynamics in the US.14 We can also examine how kids shape existing ways of understanding in new ways to fit new conditions and perhaps even change their minds about what they think altogether. But so too can we see that young people sometimes reinforce dominant racial ideologies, even in the face of evidence that contradicts these "commonsense" ways of interpreting the social world. As I show in this chapter, although some white kids during the Trump era rejected colorblind ideology, others continued to embrace it, reestablishing dominant frameworks for making sense of race.

Racial Ideologies across Time

Social scientists have long studied white people's views on race-related social issues and how these viewpoints change (or do not) over long stretches of time. One area of scholarly debate is whether white people's racial hatred of people of color has actually disappeared or whether, as the sociologist Tyrone Forman argues, "rather than an actual disappearance in white racial antipathy, there has instead been a change in its expression."15 For example, surveys of racial attitudes find that white support for segregated schools has decreased over the past fifty years.16 However, other research illustrates that white parents today continue to engage in practices that lead to school segregation, even if they do not explicitly state opposition to their children attending school with kids of color.17 Overall, when white people's understandings and personal logics about race are examined using research methods that allow researchers to access how people "justify, rationalize, and articulate racial viewpoints," such as interview-based or ethnographic research, clear evidence demonstrates that racism has not disappeared.18 Instead, racism takes new forms, shifting, as dominant ideologies do, to fit new circumstances.19 And children, the newest generation, play a powerful role in the reworking and reproduction of dominant racial ideologies.20 Indeed, research shows that during the post-civil-rights era, societal norms shifted dramatically: white people as a racial group expressed antipathy for people of color in new and subtle ways while still working to maintain privilege.21 As such, new forms of racism are understood to be implicit, more difficult to detect and certainly harder to measure than racial prejudice during the Jim Crow era.22 Overall, strong evidence suggests that colorblind racism has been the dominant racial ideology in the post-civil-rights-era US, even before the election of Obama.23

Although colorblind racism may be a new form of racism in comparison to the past, this way of thinking is really a reworking of past racial ideas and serves, as ideologies do, to justify the racial status quo.24 Colorblind ideology and discourse is documented extensively, illustrating how white people "make non-racial claims about what are indeed racial disparities."25 Colorblind ideology generally includes the following frames. First, this dominant ideology claims that equal opportunity is available to all and that people have the individual ability to make certain "choices," which is one strategy that allows white people to disregard glaring patterns of racial inequality.26 Second, this ideology relies on the notion that racial dynamics are the result of "natural occurrences" rather than deliberate forms of discrimination. For example, colorblind ideology tends to understand residential segregation as a result of the so-called natural desire people have to live near people like them, which ignores the historical legacy of redlining, housing discrimination, and racist violence; it also overlooks contemporary forms of discrimination connected to the racial wealth gap as well as social processes involving social networks and people's prior experiences with discrimination in particular neighborhoods.27 Third, colorblind thinking encourages white people to make culturally based arguments to explain patterns of inequality. This includes rhetoric claiming that certain racial or ethnic groups struggle because they make "bad" decisions when it comes to education or child rearing. This racist framing thereby "explains away inequities [while] blaming the victims of racial discrimination for their situation."28 Finally, colorblind ideology asserts that discrimination is a feature of the past and that things are far better today than they used to be. This frame argues that because racism is no longer a major problem, there is no need for institutional remedies for patterns of racial inequality.

Colorblind interpretations of the world, as popular as they may be, ignore the ways that US society is "racialized" or how US society is fundamentally organized by the placement of actors into socially constructed categories that we refer to as "races."29 Although many people believe that racial groups are based on essential biological differences between human beings, this is simply not true. As a result of a series of historical and modern-day social processes involving religion, science, law, and politics, these political groups were invented by people in response to social conflict and a desire to control resources and power.30 Once these groups were socially constructed, they then took on real social significance.31 Meanings were and are assigned to these so-called racial groups through a process called "racialization," and when negative traits are assumed to be essential characteristics of members of these socially constructed groups, the dominant group can then more easily justify dehumanizing groups they seek to control.32 Importantly, these socially created groups are organized hierarchically, and resources are distributed according to this hierarchy, with those at the top, or in the case of the US, those racialized as "white," receiving more material and symbolic resources than groups positioned elsewhere in the hierarchy.33 In the US context, these advantages that accompany the social position of whiteness are commonly referred to as "white privilege" or, as W. E. B. Du Bois put it, the psychological "wages" that accompany whiteness.34

In other words, despite the countless ways that race continues to structure everything, from how people understand their racial identity at the micro level to group interactions at the meso level to how institutions are set up and how they function at the structural or macro level, we know that colorblind racial ideology has been the dominant way that white people rationalize and explain racial dynamics in nonracial terms.35 And this includes children.

White Kids and Colorblind Racial Ideology

"I knew President Obama was the first Black president, but I didn't understand the significance of it until Trump became president," twelve-year-old Zach told me one afternoon in Mississippi. I asked him if he talked about racism at his school, which is 30 percent white. "I'm sure we've talked about it, but it's not often. We don't bring it up that often." He also told me that before Trump was elected, he believed that the United States was an "equal place for everybody." He explained to me that this was why the election of Trump was so disruptive to his sense of the world. The election of Trump made him feel "uncomfortable" in large part because it made him realize the continued significance of racism. As a result of this sense of discomfort, Zach told me he had to rethink ideas he used to have, like why Obama's election was monumental.

Twelve-year-old Sarah attended the same school as Zach and lived in a racially mixed neighborhood. I asked her if she ever talked to her friends about racism or if the topic of race ever came up in their conversations. Similar to Zach, she replied, "No, that never comes up really. . . . In one of my periods—it's my last period of the day, and it's mostly, like, Black kids, and we're always hanging out. Just because you're different races doesn't really mean anything to us, so yeah." Sarah, like Zach, told me that she noticed the racial differences between herself and her Black peers, but this was not an important distinction to her. Sarah did add, however, that since Trump was elected, "more kids are starting to talk about racism" at her school. "I thought racism was pretty much behind us before [Trump was elected]." Sarah told me she felt "bad" for not realizing how racist her country still is.

Hazel, an eleven-year-old girl growing up in Massachusetts, told me that she did not "notice" race. She told me her school had "a mix of different kids," but when I asked her if she had friends with different skin colors, she replied, "Um, I don't really know. I don't really notice that." But other kids at her same school shared more similar views to Zach and Sarah. For instance, twelve-year-old Nora talked about how "cool" it was that there were so many immigrants from all different parts of the world in her classes at school: "I feel like there is a lot of diversity in the schools, . . . and there's a lot of people that have moved here like from different places. So that's always cool, like, when you meet a new person and they tell you about where they like lived before. That's always cool to see. . . . Like, one kid in my class moved here from Egypt when he was five, and that was really cool." When I asked Nora if these kids from different places were treated the same as the white kids at her school, she told me that yes, they were and that "everyone is equal." However, she later told me that these were also the kids who got "picked on" after Trump was elected because some of her white peers "don't think they should be here." "That made me really mad," she told me.

Other kids drew on cultural rather than structural explanations to talk about things like Black children's behavior at their school. For instance, all the kids in Mississippi who attended the public school, including Amy, told me that they noticed that the Black kids got in trouble more than the white kids did. Some of the white children explained this as teachers being mean and unfair and even racist. However, other kids like Amy explained this in ways that map onto the cultural racism frame of colorblind ideology. In her words, "If they're a bad kid, they probably would get in trouble more because they've done it more, but if they're a good kid, they'll probably get off easier." I asked Amy why she thinks kids do things that get them in trouble. "Maybe because they want attention, and sometimes their parents were like that, so they kind of follow their parents." Amy also told me that she did not think some of the Black kids at her school had parents who cared about their kids doing their homework. "Maybe they don't care as much about school?" she pondered. The idea that Black parents do not care about their children's education is a popular racist myth that is informed by colorblind thinking—that any differences noticed between racial groups are to do with cultural or group-level failings rather than how society is set up or organized.36

Overall, despite growing up in racially diverse communities and attending schools with less than 50 percent white students, these children generally articulated some of the key tenets of colorblind racial ideology. They minimized racism, they drew on cultural explanations to describe why kids of color struggled more than them at school, and they did not see racism as a barrier to equal opportunity. These were all kids who spent meaningful time with children of color in their everyday lives, though, of course, practices like racialized tracking and school discipline continued to contribute to their exposure to racial hierarchies and racist ideas. And yet, many of these kids told me that the ideas they had about the US being a land of equal opportunity and a place where racism was a feature of the past were disrupted when Trump was elected. This group of kids suddenly felt "uncomfortable," "bad," and "mad." And these feelings required that they revisit their ideas about racial progress. As Paige put it, "I just felt like we were making so much progress with Obama. . . . Now that we have the new president, it's like a million steps backwards. It's like he will just burn it all down."

Reflecting on Obama

For many of the white children who told me that they were shocked and disgusted when Trump was elected to the office of president, it was not until the election happened that suddenly they started thinking more carefully about why President Obama—the only other president they could remember in their short lifetimes—was someone they admired. For example, Amy told me, "I think [Obama] did a really good job. He believes in people, and that's good." Later she told me how Trump did not "believe in people," especially people with a "different color skin."

In Massachusetts, white children told me similar things. Nora explained, "I feel like that's really good to have the first African American president. That sort of, like, pushes away some of the people that are, like, negative towards African American people. We should definitely have, like, a woman president too. That would also be nice to sort of, like, represent women and, um, so it's not, like, all male presidents." Nora told me how she did not like the white boys on her school bus who supported Trump. These were the kinds of people who were "negative towards African American people," and she told me she did not remember them acting like this when Obama was in office. "No one did stuff like that then," she said in an exasperated tone.

Lucy also shared her thoughts. "I think it was really cool how, like, he was the first African American president. . . . I didn't really feel any difference, but, um, I liked Barack Obama better [than Trump]!" I asked her what she meant when she said she did not "feel any difference." She replied, "Um, I'm not African American myself, but my best friend, she is, and I feel like [Obama] was, like, a really good role model for her, . . . because I feel like people like her feel more insecure most of the time because they feel like they're not cool enough because they're this race, but I think he really proved people wrong." Here Lucy illustrates both a sort of apathy, Trump's election did not affect her, but also a simultaneous recognition that his election did impact other kids, especially Black kids at her school. Her comments could possibly be interpreted to suggest that she thinks Black children need "better" role models in general, which would fit with the cultural racism frame of colorblind ideology. But another interpretation could be more in line with what Nora said about the need for representation: for Black kids to see themselves reflected in the power structure of the United States. In either case, though, to Lucy, Obama's election was good for African American kids like her friend. She told me that she genuinely believed that Obama's election was good for race relations in US when "he really proved people wrong."

Sarah in Mississippi also used this idea of Obama being a "good role model," but the people for whom he modeled good behavior was broader in Sarah's mind than what Lucy imagined. When I asked Sarah what she thought about the election of the first Black president, she explained, "I thought that was something that we've kind of *all* needed. I think Obama was, like, a good role model for people. The new president? He is *not*. . . . He is racist!" Here, Sarah suggested that all Americans benefited from President Obama's election, including white people who did not believe that Black people should be in positions of power. And Sarah drew a direct link between the need for more Black politicians and the racism expressed by Trump.

During the Obama years, these kids embraced colorblind thinking. But when the majority of voting Americans elected someone whom these children identified as explicitly and openly racist, the narrative that the United States was a racially just society or that the country was "beyond race" no longer made sense to them—and this seemed to result from a new set of racialized emotions felt by this group of kids. As Zach explained, the lead-up to the election of Trump, as well as the aftermath of his administration, brought out a lot of discomfort in him and deeply challenged some of the taken-for-granted assumptions he previously held about the nation. For this group of kids, they became newly aware of the level of white antipathy and racism that was still very much alive around them in other white people, and they could not help but confront emotionally and ideologically the continued significance of racism in US society.

The Disruption of Trump to Kids' Beliefs in Racial Progress

The election of Trump disrupted this group of white kids' ideas about what kind of country they lived in. Most of these kids exhibited shock and surprise when Trump was elected, and some even expressed feelings of anger, disgust, and even hopelessness.

Shock and Surprise

In Zach's case, ever since Trump was elected, not only had he seen his country from a new perspective, but he was now noticing things that he did not during the Obama years. For instance, he mentioned racist police violence. "There's this whole thing that started last year—well, no, not just last year, but I first knew about it last year—about the police targeting African Americans, right?" Zach acknowledged that this was a problem that had been going on prior to the election of Trump but that he did not know about it until more recently, when he had been paying attention to racial dynamics in society more carefully and with a more critical eye. He also told me his perspective on National Football League (NFL) players protesting during the national anthem: "Why would they stand up and act like they are proud of America when they're not because of the problems in America?" I asked Zach what problems he thought were being protested. "Well, there's tons of exceptions, but aren't like football players, like, mainly African American? So they are protesting about racism." He went on to tell me that Trump does not like these protests and added that "Trump doesn't care" about what these Black athletes are saying, evidence Zach interpreted as racist in and of itself. "And also, isn't it true that most of the people in jail, a bunch, like, are African American and the poor population? That is not right." Certainly, racist police violence or racial disproportionality in who is incarcerated in Mississippi, where he lives, has been a persistent social problem—just not one that he noticed given how his childhood was structured. But because of a change in the political landscape, this twelve-year-old white boy became aware of patterns that he previously did not know about, particularly in the realm of the criminal justice system. Interestingly, his awareness of racism within this institution increased not due to something that happened at the micro level in his community or based on a book he read or a conversation he had with his parents. Instead, this recognition was due to a shift at the macro level involving the election of a new president and national political debate about racism in the country—a shift that brought about powerful emotions for Zach as well. This is a good example of how the macro level, especially the realm of politics, was part of Zach's racial context of childhood and how it shaped his racialized emotions. Of course, he also interpreted all kinds of messages from his family and local environment. But he made sense of all of these messages in connection with macro-level dynamics including a turbulent and controversial national election and political scene. Zach was presented with inconsistent racial ideological frames and thus had to negotiate these to make sense of racism in US society. As he interpreted aspects of the political landscape and navigated through his feelings of discomfort and embarrassment for not realizing the realities of racism before this moment, his racial ideological perspective shifted dramatically.

Ten-year old Amy, the sister of Zach, had a slightly different take on things. She agreed with her brother that Trump was racist, but her explanation for why was limited to "because he thinks about color." Amy clung to the notion of living in a colorblind society. "I think [racism] must still happen because you can kind of see the patterns around. But not as much. It's way better than way back, but I think it is still—it still happens." And yet, despite her commitment to believing that the United States was a fair and equal society, she was conflicted when it came to making sense of Trump's election as well as his words and behaviors. "I'm not really sure about him. . . . When I hear him talk, I think, 'Oh wow, that's kind of racist!'" Like children discussed in chapter 5, here Amy drew on the construction of "kind of racist," which stands in contrast to some of the other white girls who do not support Trump, like Paige, who confidently asserted that Trump was absolutely "100 percent a racist person who does racist things." When I asked Amy what she would say to Trump if she could say anything, unlike some of the other white kids who were ready to march up to him and tell them everything they thought, Amy replied, "I would probably be too shy to say anything to him." Similar to some of the kids who love Trump,

Amy seemed to be in the process of trying to figure out how it was possible to have a president in a postracial society who was racist. And she was not at all confident in her views, at least at the time of this interview. This was especially evident after I turned off the voice recorder, when she confided in me, apologizing for not knowing about some of the things I asked her. "I'm sorry. Honestly, I am sorta confused right now about all this stuff," she said with an apologetic look on her face.

Eleven-year-old Hazel in Massachusetts was also shocked when Trump was elected. But she was even more shocked that so many Americans voted for him. Indeed, for Hazel and others in this group of white children, although they often associated racism with one individual man like Trump, in the case of the president of the United States, his election spoke to a much larger problem. As Hazel told me, "I had no idea the country was so racist!" She explained to me that if so many people "picked him," then that really says something about the racial beliefs of "a lot of people." "I was really surprised," she told me. "How could that happen?"

The girls in this group of kids were also shocked and horrified when it came to issues related to gender and gender-based violence. These kids were shocked by reports of Trump's treatment of women but, like Hazel, equally shocked by the reaction to these reports by so many Americans. As Paige told me, "We had an assignment to write about what's an example of a modern-day problem. . . . I said that harassment and, like, sexual assault is like a big problem in my opinion that's not really being addressed. . . . People like Trump just think it is a laughing matter." She explained to me how "disgusted" she was that so many people were "okay with having a president who does these things to women" and asked me, "What does that say about America?" Relatedly, Amy told me that she really thought a woman would finally be elected to the role as president and how excited this had made her: "There's always been boys being president, and there's, like, there's never been a girl. People think men are more powerful and stuff like that, so they don't want a woman to win an election. . . . I really thought Hillary would win, . . . but I guess people are still like, 'Nope! She's a girl.'" Amy told me how she knew a lot of people supported Trump, but she thought that the United States was finally ready to elect a woman—that maybe in this case "even people who think only men should be leaders" would choose a woman because of how "bad" of an option Trump was.

Lucy in Massachusetts articulated almost the same point. "I wanted a girl president for once. . . . Girl power! I feel like everybody was surprised [with the election results] because they thought Hillary Clinton would have won. I was [surprised]!" She told me she thought it was time for the country to elect a woman, and she said she was hopeful that since the first Black president had previously been elected, maybe now a woman would be too. Her shock and disappointment of Trump winning the election, despite all the "disrespectful" and "mean" things he has done toward both women and people of color, was still evident nearly a year after the election.

For many of the girls in this group of kids, the election of a man accused of sexually assaulting and harassing women destroyed their hopes that there would be the "first girl president" but also revealed to them something deeply disturbing about gender in the US. As with racism, Trump's election—and specifically the fact that so many people supported him despite his sexist acts—disrupted these kids' understanding of the country they lived in. The election disrupted their sense of normalcy and made them feel deeply uncomfortable, particularly in the way that Trump's election challenged their previous sense that their country was "beyond" these divisions. "I don't even know how to feel about America right now," one of the girls told me, clearly ashamed of those who voted for Trump.

Anger and Disgust

Kids like Zena not only were surprised when Trump was elected but were also angry. As described in chapter 2, when Zena woke up the day after the election, she cried. In her words, "I'm pretty sure my parents woke me up and said, 'Hey, I have something you would have never guessed would have happened.'" Zena went to school and talked with her friends about the outcome too. She described a sort of horror around her: "I'm pretty sure there were about twelve of us at school that day who were all ready to move to Canada. I mean, we were all just kind of like, you know, 'Well, crap. What are we going to do now?' I mean, we already had low standards with him. We already knew, you know, we couldn't set the bar too high. And then America was like, 'Hey, let's elect this person!' and we were all just kind of like, 'Excuse me?!?!' Like, 'Huh??? . . . It's not going to work.'" Zena told me that she and her friends, as well as her family, were still mad about the election results and horrified that Americans would select someone like Trump, "especially given how racist he is," to be the president. I asked Zena what she meant when she said this. She explained,

> Trump is *definitely* racist [sighs]. I think if you meet someone and they start their sentences off with "I'm not racist," they have a racist tendency. And I feel like that's definitely how, if Trump said something, he would phrase it. "I'm not racist *but*"—you always have to listen for the "but" because it's always going to be something about "we need to kick these people out of America because they're taking jobs" or "these people are bad and they're just going to hurt us," which is so stereotypical of white Republicans. He's just—he's not doing a good job of embracing that the world is changing, and I guess he's definitely stuck in his racist ways.

Zena believed that the United States had been on a path toward equality—that "the world was changing" and that Trump's election was an interruption to this racial progress. This did not just shock her but also angered her. And she was not alone. Many of these kids told me how the country was undergoing long-needed change in areas related to race, gender, and sexuality and that some people simply refused to get on board. Kids shared their feelings about "old" people who did not support same-sex marriage or who were concerned about gender-inclusive bathrooms. As one child put it, "Why does it matter if you're in love with a girl or a boy?" These kids told me how frustrated they were with people constantly debating these topics instead of "just moving forward." Adults, and sometimes their peers, being "stuck in the past" was a phrase these kids used a lot to differentiate themselves from those with different viewpoints on issues related to social justice.

Paige also associated her teachers' perspectives with this idea of being "stuck in the past." She attended a private religious school in Mississippi, and she had many opinions to share about some of the dynamics at this particular school. "Everyone's Caucasian at my school 'cause it's a private school, so you don't have to, like, be really, really rich, but you do have to, like, pay to go there." Paige is aware of the vast income inequality around her, as well as how this economic inequality is racialized in her community, with white families holding far more material resources on average than Black families do. Paige told me it was good that she was going to high school at the public school, which is predominantly Black, because her private school did not seem to reflect "the real world" to her. Paige really did not have a lot of positive things to say about her private school. She was particularly annoyed by her perception that some of her teachers and peers seemed unable to grasp aspects of what Paige considered to be "reality." For example, she told me about one of her teachers who refused to intervene when Trump-supporting students said things that were discriminatory during class discussions about politics: "There's these two sisters, and I'm pretty sure their grandfather's racist 'cause, like, I'm pretty sure they've said like, 'Oh, you know my grandfather's racist.' And one of them, she was going on and on about how Christianity is so much better than, like, being Muslim because, like, I don't even know what she was talking about, but just *so* out there. . . . You could look around the room and just feel the tension because she was just saying some pretty *bad* things." Paige told me that she really wanted the teacher to "do something" but that, to her dismay, the teacher "stayed out of it." Paige told me that these kinds of conversations at school happened a lot, and though she often wanted to intervene, she also did not want to get in trouble: "Whenever [the teacher] says something that I don't agree with, like, I'll try and, like, kind of ask her about it, like, 'What do you mean by that?' And she'll just be like, 'Oh, you know, it's the Catholic Church's beliefs that da-da-da-da-da.' So she is very Catholic and very religious. Like, she, like, listens to Christian radio stations every morning on the way to school. I mean . . . [lifts her eyebrows and looks over to the side, indicating that she thought this was weird.]" Paige did not seem impressed with her teacher or some of her peers, particularly due to their political perspectives on issues like race, religion, gender, and sexuality. Paige told me that although she had been having these issues at school for a long time, the Trump era heightened the political polarization at her school. "It has gotten way worse," she said. In addition, she told me she felt "mad" a lot due to the things that were said at school but, more importantly to her, by the things that were not said—like teachers not intervening when other white kids said racist, Islamophobic, or homophobic things. Both Paige's words and her body language conveyed to me that she was emotionally agitated by the political dynamics at her school.

For Paige, like many of these kids, Trump's election illustrated that there are a lot more people who are more discriminatory than she thought. Though not the focus of this study, many kids brought up LGBTQ+ kids and their experiences at school. This group of white kids explained to me that they did not understand "what the big deal is" and that they did not understand adults' fighting over issues such as bathrooms and the rights of trans and gender-nonconforming people. As one child told me, "Who cares what bathroom someone uses?" Some kids even talked to me about disagreeing with adults and, specifically, problems some of their friends were having with their parents about issues related to race and politics. As Zena explained, "Uh, yeah, I have a good friend whose parents are *really* big on Trump and everything he's doing. And she's like, 'I just don't see where they're coming from!' . . . Their parents are like, you know, 'Oh, we need to raise you like this, and you need to be a big supporter of Jesus and Trump and racism.' And my friends are like, you know, 'I'm going to need you to take a step back, Mom and Dad!'" Zena told me how angry some of her friends were with their families and how this time was really challenging, especially in a place like Mississippi, with so many Trump support-ers everywhere. But she also told me how angry she was about the state of the country under the Trump administration:

> You never see anything in the news that Donald Trump did some-thing good today. And if you did, it would specifically be in the news like, "Hey guys, we know he's screwed up a lot, but he *finally* did something good!" He's just—I don't think he takes [being president] seriously. Everything you hear in the news, it's like, um . . . you know, "Trump is trying to, like, form alliances with this country. They play golf together." Or it's, like, just another scandal about him. It's never, like, you know, "the stock market has increased because of some-thing Trump did" or, like, "there's, like, unemployment down because Trump got jobs." Instead it's all related to racial things all about him wanting only a certain group of Americans to be Americans. . . . It makes me so mad. How can he be a president?

She told me more about her thoughts on some of his behavior, spe-cifically focused around issues of racist anti-immigrant rhetoric and policies, racial disproportionality in the criminal justice sys-tem, and debates about the former Mississippi state flag, which featured a Confederate emblem: "All of this stuff is what happens when you have a bunch of old racist white men sitting in power! And I mean, like—why? Like, why would you think that it's all still okay? After the 1800s, that should have ended as soon as everybody got their head on straight. What we're doing in this country to peo-ple [of color] is inhumane and horrible." What was striking about

Zena's comments was not just what she said but how she said it. Her body language, her tone and volume of voice, and the way she sighed with frustration over and over conveyed that Zena was not just intellectually invested in discussing white supremacy but that she was emotionally invested too. Zena expressed disgust and anger and a desire to take action to change her country.

Nora in Massachusetts also talked about her feelings regarding Trump, immigration, and racism. She said, "Not letting immigrants in, I feel like that is awful. It is racist because, like, a lot of people [in the United States] are from different places." She told me that the "whole point" of the US is that people from different countries of origin can belong. When I asked her how it makes her feel when she hears Trump say negative things about immigrants, she told me it made her "very mad" and made her want a new president who cared about "all the people."

Peyton, a ten-year old boy in Mississippi, also expressed anger and disgust toward Trump's leadership. Acting as if he was speaking directly to Trump, Peyton assertively stated, "Dude. You started this war with North Korea. You really need to, like, bring them a thing of chocolates or something instead of saying something offensive to them. . . . The best thing to say is probably not, 'I'm gonna nuke ya!'" Peyton also framed Trump's dealings with other governments around race. He told me that Trump is "definitely" racist and that Trump reveals this about himself when he talks about China, Elizabeth Warren and Pocahontas, Black athletes, and Muslim people. "I've just heard multiple quotes from him that were just very racist. It's horrible." Peyton let out a huge sigh and slumped back into the chair he was seated in. He looked not only angry but also a bit demoralized. "He is just *so* bad," he added.

Indeed, anger and disgust were very strong emotions expressed by this group of white children when discussing racism. One way of thinking about these emotions is to examine them on the individual level and view them as children's own personal disposition or political ideas. But, as I made clear in chapter 2, given patterns in these data, as well as evidence that these emotions are produced through interactions with teachers, parents, other people in Mississippi and Massachusetts, and so on demonstrates their social and relational quality. And, based on what these children shared, these racialized emotions played a foundational role in shaping their ideas about both race and politics.

Racialized Emotions and White Kids Rejecting Trump

The kids described in this chapter experienced a dramatic disruption to their sense of the world and to their strongly held belief that they lived in a country that was not racist or, at the very least, a country making solid racial progress. Their sense of the world was turned upside down by Trump's presidency, and the ideals they held were overtly challenged both at the macro level of national politics and also in their everyday lives as they encountered other kids and people in their community and even family members who were "stuck in the past." For these kids, this ideological vertigo was unpleasant to them. They did not like this sense of instability and uncertainty because it disrupted their epistemological sense of how the world worked. Certainly, one way that colorblind racial ideology is powerful is that it allows white people to maintain a sort of feigned ignorance or "comfortable complicity" about racial matters or what the sociologist Jennifer Mueller describes as a "process of knowing designed to produce not knowing surrounding white privilege and structural white supremacy."37 And certainly, when these ideologies are challenged or disrupted, this disrupts the comfort of white people, as they are presented with alternative possible understandings of how the world works. Perhaps how they saw things was not as accurate as they thought.

As such, colorblind thinking operates as a cognitive process in which the glaring racial inequalities in US society are distorted. But colorblind racism also serves an emotional purpose. As Bonilla-Silva explains, "domination itself produces both material *and emotional* well-being among members of the dominant race."38 That is, this group of white kids grew up experiencing a set of positive group-based emotions connected to colorblind thinking that excused them from having to feel anything whatsoever about racism or racial injustice. The frames of colorblindness that place racism in the past and that explain racial inequality as the result of individual people of color making bad decisions, for instance, protect white people from feeling any sort of guilt or responsibility or even a relationship to centuries of oppression. Mueller's research, for example, shows that even when white college students research their own family history of wealth and learn about the racial wealth gap and their own personal connection to the legacy of racism, these students avoid coming to terms with this through a set of cognitive maneuvers that reinforce colorblindness. These maneuvers also serve an emotional purpose: colorblind ideology protects white people's emotional well-being. It provides them with a false understanding of why inequality exists in the world that excuses them from even having to think about the suffering of others and that allows them to carry on living their lives comfortably and guilt-free, acting as if the world is fair and just—or at least fair and just enough for them not to have to worry about it.

For the kids in this chapter, though, the election of President Trump and his words and actions disrupted how they thought about racism *and also* how they felt. Specifically, their emotional well-being was unsettled. They were faced with feelings like anger, shock, disgust, shame, and even guilt that they had previously never felt, at least not with respect to racial matters at the scale of their national government. And these feelings did not go away quickly. Trump's election and presidency introduced for these children a shared feeling of disillusionment: "I can't believe I didn't know people were so racist in the US. If I was wrong about this, what else am I wrong about?" This disillusionment collapsed these children's well-established sense that the world is fair and just and caused them to call into question many assumptions they had about their country, about what democracy looks like, and about what they should do with their new feelings and knowledge. These emotional experiences, thus, led these children to produce racial ideas that they previously had not held.

Reconciling and Rejecting Colorblind Logic

The emotional well-being that comes with structural white advantage—or the ability to live in the world and not think that racism is a problem—was disrupted for the white children in this chapter when Trump was elected.39 They were faced with a new reality, a new way of seeing and feeling race in the US. But how they responded to this reality differed: some of these children, in response to this unsettled sense of the world, retreated back into colorblind thinking by articulating views such as, "Once Trump is gone, things will go back to normal." These kids believed that if everyone just stayed calm, soon this "terrible time" would pass. For these children, the discomfort they felt when confronted with the realities of race led to a retreat away from unsettling racialized emotions. However, other children felt so disillusioned that their anger and disgust motivated them to want to take action to work for social change, much like the sociologists Deborah Gould and Nadia Y. Kim have found in their respective books on how emotions can mobilize social movements.40 For this second group of kids, they were done with colorblind ideology and told me that they wanted to take actions to work against the forms of injustice that the Trump era revealed for them—injustice that extended far beyond the election of this one individual. After all, a lot of people voted for Trump and supported him, which to some kids was more shocking than the words that came out of Trump's mouth. These patterns are important, as they show not only the variation in how these white kids interpreted the future of race relations in the United States but also variation in what, if anything, they intended *to do* now that they were more fully aware of the racial injustice around them.

Reconciling Colorblind Logic

One child who sought out ways to reconcile conflicting messages about race was Nora. "Trump won't be in office forever. We will have, like, a new person in charge, which will be good," Nora told me. She explained that all the things Trump did, including the racist things Trump said that contributed to the white boys at her school acting in racist ways toward Black and Latinx kids, would one day disappear when Trump was no longer president. Nora acknowledged that a lot of people would be harmed over the next few years, including kids of color and of other marginalized statuses at her school, but she expressed confidence that all of this mess would go away in the future. Though Nora was disgusted that Trump was elected and recognized that many Americans voted for him, she was committed to her belief that the United States was not actually as racist as it seemed in this moment of Trump. Nora's hope for the future, thus, was that a set of circumstances would emerge in the years to come such that she could reinstate confidently her belief that racism was not part of US society—that the racism she identified during the time of Trump was an aberration.

Paige was very negative about the racism, sexism, and homophobia that she identified as increasing in her school because of Trump. And yet, like Nora, Paige told me that she also believed that after Trump was out of office, these kinds of behaviors at her school and in her community would become less common and less accepted. Paige did not think things would completely "go back to normal"—she was very clear that she thought Trump's actions would have a long-lasting impact on US society. But she did think that the kids at her school who felt emboldened by Trump would "chill out" and would stop being so awful once a new president was in office. Paige's anger seemed very much directed at Trump himself as an individual, and as such, she believed that a brighter future was ahead, especially if he did not get reelected. Though she was unwilling to suggest that racism itself would disappear along with Trump's presidency or that his influence would entirely die down—there was too much evidence around her in Mississippi of how many people supported Trump—she certainly hoped for a day when she could return to a sense of pride in her country instead of shame and embarrassment. She hoped for a day when kids at her school would not explicitly express their racism, even if racism persisted. In this sense, Paige hoped for some kind of a return to a time when she could believe that the country was not actually as racist as it appeared to be during the Trump era—a return to a time when she "didn't have to worry about all this stuff every single day." Paige's racialized emotions were not pleasant for her, and she did not enjoy navigating them. Instead, she wanted things to "go back to normal" as much as they possibly could and protect herself from having to feel these negative emotions.

Kids like Nora and Paige, as well as a number of other children who were disgusted by Trump, believed that ultimately, even though Trump brought out the racist individuals in US society, and even if the consequences of his presidency would be long lasting, these "bad" people would not prevail—that the "good," not racist people would vote in the next election and that in a few years, everyone could go back to not having to worry about racism. In chapter 5, I discuss another group of white children who told me that they loved Trump and did not care about him being racist. I identify their thinking as being a form of what the sociologist Tyrone Forman refers to as "racial apathy."41 And though the apathy of that group of kids is extremely evident, I also found evidence of racial apathy in this group of anti-Trump kids too, as well as a desire to retreat away from any feelings of discomfort, guilt, or shame about the racist reality of their country. Though the children in this chapter experienced extreme disillusionment, for some, their response was not a rejection of previous ways of thinking but rather a longing to return to that state.

While some of the white kids who felt uncomfortable about Trump's racism embraced a new ideological view about racism in the US and were motivated to take action to challenge racism, others did not respond in this way. Instead, another group of these kids retreated back to colorblind thinking. By doing so, this protected them not only from feeling uncomfortable about racism but also from feeling guilt or any sense of accountability. In this sense, it is not that they believed something that they knew was not true; instead, their retreat to colorblind ideology protected them from feeling things that they did not want to feel. How kids produce ideological positions about race, then, is connected not only to macro-level political dynamics but also to racialized emotional dynamics.

Though these children were in middle school, this pattern of "willfully reason[ing] colorblindness" is similar to what Mueller found with college students after they were presented with information about their own family's relationship to the racial wealth gap. Like the college students, simply learning about racism or seeing racism in a new light or even feeling angered by racism did not necessarily lead them to fundamentally shift their racial ideological perspective or, most importantly, their actions. Rather, at least for some of these kids, disillusionment and the emotions that came with that experience appeared to be temporary, as their emotional desire to return to a sense of racial comfort and emotional well-being ultimately prevailed. This desire to feel good about their country and their fellow white citizens and to believe that their country was not actually as racist as it appeared in the moment led these kids to creatively rework colorblind logic in ways (i.e., "soon things will go back to normal"; "this is not normal"; "this is just a bad guy in office") that ultimately served to reproduce colorblind logic to fit new social conditions.

Rejecting Colorblind Logic

Though some of these white children appeared to be in the process of finding ways to sustain their colorblind thinking, for others, the emotions of anger, disgust, and horror related to Trump's racism had a different effect on them. For these white kids, experiencing child-hood during this sociopolitical moment and experiencing a deep sense of disillusionment with their country and fellow white citizens motivated them to take action against racism, to get involved in political organizing, to seek out resources so they could learn more about the history of racism, and to do this work alongside their peers of color. These children were outliers in this sample—only three of them expressed these views. And interestingly, all of these children lived in Mississippi.

Zach, Zena, and Peyton all told me that Trump being in office made them want to learn more about the history of racism in the US, to make changes in their schools so that other kids would learn more too, and to become involved in politics in some way, either now or in the future. Zena especially recognized the importance of the macro, structural level of law and policy as a place where social change emerges:

> I think that we're 100 percent not past racism. I think that, like, es-pecially with, like, um, everything you see on the news with, like, the police, . . . like, with white cops shooting African American people and not having reasons other than them being Black or African American people getting, like, sentences in prison that a white per-son would just have to do community service for, . . . I feel like I've had this realization that, you know, like, we're not past this racism because there are people who are standing at the door saying we can't pass this change—the people who sit in the big chairs and say, "No, I don't want that law passed." It's just—it's a problem because people have the power [to create change], and they use it for the wrong reasons, . . . and that sucks. We need new people in power.

Zena talked with me about how she thought racial representa-tion was really important and that more Black people needed to be elected to leadership positions, especially in Mississippi. But she also told me that she thought more white people who care about inequality also need to become more active on the political level. After our interview, she chatted more casually with me about her own aspirations and hopes for the future. She mentioned that her mom was involved in local politics and that she found herself as a kid considering whether she should follow in her mom's footsteps. She talked about needing to think more about how she could strategically use her position as a white person in Mississippi to help pass the kinds of policies she believed were necessary to deal with discrimination, racism, and specifically, voter disenfranchisement. "Maybe I should try to sit in a big chair one day?" she posed to me. For Zena, growing up in the era of Trump meant that she not only saw the country in new ways but also felt a sense of responsibility to her country—and to the ideals she says she holds—in new ways. Importantly, she imagined herself acting differently in the world in community with others—not just talking a big game and performing to other white people how antiracist she was, a common problem she identified among some of her peers. Overall, feelings of anger and disillusionment about colorblind ideology led Zena to reject this way of thinking altogether and instead to think in new ways about what was needed in US society if the nation were ever actually to become a land of equal opportunity, justice, and freedom.

Zach also articulated his newfound understanding of what needed to change in the world around him. He told me that he knew he needed to learn a lot more about racism. He told me that growing up during this time made him realize the importance of being able to think for oneself, analyze news stories critically, confidently argue one's position, "take a stand" on important issues, and "learn more about history." He also told me how important he thought it was to travel and "see how other countries do things," an experience he had the opportunity to do quite frequently, as his parents frequently traveled internationally with him. Zach outright rejected the idea of US exceptionalism and was frankly "fed up with" US politics under the leadership of Trump. Like Zena, his reactions were directly tied to his emotional and ideological interpretations of what was happening at the macro level of society and how these things mattered in his local community, particularly with respect to racism among kids. "Discrimination happens here, and we need to do something to stop that!" he told me, emphasizing that the actions at the level of national politics were not some distant and unrelated phenomenon but something that shaped factors at the very micro level, including how people in his community interacted with one another. Though Zach did not explicitly state his interest in going into politics, he did highlight his belief that actions must be taken to create change—that simply going along with the status quo will not lead to the kinds of social changes he believed were necessary in the United States.

Finally, Peyton also demonstrated a strong commitment to his rejection of colorblind logic. For Peyton, the disgust he felt about racism was directed toward other kids at his school as much as it was directed at Trump. Peyton told me that some of the older, popular white girls at his public school whom he used to try "really hard" to be friends with had been saying and doing racist things ever since Trump took office. As he explained, "I don't like the whole racist thing. Those girls sound like monsters, like white supremacist people back in the fifties. . . . Those girls are going to lose friends and probably regret what they are doing later." Peyton told me he wants all the kids at his school to get along but that these girls were causing major problems, especially given that the majority of the kids and adults at his school are Black. He told me he had stopped talking to them because he cannot be friends with people like that, even though he places a lot of value in being popular himself. Though it may seem like a small move to adults, for Peyton, this decision was big for him as he navigated the social hierarchies at his school. Though Peyton decided to reject the girls' racism even if it cost him popularity points, he also told me he generally feels pretty hopeless about other things he can do in this moment that will reflect his ideals and lead to the kinds of changes he wants to see. "What I have learned is that Americans do a lot of racist stuff." He then mumbled something under his breath that I had to ask him to repeat. He sighed deeply with a depressed look on his face and hesitated. Finally, he responded, "We are horrible people—in many ways. I mean, we kill manatees. I like manatees. It's just all unacceptable." Peyton told me he wanted to change a lot of things in the world—everything from racist policies and practices to issues related to his concerns about the environment to the large number of impoverished people in Mississippi to the rights of manatees not to be mangled by selfish humans. He told me that he felt pretty demoralized when he thought about all of these social problems at once, and he was not entirely sure what he could do as a kid to try to make these changes happen. "I mean, I can't even vote," he told me. "I will as soon as I can. But for now, what can I do?"

Peyton's emotional expressions were those of anger, sadness, hopelessness, and frustration. These emotions were racialized emotions, produced as a result of his social interactions with peers and in relation to the broader racial structure of US society. As a result of how he felt, he was absolutely unwilling to reconcile colorblind logic in a way that would allow him to regain any sort of comfort or emotional well-being. Instead, he was disgusted by the things he saw around him, and he told me that white people like Trump but also white people like the popular girls at school were one major source of these problems. To Peyton, this had to change somehow, even if he was not yet sure what he could do, other than arguing with or, in his words, "going for people" on the school bus when they said racist things or refusing to be friends with white kids who acted in racist ways.

Will Colorblind Ideology Prevail?

As a result of what they viewed as racism in the national political landscape, Zena, Zach, and Peyton were all white kids who produced a set of emotions tied to a new recognition of the racialized nature of US society. Because these kids felt race in this new way, they embraced a new and alternative racial ideological position. They believed that racism is more than an individual-level problem or even a problem tied to one racist individual in a powerful position. They told me that things would not go back to how they used to be once Trump was out of office. In fact, Zena told me that she has now learned that things "should not go back" to "how things were" because "how things were" was also bad. Instead, these children all cited the macro level of electoral politics, political leadership and rhetoric, and law as important features of racism today—and as features that shape their own lived experiences at the micro level, like interactions they have on the school bus.

These examples are important theoretically because they demonstrate that growing up during the Trump era shaped kids' racial learning. Specifically, the political landscape informed how they felt about race, which shaped their ideas. These new feelings led them to think ideologically about racism in new ways and encouraged acts of resistance in the future. Kids can reject dominant ideological views as they interpret and try to make sense of the everyday world around them. But this is challenging for kids to do, especially as dominant ways of feeling race and thinking about race surround them constantly and are reinforced persistently in everyday life. This is probably why cases of kids rejecting colorblind logic altogether and maintaining this perspective as they thought ahead into the future were few and far between in this research.

More commonly, I observed these white kids express horror, disgust, and anger related to Trump but then work to reestablish colorblind thinking as they looked ahead to the future. Even children whose worlds were turned entirely around—kids who were angry and disgusted by their elected leader and many of their fellow citizens and who saw the US in an entirely new light as a result—seemed to prefer to return to the comfortable complicity that comes with colorblind logic. In this sense, it is very likely that colorblind logic, though cracked open a bit during the Trump era, will be repaired and ultimately prevail as a dominant way of making sense of racism in the US.

And yet, for a few of these white children, dynamics at the macro level of US society, involving Trump, laws, policies, public debates, public outrage, current events, and so on, profoundly shaped their sense of who they are, their interpretations of the problems the country faces, and their ideas about what they need to do about it as a white person. For these kids, colorblind ideology simply no longer made sense—it did not explain the world as they saw it or how they felt it.

As Bonilla-Silva argues, "the constant retooling of the racial self usually produces more of the same, but it also creates the space for rupturing racialized habits."42 The white children in this chapter powerfully illustrate his point—both the kids reproducing more of the same and the kids who cannot forget or unsee what this moment of growing up in the Trump era has taught them about the reality of white supremacy in the US. Overall, these kids illustrate that despite the continued dominance of colorblind logic, other ways of making sense of racism in the US also exist.43 And it seems that racialized emotions are what guided Zena, Zach, and Peyton to these other ways of understanding racism.

4

"He Likes the People with the Lighter Skin Better . . . and That's Not Me"

Racial Fear and Solidarity

"Trump does some bad things!" ten-year-old Kenny, a Black child growing up in Mississippi, told me one afternoon. "Trump talks about racist things, . . . and he does racist things! He puts inappropriate things on Twitter. Like, people won't admit it, but saying, 'I'm going to build a wall from Mexico,' and saying bad things about Mexicans is racist, and [people] won't admit it!" Kenny paused, looked down to the ground, and shook his head with disbelief and disgust. "To me, that's something." He reflected a bit longer before he looked straight at me and said, "You know, when Barack Obama was the president, I wasn't thinking about politics. I didn't really talk about Barack Obama because there's nothing to talk about! He didn't do anything bad. He didn't start anything. So, I mean, when he was president, I didn't get into politics because I didn't have to, because he was a good president." We talked some more, and as the interview ended, I asked Kenny what he believed was a major problem in US society right now. Without hesitation, he confidently stated, "Racism. Racism is one of the main things that this country has always had problems with. And I'm scared Trump will make that worse."

* * *

The racial and political climate of the Trump era had devastating consequences for children of color.1 We know from existing research that these consequences included negative childhood mental health outcomes, deprivation of resources, stigmatization, trauma and stress, and increases in hateful speech and behaviors of children in schools across the nation.2 But we know less about how kids actually felt and how they made sense of the political and racial landscape that defined this time in their childhood. This chapter highlights the perspectives and reported feelings of kids of color growing up during this time in the two communities studied. In Mississippi, the children interviewed identified as Black or "a mix," while in Massachusetts, the kids classified themselves as being either Black, Cape Verdean, biracial, "a mix," brown, Hispanic, and/or Mexican American.3 These demographics reflect those of the two communities studied.

Overall, patterns in this interview data illustrate that most of the children of color expressed racialized emotions of *fear and anxiety.* As this chapter explores, the fear experienced by these kids was connected both to macro-level dynamics, such as Trump's encouragement of anti-immigrant and anti-Black rhetoric and actions, and micro- and interactional-level dynamics, such as kids experiencing racist violence from their white peers who felt emboldened by the election of Trump or witnessing family members encounter racist white people in daily life.

Patterns in this research also highlight the righteous *anger* experienced by this group of children and how this anger functioned in their lives, including how it provided them with a sense of *agency.* Unlike racist stereotypes of "angry" Black people that serve to delegitimize emotional responses to racist violence or teachers who accuse Black youth of being "inappropriately" angry and in need of punishment and control, the data presented here show the thoughts and feelings of kids in response to being the target of explicit acts of racism tied to Donald Trump's presidency by their white peers. These children's racialized emotions connected to anger were at times useful to them, as it brought a sense of group solidarity with other people of color that kids drew on for hope and motivation to work for change.

This sense of agency led these children to seek out more information about aspects of the macro-level dynamics, such as Kenny deciding to start paying attention to and learning more about politics. But this sense of membership in a larger group also appeared to increase the confidence these kids needed to confront racist peers at school and generally feel connected to larger social movements for racial justice. To be clear, I am not suggesting that the Trump era brought an increase in the emotional well-being of kids of color—certainly these children experienced enormous emotional and psychological trauma that should not be ignored or minimized. However, from what these kids expressed, their racialized emotions—and how they felt about their own sense of agency and freewill—are indeed complex and include more than trauma alone. These children's racialized group-level emotions reflected both trauma and also a "potential" or, as bell hooks writes, a "passion for freedom and justice" that can make "redemptive struggle possible."4

Overall, while many social scientists across disciplines have developed a wide range of theories of childhood emotions, this chapter focuses narrowly on the impact that the racialized sociopolitical sphere in US society has on how kids of color think and feel about racism in the US. This chapter explores the positive and negative racialized emotions experienced by this group of children and argues that these racialized emotions—expressed by kids *in their own words*—are an important part of racial learning processes for children across racial groups. Finally, kids of color are some of the best experts on the racism of white kids. Listening to this group of children share their experiences, feelings, and thoughts about their white peers not only offers insight into how kids of color understand racism in everyday life but also reveals more about the racism of white kids and what kinds of ideas and feelings white children have about race, what they do with these ideas and feelings, and the harm that results.

Perceptions of Trump

The kids discussed in this chapter did not like Trump. They thought he was a racist individual with a great deal of institutional power who threatened them and their families every single day he was in office. For example, thirteen-year-old Alexis, a child in Massachusetts who identified as "biracial or mixed," stated, "I think, um, he was dropped." When I asked her what she meant, she replied matter-of-factly, "He was dropped as a child." "I just think that he's really not fit for the presidency, and I don't think he understands what he needs to accomplish and how many lives he's ruining." Juliana, a Black child, shared a similar perspective. "I don't like him," she told me assertively. "He is doing a terrible job, and I want Obama to come back." Juliana also told me that she believed "Trump is racist" and that he only cares about people who are white like him. "He is an example for people of how to be crazy," she continued, explaining that to her, his terrible, racist, crazy behavior was an invitation for others to behave similarly. "He should *not* be the president," she added emphatically.

This group of children also viewed their own perspectives on Trump as aligned with that of their larger racial group, and they spoke about this often. Ria, an eleven-year-old Black child in Mississippi, said that she did not like Trump personally and that she thought that "most of the Black people" she knew also did not like him. Instead, she explained, it was the white kids at school whose parents voted for Trump. In her words, "I know that, like, at my school, more of the, like, white kids' parents voted for Donald Trump." She expressed that she wished Obama was still in office because, as she explained, "I *know* that he was less racist than Donald Trump is!"

Similarly, Mariana, a ten-year old in Massachusetts who described herself as Mexican American, told me that she "really did not like Trump." I asked her why she felt this way. She replied, "Well, he's trying to kick, like, all Hispanic people out [of the United States], but actually his wife is an immigrant and his mother was too. So, like, I don't get why he's trying to kick us out. I don't get why he's trying to kick us out if his family is one too, so . . ." She trailed off, demonstrating that she believed his logic was inconsistent. Mariana's use of the word "us" reflected her own identification with a group attacked by Trump, which illustrates powerfully how the emotions that she felt were connected to her sense of her own racial/ethnic group membership.

Mariana also added her disgust with Trump's behavior toward women. "He made, like, girls do something bad. . . . He sexually assaulted somebody and stuff." For this ten-year-old, the president of the United States was someone who threatened her not only on the basis of race and ethnicity but also on the basis of gender. Indeed, many of these children told me about their horror with respect to how Trump treats women. As Devion succinctly put it, and as described in chapter 2, "He has said racist things. He has abused women. I don't think that's right for anybody to do, especially not the president!"

Overall, not one of the children of color interviewed in this research approved of Trump or believed he was acting in the interests of people like them. Instead, these children shared how over and over Trump made them feel threatened and fearful. And this was primarily due to their identity as a member of a racial group that was not white. As twelve-year old Monique poignantly put it, "He likes the people with the lighter skin better . . . and that's not me."

Feeling Race

Children perceive of race and *feel race* before they even have a full explanation of what it is or how it works in society. As discussed throughout this book, racialized emotions are experienced by all racial actors, although the seriousness with which these emotions are considered in society is organized hierarchically, with the dominant group's racialized emotions normalized and more highly valued.5 For instance, despite the long history of textbooks and lesson plans designed to fit a nation-building narrative that forgets the white supremacist past and erases atrocities that continue to shape how our society is organized and functions today, many conservative pundits and politicians worry that schools spend too much time teaching about racism. These debates about whether kids should learn the history of racism in public schools often center the feelings of white kids (or their parents) while avoiding thinking about how kids of color feel (and have long felt) when the history of racism in the US is routinely ignored and systematically altered.6

Indeed, racialized emotions are a key part of how young kids of color start to form their interpretations of the social world, of hierarchies, and of power. It is for these reasons that parents raising children of color often think so carefully about how to engage in racial socialization practices within the private realm of the family—how to prepare their children to encounter a fundamentally racist world while still maintaining a confident sense of self, pride in who one is, and positive mental health and well-being.7 For instance, as the sociologist Dawn Marie Dow discusses in her book *Mothering While Black*, the middle-class and upper-middle-class Black mothers she interviewed described teaching their Black children emotion-management and image-management strategies in order to help their kids express themselves in ways that would "ensure they were treated well." As one mother told her, "I talk to [my son] constantly. . . . If the police ever pull you over, how do you need to react? So, we do scenarios for all of that; it's just prepping for life." As Dow argues, "The societal institutions that are often viewed as resources for middle- and upper-middle-class white families were instead viewed with some level of circumspection and fear by the mothers in this research. The labor these mothers engaged in for their sons and daughters *to feel* confident, safe, and valued is largely rendered invisible to the broader white society."8 As Dow and other scholars studying racial socialization in Black families document, many parents raising Black kids consider and even anticipate the racialized emotions of their children as they communicate with them about race and racism. These parents think strategically about how to help their children navigate their racialized emotions, particularly as they encounter authority figures such as police officers, teachers, doctors, and so on.

In addition to family-based research, recent research within the sociology of education helps make visible how racism shapes not only the academic experiences of kids of color but also their racialized *emotional* experiences.9 In the sociologist Eve Ewing's exploration of what happens when the city of Chicago closes public schools in the historically Black neighborhood of Bronzeville, she finds that school closures here are a "devastating event that leaves an indelible emotional aftermath" for the Black community.10 She documents how these school closures are linked to a long history of racism in Chicago and how integral these schools are to the Bronzeville community. She documents how hard people fight to keep the schools open as well as how these closures result in "great harm to black children—regardless of intent."11 Though not framed or theorized explicitly as examples of racialized emotions, Ewing's interviews with community members reveal that their emotions of grief, sorrow, and "institutional mourning" are part of a "collective phenomenon" and are "transacted between actors who are already shaped by social relationships and history."12 In many ways, these reactions can be understood as racialized emotions.

Ethnographers have also studied the messages about race that kids receive in classrooms and schoolyards. For instance, in the sociologist Amanda Lewis's rich ethnographic account of three elementary schools, she captures moments in which teachers mock kids for responding in Spanish instead of English by making comments to students like, "Look, Becky, you're in America now, let's use English, not that Spanish stuff."13 It is unsurprising, then, when some of the Latinx children in her research expressed shame about Spanish being their first language. Throughout *Race in the Schoolyard*, as well as many other school-based ethnographies about kids and racism, Lewis documents the way children express emotions related to their experiences of encountering and interpreting racist ideas at their schools.14

Like family-based research, school-based research offers rich evidence that racialized emotions of kids of color exist and shape their sense of the world. And yet, scholars have done less work to directly incorporate kids' racialized emotions into theories of racial learning, particularly with a focus on how this learning is connected to the larger macro-level sociopolitical climate. As a result, more could be learned about how children of color in the US *feel* race. In particular, more could be learned about how these kids feel race in connection to the geographical and political contexts that define their childhood.

What I can show based on interviews with the children in this study is that racialized emotions and "feeling race" are key components of racial learning processes—and that the development of these racialized emotions cannot be adequately understood without accounting for the political and racial landscape defining the context of kids' childhoods. A child's racial context of childhood includes more than just where they live and spend their time. It includes more than their family and friends and peers and media. A child's racial context also includes the political moment in which they experience childhood. And racial learning includes how kids feel race, or the racialized emotions they experience, in response to the racialized context in which they come of age.

"I Am Scared": Racialized Emotion of Fear

Most of the children of color with whom I spoke expressed fear with respect to the election of Trump—but this fear was connected to their larger sense of living in a racist country. These fears manifested themselves in different ways, but for all of these kids, their ideas about race and their racialized emotions were connected to the political realm of society. Some kids were worried Trump would make them fight in a war or leave the country due to their racial or ethnic identity. Others were concerned that Trump being in power would lead white police officers to shoot even more Black people. And still others were worried about how people standing up against racial injustice would be treated by the Trump administration, like Colin Kaepernick kneeling in protest of racism at NFL games. Finally, other kids were scared that their family members would be deported while they were at school, never to be seen again. Across the board, nearly all of the kids interviewed in both Mississippi and Massachusetts expressed a group-level racialized emotion of fear connected to racism and politically induced stress that they identified with the Trump administration. Trump's election and presidency created a sense of emotional racial distress and racial trauma for this set of kids—and this stress and trauma were experienced at a group level in addition to an individual one.

For instance, in Mississippi, twelve-year-old Marcus, who is Black, talked in very concrete terms about two specific reasons he was scared when Trump won the election. "It was bad when he won because [Trump] wants to send us back to where we came from." By this, Marcus meant that because he is Black, he believed Trump may try to make him leave the United States and send him and his family and anyone else who was part of his racial group "back to Africa." "But," Marcus continued, "he doesn't have enough power to [do that] 'cause the Supreme Court would shut him down." Marcus seemed relatively convinced by this argument but still concerned. Marcus also had a second fear:

> They said it might be a World War III against North Korea, and then like some people, like me—like, I asked my stepdad one day about the draft. And I asked him if we are going to have enough people to fight against North Korea. Will I have to go [to fight] even though I'm, like, twelve? And he said no 'cause, like, I'm the only son that my dad has, and I'd be the last to get picked, and then he said Donald Trump is just saying all of this stuff on social media and not to worry.

Marcus explained in a concerned tone that he continues to worry that he himself, as a twelve-year-old, will be drafted and have to go fight in a war of a president who thinks Marcus is not a real American because he is Black.15 The fear of violence experienced by these children took both the form of racial violence in their communities and also the fear of another large-scale international war that would involve them.

Twelve-year-old Keshunna, also a Black child growing up in Mississippi, believed that Trump was racist and, like Marcus, was worried that Trump might "send us back to Africa." She said she was concerned about Trump not only because of what he said but also because of "his actions." Keshunna brought up Trump's border wall and things he said about Mexicans as an example of his racist actions and words. She added, "He's definitely wanted to put a travel ban, so not allowing people to fly, um, if they were Muslim or from those countries. . . . I feel like he just needs to quit!" Keshunna shared that she longed for the days when Obama was in office, not because she was particularly interested in politics or current political events but because Obama made her feel "normal," whereas Trump makes her feel "worried" and anxious. Obama did not talk badly about entire groups of people, she said, and "he didn't talk like Donald Trump do now! [Obama] didn't talk all that." Keshunna's expressions illustrated not only that she believed that racism was flourishing in the US due to Trump being in office but also that she felt a sense of fear, a sense that things are not normal, a sense that something could go very wrong at any moment. And this uncertainty was emotionally unsettling to her. Keshunna also recognized her own vulnerability as linked to that of members of other marginalized groups, such as Mexicans and Muslims, and expressed a form of solidarity with all of those targeted by Trump's exclusionary words and actions.16

Many of the Black children interviewed also spoke explicitly about police officers shooting and killing Black people, including other Black kids. For twelve-year-old Maya, she explained that when Trump was elected, many of her Black friends at school "felt dead inside." Like Kenny, Maya said that when Obama was president, she did not really have to worry very much because "he really wasn't that crazy and stupid like Trump." Obama did not "start with North Korea's president" and put the country at risk of another war, which was also a concern of hers. Maya explained that when Trump was elected, her parents talked with her about it and asked her if she had any questions or worries. When she told them her concerns, they told her not to worry about him or even think about him. As a result, she explained, "I really don't pay attention to Trump. I keep forgetting that he be in office!"

However, the thing Maya said she was most fearful about was herself or someone she loved who was also Black being shot by a police officer. She said that unlike her worries related to Trump, which she could find ways to ignore, she could not ignore this fear. It was too scary. Maya explained that gun violence, including community gun violence that did not involve police officers, was the "biggest problem" facing the US today. She mentioned a number of different shootings that had happened nationally and locally, especially those involving Black people and the police. Another twelve-year old, Brit, shared a similar perspective: "I know there will just be a bunch of stuff dealing with the police chasing [people in] cars and stuff, and then [the Black person] will get out, and they'll be unarmed, and then police will start shooting at them. And then when it comes time to go to court, the police officers change the story up to make them[selves] seem innocent." Both Maya and Brit talked about this pattern of police violence in racial terms—it was not their view that the police were engaging in this practice across the board. Rather, these girls talked about how Black people were specifically targeted and murdered by the police.

Black boys in this research also shared similar concerns, and these worries were very much linked to their identity as specifically young Black boys. Kenny explained his point of view:

I have heard stories about Black youth getting shot by police officers and people figuring out that they got shot by a police officer three years later. . . . They don't like us wearing hoods in school because they think we're not listening. But they're scared of the story about a Black kid . . . who was wearing his hood walking and the security guard called the police saying, "I see this suspicious Black kid walking around," and [the police] were like, "Just leave him alone." And then the armed security guard dude followed him and ended up shooting him because he thought he was a suspicious character but he had no weapons. So . . .

I asked Kenny how he felt when he heard stories like this. He responded, "It makes me feel like this is probably the worst country. Just the way people look at North Korea and say, 'Oh, North Korea is so bad because they have, like, uh, a dictator.' . . . But we kill our own people because of their skin color and the way they look! If that would've been a white kid walking with a hoodie on, he would have not been shot!" Although violence against Black people and communities has been a problem in US society for hundreds of years, these kids overwhelmingly interpreted the violence—and protests against it—in the Trump moment as more intense and more common than during the Obama years. These children made this argument on the basis of Trump's hateful rhetoric and his supporters' explicit denunciation and humiliation of people like Colin Kaepernick or Black Lives Matter leaders speaking out against racism. As Kenny said, "These athletes kneel because they think that Black men should have more rights than they do and they shouldn't just be getting killed in the street by police officers who think they are suspicious, even though they don't have any armed weapons on them." Kenny explained his thoughts on the protests and said that while he approved of them, he was not so sure he would be brave enough to participate. "Even though I think they should do that, it's not something that I would do. I don't think it's a good idea to do that, especially in this kind of community." When I asked him what he meant by that, he talked about the community context of Mississippi but also the political context. He mentioned the white supremacists in Charlottesville, Virginia, and the protester who died. "This is a scary time," he told me.

Keshunna agreed. As she explained, "I heard about a man. He got shot—a Black man got shot for no reason. . . . It makes me feel like the police officer—they're racists! Because if you shoot some-body that's Black for no reason, then you're racist." Like Kenny, Keshunna identified the racism of the police as connected to Trump, particularly given Trump's explicit hate toward the Black Lives Matter movement altogether. "I know that a man in St. Louis, he went to jail for protesting [and holding] the signs saying, 'Black Lives Matter,'" Keshunna said. She explained that Trump and people who supported him did not like people protesting against racism: "Trump hates them." And as a handful of children said, each in their own way, from their vantage points, Trump does not value the lives of Black people. And this was very scary since they are Black people.

Kids interviewed who identified as Hispanic, Mexican American, or "a mix" also expressed fears about Trump and his supporters. For these kids, though, their fears were primarily connected with the hateful anti-immigrant rhetoric they heard from the presi-dent, which was then repeated in their schools and communities by white children they had to see every day. This group of young people said they were certainly scared about other kids at school and tried to avoid them but that most of all, they were fearful about law enforcement, particularly immigration enforcement officers. For instance, Mariana shared the following with me: "When Trump got elected, I was actually kind of nervous. My dad isn't a citizen. If [Trump] sends him back, he's not going to be able to come back, and I won't be able to see him. . . . Like, like [one time recently], we were just driving and the police were behind us, and I got scared because if he were to get pulled over, they would arrest him, and they'll send him back. I am scared." She told me that the fear she felt was constant and every day—she told me that every morning when she left for school, she worried about whether her dad would be there when she got home. I decided to end this part of the interview early because Mariana was so upset and on the verge of tears, and I did not believe it was ethical to continue asking her about this trauma. Sociologists like Joanna Dreby and Roberto Gonzales have studied this issue at length, finding that Mariana's experience is similar to that of many other youths across the country.17 This is particularly true for kids living in areas within close proximity to immigration raids. For instance, sociologists found that children's mental health suffered tremendously following the 2019 raids of chicken-processing plants in Mississippi by immigration enforcement officers—raids that happened, incidentally, on the first day of the new school year, meaning that kids returned home from school to find their parents gone, as discussed in chapter 1.18 Although statistically the Obama administration deported more immigrants than the Trump administration did, the popularization of anti-immigrant rhetoric during the Trump years seemed to enhance the fear felt by the kids in this study who identified as either Latinx or immigrants. The outrageous things the president said about Mexicans, for example, were heard by children themselves, which impacted their racialized emotions and, in particular, heightened their sense of fear. Popular political rhetoric thus seemed to shape these children's racialized emotions and, in turn, how they interpreted what was happening in this moment with respect to racism, politics, and specifically, deportation efforts.

The fear that the children expressed was directly related to their own identity as members of particular racial or ethnic groups. Similar to what the sociologist Nilda Flores-Gonzáles finds in her book *Citizens but Not Americans: Race and Belonging among Latino Millennials*, these children's sense of belonging in US society was challenged by the continuous racist rhetoric and acts of a president and his supporters who did not see these kids as "real Americans."19 Growing up in a country where they did not feel that the leader valued their existence, or even viewed them as full citizens, speaks volumes to the racial trauma experienced on a regular basis by kids of color in the United States. These children's perspectives also reflect larger processes of the long-standing historically rooted racialization of kids of color that deems them less important, less valued, less innocent, less intelligent, less in need of protection, and even less in need of pain medication than white kids are.20

Indeed, the fear experienced by kids of color in the United States is part of what Bonilla-Silva refers to as "feeling race."21 The kids in this research absolutely felt race. But the fear that they felt was not only an individual-level phenomenon. Instead, these expressions of fear were group-based and relational. They were experiencing "racialized emotions" in connection with Trump being elected to the presidency. And these racialized emotions shaped how they interpreted the social world around them and how they believed (or not) that they could act in that world. As James Baldwin wrote, "Long before the Negro child perceives this difference [socially imposed white superiority and Black inferiority], and even longer before he understands it, he has begun to react to it, he has begun to be controlled by it."22

"Bullying" or White Kids' Racism?

While Aiden, a ten-year-old white boy, told me that he had to ignore "disrespectful" kids at school the day after the election because "they were saying mean things about [Trump]" and claiming that the president was "racist," it was impossible for eleven-year-old Devion to ignore the white kids at his Massachusetts school whom he viewed as "disrespectful." But the two forms of disrespect are not identical. For Aiden, "disrespect" meant hearing accusations of the president being "racist." But for Devion, "disrespect" referred to the fear of verbal and physical assault on his own person. He told me a story about a boy in his class who stabbed him: "I was just *fully ashamed* by this kid 'cause he was saying some racist stuff after

Trump won, and that was the kid that has [previously] said racist stuff to me. . . . I know what it is like to feel pain because that kid stabbed me in the back about two or three inches with a sharpened pencil." Devion was particularly mad because the other kid was not suspended, even though he used racial slurs and stabbed Devion with a pencil. Instead, Devion was forced to stay home for a week. He told me that the teacher blamed him for antagonizing the white boy. From Devion's perspective, this conflict was not just a typical example of kids getting into spats at school. He told me that it had everything to do with racism. With tears forming in his eyes, Devion told me how he felt that day after the election: "Trump said stuff about Mexico, and he's basically just racial-profiling people! . . . And people have been joining him! I've heard some things on the news, and what he says isn't right!" Devion then shared another story with me about white kids at his school shouting "Build the wall!" and harassing Latinx kids at recess. "I honestly think that it's crazy that kids would say that. But they do. It makes me so mad." Devion told me that he believed the election of Trump emboldened the already-racist kids at his school and that things were only going to get worse as these children enforced and reproduced existing forms of social inequality.

Dominick, who identified as Black and Cape Verdean, also shared a similar story with me about the behavior of his white peers in the aftermath of the election of Trump: "Right after the election, in school this girl said that everybody who—so we were at gym—and she said to everybody that was Black, 'You're a slave 'cause you're Black.' . . . Nothing happened to her. . . . I did not feel good then." I asked Dominick why he thought none of the other white kids or the white teachers said anything to the white girl. "They don't care!" he said with an angry tone. "It's really bad. We have racist bullies in our school, but [the adults] don't do anything." Like Devion, Dominick told me that although this type of behavior had happened before Trump was elected, he felt that now that Trump was in office, his white peers felt like they could "get away with this" behavior and that they had permission to say and do explicitly racist things and face no consequences.

These two boys, as well as many of the other kids interviewed, used the word "bully" to describe the language and behaviors of their white peers. Certainly, in school-based contexts, the concept of "bullying" is commonly discussed, with many antibullying programs in place that focus on reducing individual-level behaviors that lead to hurt feelings. But much of this discussion about bullying focuses on individual behaviors and how "anyone can be bullied for anything."23 However, for these children of color, the peers they identified as bullies were described specifically as "racist" white kids. That is, the behavior of these peers was linked directly to group positions within a racial hierarchy. Evidence of this kind of racist bullying is not just found in my own research. In a recent volume focused on how racist rhetoric impacts education, John Rogers and Michael Ishimoto discuss politically induced emotions and stress in high schools during the era of Trump:

> Students frequently made outlandish or mean-spirited claims, particularly in relationship to social class, race, or gender. [Teachers interviewed stated] that teenagers "will make comments just to shock, they'll make comments just to make someone angry." But [they] experienced the 2016–2017 school year as fundamentally different. [One teacher] noted: "I had never seen behavior this brash. . . . I saw this dynamic happening on the national level and was amazed to see such a mirror of the same thing with [my students]. . . . [They were] just flat out hostile to each other."24

While these behaviors were not new, clearly these teachers, like the kids in my research, identified the macro-level political moment as contributing to an increase in these behaviors, and particularly racist behaviors, in school environments. Education researchers use the term "racialized bullying" to get at how these kinds of behaviors "compound the stress and trauma communities of color experience from racism outside of schools and create toxic climates in classrooms and schools," as well as how experiencing this kind of bullying "threatens to silence the voices of students of color and to embolden authoritarian and antidemocratic sensibilities of the victimizers."25

Moving away from the idea that bullying is simply one person deliberately hurting another person's feelings, the sociologist C. J. Pascoe argues for a more sociological analysis of these peer dynamics, including the recognition that young people actively participate in the reproduction of inequality through engaging in these behaviors. But "these interactions also shouldn't be understood as the sole province of young people." Instead, she argues that "shifting the discussion in this way would place social forces, institutionalized inequality and cultural norms that reproduce inequality at the center of the discussion." Taking this discussion even further, Pascoe argues, "Our culture-wide discussion of bullying needs to shift focus from individual behavior to the aggressive interaction itself. It also needs to attend to the social contexts in which bullying occurs as well as ask questions about meanings produced by such interactions."26 In other words, rather than writing off behaviors like a white boy stabbing a Black boy with a pencil or the use of racist slurs as simply "bullying" behavior, we ought to recognize how these behaviors are informed by and reproduce broader unequal structural arrangements in our society.

Kenny and I talked about this distinction between "bullying" and white kids' racist behaviors. I asked him if he had heard anyone at his school chant "Build the wall" at recess or on the school bus, as some of the white kids described to me. I wondered if white kids were engaging in these behaviors around their Black peers or only in spaces with other white kids. And were Black kids participating in this anti-Mexican and anti-immigrant rhetoric? Kenny told me with a very serious tone, "We don't play around about that," implying that the Black kids at his school definitely do not engage in this behavior. He went on to tell me that while he could see how some kids might think it is funny to listen to someone imitate Trump's voice and speech patterns in a mocking way, there really was not much else to laugh about. "Really, it's kind of serious that he's going to build a wall. . . . Some kids say that he should build a wall because they think that Mexico should be kept out of our borders even though they're one of our allies 'cause they're connected." Kenny told me that while some of the white kids at his school thought chanting "Build the wall" was funny, he certainly did not—and when he heard kids doing this, he told them to stop. "It's not right," he told me. Like many other children discussed in this chapter, Kenny saw his own experiences as linked to those of other racial groups who also faced racism.27 And likewise, kids like Mariana identified Black children as targets of law enforcement too—not for immigration enforcement purposes but still for racist reasons nonetheless.

Racist Interactions in Neighborhoods and Communities

Racist behavior of white kids is not found exclusively in school contexts. Kenny told me about his experiences with racist white kids in his school but also in his Mississippi neighborhood: "There's some kids who like Trump, . . . like my neighbor, actually. He, um, just goes around—he says stuff that's not smart. He says that Black people can't marry white people, and he says a lot of stuff that's not really good. But he has an aunt that married a Black person! He just says stupid stuff." Kenny then told me a story about how this white child blamed Kenny's brother, who is Black, for an accident that happened in the backyard when the kids were playing: "This kid told everybody in the neighborhood that my brother hit his brother in the eye. But everybody knew [this kid] did it. The parents knew he did it. They just didn't want to admit it. Then, when the brother [who got hit], when he woke up [the next day], he said his brother did it and not my brother. But the parents still said that he didn't do it." Kenny gave more detail about this incident and expressed how angry he was that this neighborhood kid would blame his brother for something stupid that he did. Kenny also expressed his disgust at the parents of this white child for refusing to hold their own son accountable for his behavior, both that day of the accident and also in general, like when this kid said racist things to the Black kids in his neighborhood. "That kid is eight years old. He's only eight!" Kenny added with a tone of disbelief, emphasizing how disgusted he was with this child, being so young but acting so badly. Kenny told me that he stays away from that kid now but that he is still very upset and angry about what happened.

Twelve-year-old Brit also shared a story about something that had happened recently to her mom involving a white person and that made Brit angry:

> One day, my mom came—she came home from work, and she wasn't, like, she didn't look good. . . . Like, she looked like she had a bad day and stuff like that. So I asked her what happened. She was like—she was working with a customer, and it was an old white lady. [And then she got upset for some reason and left the store], and she was outside of the store, and she was just yelling out [the n-word], and she was spitting on the window! Yeah, so they ended up calling the police on her.

These kinds of stories were told by these children over and over both in Massachusetts and in Mississippi. For these kids, unlike their white peers, the notion of living in a world in which no one notices race or where racism no longer exists did not make much sense even before Trump was elected. However, given that these children perceived racism to be on the rise, the moment in which these interviews were conducted was an unsettling time for them and a time when many of these kids expressed the racialized emotion of anger. This anger is important. "Anger has gotten a bad rap in the sociology of emotions and mental health, yet 'silencing anger justifies and perpetuates domination by silencing the voices of the oppressed, labelling anger as "loss of control," as "emotional," or as "neurotic.""28 "Anger is an indispensable emotion for the cognitive and emotional liberation" of members of racially marginalized groups, "as it increases group identification and solidarity."29 In short, as the cultural studies scholar Sara Ahmed suggests, anger is literally "a call for action."30

As Bonilla-Silva points out, however, it is important not to "glamorize" anger since anger can becoming "all-consuming" and contribute to further trauma and negatively impact people's emotional well-being.31 It is also critical to remember the ways that anger is often applied to Black children in contexts involving authority figures, or what psychologists refer to as "anger bias," which reinforces racist ideas about Black youth and shapes how they are treated.32 Despite these important points, though, anger can have the potential to contribute to group solidarity and collective social action, which is what I found with these children.

Feeling Group Solidarity and Taking Action

Many of the kids in this research mentioned their desire to do something about the racism around them—and they told me it was their disgust and frustration with what they witnessed and experienced in everyday life, especially with Trump in office, that inspired them to try to do what they could to make a positive difference. They told me they felt solidarity with the Black Lives Matter movement and protesters like Colin Kaepernick. And they told me their anger inspired them to care about politics in ways they previously had not.

Twelve-year-old David, a child who identified as "white/biracial/mixed" in Massachusetts, told me that he felt a lot of anger but that his anger had less to do with kids at school and far more to do with Trump being elected as president.

In the morning, when I had to go to school, I asked my cousin—I was like, "Who won?" and she was like, "Donald Trump did," and I was like, "*Ugh.*" I was like, "Ugh." I was mostly angry and shocked 'cause I did not want him to be president, but I was like really, really hating him. And I still am. I don't like him. He is doing a bad job. He is racist and makes fun of other cultures, . . . and I don't like the way he talks about other countries and people from other countries.

As David explained, his anger was primarily due to the fact that he could not believe that such a racist person could be elected. Later in our interview, David also told me that he has noticed that "a lot of people are making fun of Black people" since Trump was elected. He mentioned Black Lives Matter and how he supported this group even though he did not identify as Black. "It is true, because [Black lives] do matter. They're exactly like me but just a different skin color." But, as he explained, a lot of white people do not see things this way and engage in racist behavior, including even members of his own mixed-race family. He told me about having to "call out" his white brother for making fun of someone who was Asian. "I was like, 'That's racist.' And he was like, 'Okay, okay, I'm sorry.' He didn't do it again." David told me that he feels empowered to stand up to family, peers, and even strangers when it comes to people being racist but that he really had not felt this way until very recently, when Trump took office. David saw himself as connected to people beyond his own racial group's boundaries. David saw his own fate as "linked" to other people of color generally.33 Clearly, the political landscape of David's childhood shaped not only his racialized emotions but also the way he decided to act in the world. David also told me that he was disappointed because he thought many people around him were scared to do this. "Sometimes they don't want to stand out, so they don't speak up. I wish they would," he stated, suggesting that working together as a group in solidarity with one another would be a powerful way to combat racism in society.

Indeed, many of the children of color told me that they wanted to protest Trump and racism—they felt that "call to action"— but that the fear they also experienced outweighed their anger. Specifically, examples of violence such as that which took place in

Charlottesville, Virginia, in 2017 involving the "Unite the Right Rally" were frightening to these kids. As twelve-year-old Maya stated, "There's a whole lot of KKK over there and stuff. We shouldn't be going nowhere near there, Virginia!" Similarly, Ria pointed out that there was white racist violence not only in Virginia but also in other places. "In Charlottesville, Virginia, a few months ago, that was when a car drove through the people that were protesting. That made me very upset. . . . I also remember when a guy went into a church and shot Black people in South Carolina." Many of the children in this study, across racial lines, shared their fears of gun violence in the US, but for these kids of color, part of that fear was connected to fears not only of police officers shooting people like them but also of white supremacists doing the same. Much like with fears of bullying, these Black and brown kids understood violence as being about group interactions, group membership, and how racism operates in the US, rather than simply as being about individuals. This fear was what some kids identified as why finding other ways to take action, rather than directly confronting white racist people, was a safer and more strategic option. "There's a lot of crazy white people out there," as one child told me repeatedly, indicating that she wanted to stay far away from them.

However, when it came to standing up to white kids in their schools and local communities, many of these kids felt empowered to do so. For example, Juliana shared her thoughts about interactions she has regularly with white kids who say racist things and who support Trump: "Sometimes, I'll just be walking in the park, and those white kids will say things to us, and me and my friends will just ignore them. 'Cause it's just not okay to be racist. . . . But sometimes, I do say something [back]. When I say something to them, I get in a fight. I sound like my mom. It's funny because she has this thing on our dining-room table that says, 'Sometimes I open my mouth and my mom comes out' [laughs]. And it is so true!" Juliana explained that she found it hard not to speak up when the white kids at the park or at school said or did racist things. She felt like she needed to speak up, even though her mom consistently warned her to be cautious about doing so. "My mom will say, 'You got to be careful in the world because, one, you're a girl and, two, you're this color, so you have to be careful.' I'm like, 'Trust me. I know.'" But Juliana told me that even though she tries to ignore those kids, it is sometimes too difficult because they make her "so mad." Another thing that Juliana also told me made her really mad was that her "mom got fired from a job because of her skin tone and had to take a new job." The new job required her mom to work late and not get home until nearly midnight, meaning Juliana did not get to see her as much. Juliana identified a number of examples of not only how racism made her mad but also how it made her want to do something to try to change it—and for her, the most obvious thing she could do, even though she tried to be careful about it, was confront her white peers in the park and draw attention to their racism.

But when Devion stood up to racist white boys at his school, he not only experienced physical violence but also ended up getting suspended from school. He really wanted to tell me about being suspended and what followed. "Since I was assaulted in that school and everything, my parents did not want me to go back." Following his suspension, which his parents unsuccessfully tried to fight, his parents pulled him out of school and began to homeschool him. "I have a tutor that comes to my house every day, and then in the afternoon, I go to my after-school program for social time." I asked Devion how he felt about no longer going to the public school. "I honestly think it's better because I get to learn about some stuff that we may not get to learn about in school, . . . like Black history. I really like to learn about that. I just like to learn about the Black people that were here a long time ago and what they did. . . . My friends [at the public school], they don't learn anything about this stuff." We talked some more, and Devion told me more about how he feels, particularly with respect to his relationships with his peers:

I mainly hang out with mostly just darker-skin people. . . . I just feel more safe around them 'cause of, like, what has been going on the few last years. I just feel more safe around them because . . . I've had the racism comments. . . . They called me the n-word. They've done a bunch of rude stuff. . . . And I trust most people, but I don't trust the white kids that have harassed me. I don't trust them and their friends. And I have anger issues with them and get in fights. . . . So my parents just thought it would be good to put me in homeschool.

From Devion's perspective, the white kids at his school were so awful to him that he could not control his feelings and consistently got into fights with these children. Yet, he learned that fighting with these children led to his own removal from the school. The "anger issues" he mentioned may be based on how he actually feels, or they could also reflect what teachers have told him is "wrong" with him—that being angry with white kids for being racist is somehow an inappropriate response. What seemed to empower Devion in new ways, though, was learning Black history. And he was not alone.

In Mississippi, Kenny also shared with me his passion for studying Black history. He explained, "I have to do a lot of learning outside of school because Black History Month is the only month we talk about it. . . . We never learn about Black history other than in February. The only thing we learn about is Civil War and all the right white people." Kenny told me that his parents provided him with many other resources outside of school so that he could pursue his interests in history and learn as much as possible. He told me specific titles of books he had read recently, facts and figures he had learned, presentations he gave at school, films he had watched, and discussions he had with his father, who also was passionate about the subject. When he talked about this interest, he sat at the edge of the chair excitedly. At the end of the interview, after we turned off the recorder, he went back to the topic and told me about a presentation he was preparing to give to his class about Black politicians in Mississippi. For Kenny, part of taking action to fight for the liberation of Black people included knowing history well and educating other people about it, even when it was not the month of February or when he was not the teacher. In this sense, for both Devion and Kenny, learning Black history was a powerful way to stand up to the racism they witnessed in white children around them, in their schools and communities and even at the level of the nation's political leadership.

Overall, these children told me that they identified as people whose individual interests were tied directly to those of other people similarly positioned in society, including members of their own racial group(s) as well as those of other nonwhite groups.34 For the kids interviewed in this study, it was this sense of belonging to something bigger than just themselves that provided them with the confidence necessary to take action—whether that be in the form of direct confrontation with racist white peers or engaging with politics or studying Black history—to challenge the injustice they identified in their lives.

Developing Racialized Emotions

In Jonathan Kozol's best-selling book *Savage Inequalities*, he interviewed children across various US cities about their experiences of educational inequality in the so-called land of equal opportunity. He conducted these interviews in the early 1990s. And yet, despite claims of racial progress during the past few decades, many of the things the kids of color shared with Kozol resonate with the experiences, thoughts, and feelings shared by the children in my research nearly thirty years later. One girl whom Kozol interviewed shared the following: "Only one other student in my class was Black. I was in the fifth grade, and at that age you don't understand the ugliness in people's hearts. They wouldn't play with me. I couldn't understand it. During recess I would stand there by myself beside the fence. Then one day I got a note: 'Go back to Africa.' To tell the truth, it left a sadness in my heart." Another boy then chimed in after her and stated, "It does not take long for little kids to learn . . . they are not wanted."35 Clearly, the thoughts and feelings of children depicted in Kozol's book parallel those of the kids described in this chapter in their recognition of how racism shapes their lives and how they *feel race*, generation after generation.

Racialized emotions are a key component of racial learning processes. That is, growing up in a racialized society means that "racial actors, both dominant and subordinate, simply cannot transact their lives without racialized emotions."36 As Bonilla-Silva explains, "while whites believe the system is fair, the racially subordinate experience the unfairness of the system, leading each group to develop emotions that match their 'perceptual segregation.'"37 The children in this book formed ideas about race as a result of the emotions they felt related to their racial classification. Accordingly, "races fashion an emotional subjectivity generally fitting of their location in the racial order."38 Part of figuring out how race works in US society, then, means developing emotions that fit the material circumstances of one's life, including one's own material interests, which are shaped by one's position as a member of a particular group in the racial hierarchy. This is clearly an important, foundational part of the process of how people learn race. And this begins in childhood.

Despite the evidence that racialized emotions are central to childhood racial learning processes, sociological studies rarely attend to the powerful role that these group-based, relational racialized emotions—not just individual-level emotions—play in theories of how the newest members of society interpret the system of race that shapes all of our lives. These emotions have not always been ignored, but they have been undertheorized. I argue that adults generally, and sociologists in particular, need to take the racialized emotions of children more seriously in both research endeavors and in applied settings, like schools. We need to recognize how racialized emotions shape the ideas that young people produce about race, racial inequality, racism, and racial privilege. Further, we need to do a better job of acknowledging the long-standing patterns across time in how kids feel race, and we must attend to the nuances that come with each child's unique context of childhood, defined by both micro- and macro-level dynamics and how they interrelate.

Overall, the particular political environment that defines kids' childhoods matters for the way kids develop their feelings and subsequently their ideas about racism—as well as their sense of where they and others fit (or do not) into what is supposed to be a democratic, fair, and just society. The turbulent post-Obama era provides a unique opportunity to explore how racial learning processes are connected to dynamics operating at the structural level, including national politics and political rhetoric. Recognizing these factors as important for racial learning helps lead to stronger, sociologically informed theories of how children learn *and feel* race.

5

"Racism Is Fine"

Racial Dominance and Apathy

> INTERVIEWER: Some people say that there's a lot of racial tension
> in America right now—what do you think?
> GRACE: I honestly think it's fine [laughs]. I don't really care
> [laughs].

Very little is known about the kids who experienced Trump's election and time in office positively. In fact, I am unaware of any research conducted during this political moment that described or analyzed the ideas and feelings of white children who expressed support for Trump—including those who identified his words and actions as racist but still supported him anyway. What were these kids feeling and thinking? And what does this tell us about racial learning processes?

"I don't really care that Trump is racist" was a popular expression of the white children I interviewed. Many of the young white people who supported Trump said that while they thought Trump was racist, or at least "sorta kinda racist" or "did a few racist things," they ultimately did not really mind. Grace's words in this chapter's epigraph illustrate this point, but she was not alone in this view. For instance, Lucy, who was twelve years old, white, and lived in Massachusetts, told me that she was very "into politics." She explained to me that she loved knowing what was going on in the world. In fact, before school every morning, she got up early to drink a cup of tea and watch the news. "I feel like I've heard stuff on the news about [Trump] being racist, but, like, the [news anchors] exaggerate stuff. But I don't really think he's all *that* racist.

I think when he does one thing wrong, people turn it against him. Overall, I'm not saying he's the best president, and he's definitely not the worst. But he's not racist. I mean, there might have been one or two incidents when he was racist, but he's not racist—most of the time." Lucy acknowledged that Trump *is* racist, even as she tried to explain it away as an exaggeration of the news media. She ultimately resolved this tension by simply stating, "Trump is fine."

Jackson, a twelve-year-old boy in Mississippi who identified strongly as "Caucasian," told me that he "felt good" after Trump was elected because he supported many of Trump's positions, especially the immigration policy of extending a wall between the United States and Mexico. "Yes, racism exists," Jackson told me confidently. He went on to explain how racism relates to his position regarding football players like the former football quarterback Colin Kaepernick kneeling during the national anthem at NFL games: "Some people are [kneeling] because they don't like the president. They don't like racism. They don't like the way some people are getting treated. . . . But if [they] want to live in America, why [are they] kneeling instead of, like, loving our country that people fight for every day so we can be free? If they don't, like, wanna stand for the Pledge of Allegiance or the national anthem, why are they living here?" Jackson made it clear that he understood these athletes' protests to be about real racism in the US, and he saw protests against Trump and protests against racism as linked. Importantly, he did not deny that racism existed or even deny that it negatively impacted "how people are treated." However, his conclusion was that even if racism negatively impacts people in significant ways, it is still not a legitimate enough reason to merit protest in this country. Standing up for the national anthem—and for the president—is simply more important. As Jackson made clear, being American means not protesting ongoing forms of racism or racial discrimination, a definition that suggests that to Jackson, being American ultimately means being white.

These kids did not deny that Trump said or did racist things; rather, this group of kids generally acknowledged the existence of racism and classified Trump's words and actions as "sorta racist." But, to them, racism was "fine" and something they told me they did not care about.

And yet, although these kids *said* that they did not care about racism, their expressions of how they *felt* about race-related social issues revealed something quite different. Based on how these kids talked about their racialized emotions and based on how they described the games and jokes they created and played with their peers centered around race-related issues, it appeared that they actually cared quite a bit about racial hierarchy, race relations, and most of all, maintaining racial dominance. The Massachusetts kids' expressions of disgust when talking about the Black Lives Matter movement and the Mississippi kids' expressions of horror at the thought of Confederate monuments being taken down suggested that they cared a lot about race-related current events. Their expressions of anger and aggression implied that they cared deeply about the perceived threat of "people from the Middle East" attacking them and taking away their religion and way of life. Their expressions of fear and rage about "people from Mexico" coming to the US to "take" what belongs to them indicated that they are absolutely invested in race-related social issues. And the pleasure and delight these kids took in making racist jokes and playing games related to Immigration and Customs Enforcement (ICE) officers and immigrants, as well as imitating Trump affectionately, suggested that they were processing a lot of ideas and emotions about race-related issues in the US, even as they said they did not care about racism.

I highlight here the contradictions between these kids' statements that they do not care about racism, or their "lack of feeling" regarding race-related issues, and their explicit expression of racialized emotions, or feeling race. I explore the interconnected negative and positive racialized emotions expressed by these kids, including anger, aggression, fear, pleasure, and delight. And I examine not only how these kids express these emotions verbally but how their behavior, especially through peer interactions with other white kids, reflects their concerns about race-related issues, especially those issues related to maintaining their own group position of racial dominance. By focusing on their descriptions of how they felt, we can see how racialized emotions are foundational to how children produce racial meaning.

"Racism Doesn't Really, like, Affect Me": Racial Apathy

"There's not really any [racism] going on in Mississippi," twelve-year-old Katie explained one afternoon a few months after Trump was elected. "But there might be in, like, other states. . . . I don't really know. . . . It's not something I care about," she added with a shrug. Katie, a child who attended a private school that was established as a segregationist academy in the early 1970s, understood that racism probably exists somewhere but does not recognize it in her community. She did not think racism shaped her life in any meaningful way.

Other kids also told me they recognized the existence of racism in US society but that, like Katie, it was not really something they cared about or knew much about. For example, eleven-year-old Cammie in Massachusetts told me, "Yeah, I think there are, like, racist people, but I am not too worried about it." Eleven-year-old Carter in Mississippi expressed a similar position. When asked if he thought racism was still a problem, he responded, "Probably. . . . I've never actually thought about it." And thirteen-year-old Brayden responded to the same question by saying, "Yeah, . . . people are treated differently," but then refused to say much more about it, completely disengaging from the discussion and shutting down.

These kids' expressions are striking examples of what the sociologist Tyrone Forman describes as "racial apathy," which "refers to lack of feeling or indifference toward societal racial and ethnic inequality and lack of engagement with race-related social issues."1 Instead of an explicit dislike or antipathy for people of color, "racial apathy captures the possibility of insidious indifference—of whites disengaging from racial inequality and expressing disinterest in the poor condition or mistreatment of others."2 Racial apathy can be seen in the children's expressions of "I don't know" and "I don't care" to questions about racism in US society.

But these expressions of racial apathy also extended beyond simple statements of not thinking, caring, or knowing about racism *generally*. In fact, these children's expressions of apathy were especially common and pronounced when they talked about their reflections on Trump's racist words and actions *specifically*. For example, when Nathaniel, a child growing up in Massachusetts, was asked what he thought about Trump doing or saying racist things, he replied, "Yeah, I don't pay attention to that stuff. . . . Racism doesn't like really, like, affect me. I don't like to think about it." Similarly, when Blake, a ten-year old, was asked if he thinks Trump is racist, he responded, "I don't know 'cause I've never heard him be racist. But he did say, um, that we'll build a wall between Mexico. . . . Mexico is, like, part of our world, so you shouldn't try to keep them out. . . . That is kinda racist." And when ten-year-old Amy in Massachusetts talked about Trump, she told me, "Um, I think he's a little racist. 'Cause he thinks a lot about color. But I don't really think about him too much either. He's just the president." I asked Amy if she could think of any examples of Trump being "a little racist." She replied, "Yeah. Sometimes. No, I can't remember anything. I just remember that I think, 'Oh that's kind of racist,' but, um, then I don't think about it really." Cammie told me explicitly, "Trump is racist, but I don't really care." Over and over, these children expressed forms of racial apathy when I asked them what they thought about racism in the United States and especially when I asked them about President Trump.

However, as the interviews proceeded and the kids began sharing their thoughts about specific events related to the political realm, it became clear to me that in many ways, these kids were *preoccupied* with race-related social issues. Even as they explained their indifference ("I don't care about racism"), they also expressed racialized emotions ("I am angry about Mexicans coming and taking what is ours" or "It makes me mad that Black people are protesting" or "I like joking around about the wall!"). It seemed to me, then, that these children experienced strong emotions related to race and racism even as they claimed not to know or care about it. This became particularly evident when kids talked about the jokes they created and the games they played with their white peers. Here, I try to make sense of this disconnect between these two findings.

Racist Play: Racialized Emotions in Children's Jokes, Costumes, and Games

This group of kids was delighted by Trump. They told me that he "stood up" for them, and they shared how happy they were that he was elected. They said they "loved" him and described how fun it was to laugh with their friends about Hillary Clinton, whom they viewed as a criminal and a "loser." These kids also told me about using (and sometimes shouting) a phrase they found extremely amusing: "Build the wall!" They also told me about "fun" make-believe games they played with their friends or witnessed other kids play involving imaginary immigration walls. Instead of playing games of the past like "Cowboys and Indians," new versions of the same sort of play involved kids acting out roles of immigration-control officers and immigrants engaged in make-believe gun conflict. Kids also expressed their delight at the funny costumes they observed people dressed up as for Halloween connected to race and politics, like people in Trump costumes holding signs that said "Make America Great Again" and affectionately imitating his hair and voice. Most of these kids, while sharing stories about these jokes and games, laughed out loud as they recalled the incidents they observed or participated in, clearly delighted as they shared these stories.

"We Just Like to Joke Around"

When kids at twelve-year-old Katie's school in Mississippi chanted "Build the wall!" on the playground at recess, Katie said that she thought it was "funny." Although she acknowledged that there might have been some kids at her school who did not think it was funny, Katie "did not really care" what they thought. At this moment in time, the "Build the wall!" phrase was regularly used in a larger political context as a direct attack against Latinx immigrants and often against Latinx people in general, regardless of their immigration status. Thus, when Katie indicated that she did not care about this possibly hurting other kids' feelings, the implication was that she did not care about hurting Latinx kids' feelings. Rather than expressing concern for the suffering or struggle of Latinx peers faced with anti-immigrant rhetoric and even violence during this time, the scenario of the kids chanting made her laugh and "feel good" about Trump winning the election. That was what was important to her—how she felt.

Katie was not alone. Many of the children in this study told me about kids at their school—sometimes their friends, sometimes their enemies—participating in this style of "joking" about the politics of immigration. Katie and others described in this chapter told me that they did not feel bad about engaging in these behaviors. It was fun for them and "just a joke." They found pleasure in their "kidding around." The following dialogue with twelve-year-old Joshua illustrates how he interpreted this kind of "joking" behavior:

INTERVIEWER: When President Trump was elected, some kids at other schools would say things like "Build the wall!" Did kids here say anything like that?

JOSHUA: Oh, yes ma'am! [laughs].

INTERVIEWER: When kids said that stuff, what was happening?

JOSHUA: Oh, they're funny! And, like, one dressed up as Trump for Halloween [laughs]. But they all just kid about it.

INTERVIEWER: What if there were kids that were saying it to be mean—what would you think about that?

JOSHUA: I think—I don't think it's wrong. . . . After the election, it is what it is.

Like Katie, Joshua expressed his belief that shouting "Build the wall!" on the playground was "just" a joke and "just" kidding around. And yet, when pressed to think about how this phrase could be used in a way that was mean-spirited or hurtful, Joshua's response of "it is what it is" indicated that he had reached the end of his thinking about it. In an ironic way, Joshua himself constructed his own wall in this moment, disengaging from the discussion of how this phrase can be harmful. Joshua did not want to feel bad about himself or his friends' behavior, and when pressed about how these words may be hurtful, he utilized a rhetorical strategy to evade feelings of shame or remorse. "It is what it is" is a phrase that is used to shut down the possibility of further thought by offering a tautology, or a circular argument, in which there is no possibility of one taking any sort of responsibility or accountability for reproducing racism. This strategy is like what the sociologist Glenn Bracey refers to as the concept of "rescuing whites," in which white people rely on discursive strategies that, as the sociologist Jennifer Mueller explains, "stifle direct critique of whites, as racialized actors responsible for white supremacy and racism."3 It would be inaccurate to suggest that Joshua did not actually care about issues related to immigration—at other moments in the interview, he expressed strong opinions about this issue. Instead, Joshua did not want to think about the suffering of other people in relation to this phrase and his own culpability in relation to it.4

These kids have learned the rhetorical and emotional strategy of "culpable ignorance" or, as Sandra Lee Bartky explains, "the willful not-knowing of what is staring them in the face, the bad faith of pretending not to know, . . . and the retreat under the two-pillared shelter for whites endangered by the possibility of guilt."5 Indeed, when

Joshua and other kids like him deny that their joking about the wall is in any way harmful, they eliminate their own responsibility for engaging in this behavior and avoid having to feel any sort of shame or remorse. This is a strategy that they are learning and practicing in childhood, and as such, it is part of their learning of how to navigate the world as a person in a position of racial dominance—and in a way that reinforces that dominance.

"That Costume Was Really Funny!"

Like Joshua, lots of kids in this study shared stories of witnessing people around them dressed up in costumes depicting Donald Trump or Hillary Clinton. Most of the kids explained that these costumes appeared around the time of Halloween, presumably right before the presidential election in early November 2016. Ten-year-old Ian described what he remembered from this time in Mississippi: "I wasn't watching the news a lot about it, so all I knew is that [the election] was in between Donald Trump and Hillary Clinton and everybody hated Hillary Clinton. In fact, [laughs] at the band rehearsal, where everybody got to dress up for Halloween, I saw one guy dress up as Hillary Clinton in a jail suit! It was really funny!" Though none of the kids in Massachusetts told me that "everybody" was opposed to Hillary Clinton winning the election, many of the kids in Mississippi believed this to be accurate. Regardless of where the kids lived, though, they took a lot of pleasure in watching people mimic and belittle Clinton.

Kids also told me that they "loved" seeing people imitate Trump's hair and the way he spoke. Eleven-year-old Cammie in Massachusetts told me that she especially liked when people would wear a wig that resembled Trump's hair and would imitate his voice. I asked her what kinds of things people in Trump costumes would say while giving their impression of him. "Uh, Build the wall!" she said with an expression that conveyed that she thought I should *obviously* know this. I asked her if she thought people were making fun of Trump when they dressed up like him. "Oh no! It's not that," she said confidently. "It was just, like, a fun thing. We love him."

Kids like Joshua, Ian, and Cammie interpreted the mockery of Clinton and the affectionate imitations of Trump that they observed with pleasure and delight. In the case of Trump costumes, this group of children appeared to find the mimicry empowering and a celebration of the politician they supported. When they saw adults around them wearing these costumes, like at a community band rehearsal, these costumes also reinforced notions about the political climate of their local community. They liked Trump and wanted to be like him. Importantly, people in Trump or Clinton costumes were not simply read by the kids in this study as individual expressions of the costume wearer's personal politics. Rather, these costumes and imitations also appeared to play a role in establishing group boundaries, reinforcing dominant political narratives and ideas, and establishing a collective sense of political cohesion. For example, the kids who supported Trump said seeing pro-Trump messages made them feel "good" and like they were "part of something" such as a larger group or community—they took pleasure in these moments. These kids understood their group as one in which "everybody hated Hillary Clinton," one in which chanting "Build a Wall!" was appropriate and desired, one that celebrated the ideas and actions of Trump, one that was politically conservative, and one that was white. For kids in Mississippi, they also stated that they identified strongly as "southern" and "Christian" and said that being Republican and being southern were synonymous.

Overall, these Halloween costumes appeared to play one small role in a larger process of racial learning about what it meant to be part of this particular "racial regime," a regime connected not only to support for a politician but also to ideas and feelings about race in the US—and feelings of affection toward one's own group.6 This group cohesion created a clear boundary between their group and groups that did not share their political views. When kids laughed at imitations of Clinton in a jail suit, their laughter was different than laughing about a silly Trump wig. That is, the laughter associated with Clinton impressions was about mocking someone or something that these children did not like or found to be threatening, whereas the affectionate laughing about a Trump hairstyle reflected children's playful delight not only in his appearance but also in his politics. These costumes delighted the kids, not just because costumes are silly but because they made the kids feel particular racialized emotions—in this case, positive emotions of pleasure and delight that come with racial dominance.

Playground Games

Another way that these children expressed how much they seemed to care—and feel—with respect to race-related issues was through make-believe games with significant racial connotations. These games were primarily played on exclusively white school playgrounds or in white neighborhoods.7 In one such game, some of the kids would pretend to be people trying to cross the border from Mexico into the United States, while other kids were border control officers, on the hunt, with objects they pretended were guns, to find the undocumented migrants. "You try to get the Mexican person, or they try to run away from you," one child explained. In another game, kids pretended to construct a wall on their playground using the play structures available to them. Because I did not observe these games as they were played, I do not know exactly how they worked, but multiple kids told me that shouting "Build the wall!" and "Trump! Trump! Trump!" were key features.

This form of play seemed to be about more than just kids using their imaginations to have fun. Rather, through these games and their descriptions of the "rules" of these games, these children appeared to be doing the important developmental work of processing elements of the social world around them. The emotional and ideological work that is accomplished through this type of play provided these kids with the sense that they belonged to a particular social group and helped them make sense of perceived threats they believed faced their group's dominant status, like perceived threats from immigrants. These games reinforced a sense of group cohesion, helped kids deepen their ideas about group boundaries, and reproduced existing social hierarchies.

The kids' creation of these jokes and games without any adult intervention reflects what the sociologist William Corsaro refers to as a process of "interpretive reproduction," which is a way of understanding childhood socialization that accounts for the active role kids play in their own interpretations of aspects of the social world around them, including patterns they see, messages they hear, and behavior they see, as well as how kids are "affected by the societies and cultures of which they are members."8 Interpretive reproduction is also a way of understanding how children "negotiate, share, and create culture with adults and each other" and highlights the "importance of collective, communal activity" among kids.9 This model of socialization emphasizes the agency that young people have. And the central component of interpretive reproduction includes "a stable set of activities or routines, artifacts, values, and concerns that children produce and share in interaction with peers."10 This includes activities that kids share with each other that help them interpretively reproduce ideas—including ideas *and emotions* about politics and race. In this sense, even if kids cannot vote and even if many adults think they are clueless about politics or racism, they nevertheless participate in society through their own understandings and refinement of dominant ideas, evidenced in their creative play. In other words, the jokes and games kids create represent their own unique forms of political and cultural participation.

Positive Racialized Emotions

Children in various parts of the United States have been documented participating in similar kinds of "games" with their friends, including games that take place in virtual spaces. During the

summer of 2021, for instance, kids in Traverse City, Michigan, conducted a "mock slave trade" in a private Snapchat group in which
they assigned monetary value to their Black classmates. Explicitly
racist messages were also shared in the group.11 Much like the kids
in my research, these high school students in Michigan engaged in
behavior that they viewed as "a joke" or "a game" to reinforce the
existing hierarchy at their school, in which they were at the top.
This unfolded amid perceived challenges to white dominance by
new demands for the teaching of the history of racism in the US
or what some members of the community labeled (erroneously)
"critical race theory." Across the country, school administrators
have struggled in recent years to figure out how to manage racist
behavior of students on social media, especially on Snapchat, where
the messages kids share with one another quickly vanish from view.
Anecdotally, almost every school leader I spoke to while sharing
my research on this subject over the past few years mentioned
incidents involving white kids using social media to dehumanize,
belittle, harass, and inflict violence against their Black and brown
peers. And certainly, data from the research discussed in chapter 1
of this book offer further evidence for this kind of behavior on the
behalf of white kids—behavior that so often is written off as "just a
joke." As such, it is crucial to recognize what goes on beneath the
surface of these games and jokes and to acknowledge the racialized
emotional and ideological work of white racial dominance unfold-
ing when white kids engage in this kind of racist play.

Most research on racialized emotions focuses on "negative" emotions like hatred, anger, anxiety, and shame, but as Bonilla-Silva
suggests, this "limits our understanding of racialized emotions, as
all actors experience the full range of emotions," including emotions
like pleasure and delight.12 Through analyzing the jokes related to
race and the election that these white children thought were funny,
as well as through exploring the games kids created as part of their
everyday play, it is evident that "positive" racialized emotions like
pleasure and delight played an important role in how these white

kids came to understand the racial order and their group position within it.

Indeed, humor plays a central role in the reproduction of racist discourse as well as group bonding among white people. Understanding that a key social function of humor has been in facilitating social affiliation and social distance within and throughout human societies illustrates that social humor has social power. Moreover, humor is a rhetorical and political tool that can challenge, reflect, and reproduce asymmetrical power relations in society.13

Laughing as members of an in-group about another group decreases the social distance between members of a particular social group. And specifically, as the sociologist Raúl Pérez argues, "race-based humor and laughter . . . play an active role in group formation and boundary maintenance, as humor and laughter can simultaneously function as a uniting and divisive social activity."14 Similarly, as the sociologists Leslie Picca and Joe Feagin explain, when people in "backstage" spaces test out their racist jokes, they demonstrate the feelings and viewpoints that they hold but that are otherwise "repressed because of social pressure."15 These jokes then demonstrate the "more serious racial feelings and/or views that they may harbor."16 These jokes offered a way for white kids to bond with each other and establish boundaries between "people like us" and "people like them." Certainly, these kids' jokes and games illustrate the importance of racialized emotions—especially positive ones— for the way kids make sense of the racialized world in which they are growing up, develop racial ideological positions that either reinforce or challenge dominant ones, and come to learn their group position within the racial hierarchy.

"But Kids Don't Even Know What All This Stuff Means": Challenging Notions of White Children's Innocence

One common myth about childhood is that kids are unaware of current events, are disinterested in politics, and do not care about ongoing public debates about topics like immigration or racial inequality. This popular line of thinking leads to the assumption that if children use a phrase like "Build the wall!" while playing with friends, they are just "having fun" and "joking around" and innocently parroting something they heard from adults around them. Children are "just kids" and therefore cannot have any real thoughts to share. While it is true that some of the kids in this research told me that they do not pay attention to politics or view themselves as politically well informed, all the kids expressed political ideas at some point during their interview and had opinions and strong emotions about political matters, especially those involving race.

This myth about kids not knowing about "all this stuff" also leads to the assumption that when kids create make-believe games in which they use their imaginations to play out what they think happens at the border between migrants and immigration control officers, that they cannot possibly mean any harm by it—they are "just kids" playing, after all. This myth is, in part, what leads some white parents to claim that their children are "naïve" about issues such as racism—and should remain that way. This myth has even led some conservative white parents to oppose the teaching of the history of racism in the United States in their children's schools under the pretense that this kind of education will somehow harm their children. The suggestion is that by teaching about racism, educators will disrupt popular narratives of US exceptionalism and make white people, and white kids, feel as if they are "under attack."

However, despite these popular myths about children, I found virtually no evidence that the kids in this research were unaware of current events or were politically disengaged—even the kids who had parents who did not talk openly with them about these topics and even the kids who told me they did not think much about politics. In fact, I found the opposite—all the kids in this research were aware of the big current events of the day and talked about engaging in lively political discussions with their peers regularly. They had strong opinions—and positive and negative emotions—about political topics, especially those involving race, and they shared these ideas and emotions with each other openly. In fact, kids were so engaged that sometimes their passionate perspectives even led to verbal or physical altercations between children in kid spaces, like on the school bus or the playground. And these ideas and emotions were incorporated into the jokes they told each other as well as the make-believe games they created.

Take Ned, for example. He shared that making jokes about Trump's border wall—like shouting "Build the wall!"—was a regular part of kid culture in his community and described this as "just a joke" at his school. But Ned, like many of the other children interviewed, *absolutely* knew what this phrase meant and where it came from: "[The wall] is Trump's plan, but it might not happen. But, like, our wall that we have right now, he probably doesn't think it's good. . . . I've seen pictures of it. It's like this little chainlink fence, kind of. I think that's what it looks like—like the fences on our playground. . . . And I don't think he wants, like, people who come in illegally. 'Cause he doesn't want that. 'Cause he doesn't believe that people should just come to America and be free and not, like, get a visa." Ned not only knew about the wall plan had seen photos of current fencing along the border and drew comparisons to other fences he had seen. His words made clear that Ned adopted the assumption of US exceptionalism and the superiority of the United States more broadly. And it was clear when he referred to the existing structures along the border as "our" wall that he has developed a strong group identity as an American and a notion of "us" versus "them."

Ned also shared that he supported the plan generally, though he did have one specific concern: "I think it might be a good plan, but, like, what if, like, they find a way to get over, like, they dig a hole under it or, like, get a ladder?" To suggest that Ned was unaware or naïve of what the wall is or what its intended purpose is disregards the fact that Ned had thought a lot about this and was engaged politically with it. Ned had thought through the details of the wall and even had concerns about how the plan might not achieve the desired outcome. Ned also knew that there were debates about this wall present among kids at his school: "Some people would be like, 'I think they should build the wall because, like, our country wouldn't have that many people and, like, there wouldn't be so many people unemployed and stuff.' And then this other person would be like, 'But we need more people for soldiers and stuff.' And, like, they would debate it. And I would just be like, 'Mm, guess so.'" In Ned's mind, the debate about immigration was really about two things: the economic anxieties of those who believe their jobs are threatened by immigrants and the need to increase the size of the US military. Even though Ned did not directly address race in this comment, Ned's perspective on this issue was deeply informed by how he understood himself as a member of a racial group as well as a political one.

Overall, the myth that children cannot possibly know what is going on politically or with respect to current events—both nationally and regionally situated—minimizes the reality that kids are political participants, even if they cannot vote. This myth also renders invisible kids' racialized emotions tied to these events—including those "positive" emotions of pleasure and delight—play in their overall process of learning about race, racism, and racial identity. The pleasure and delight these children took while engaging in these "jokes" and imitation work reflected a form of "satisfaction and even pleasure in domination."17 And just because they were "joking" did not take away from the fact that they were thinking in more serious ways about these issues. What was beneath the surface of these jokes and games?

Behind the Laughter: Fear

What motivated these kids to engage in these jokes and games was largely fear. Many of these white children felt fearful of Black people and Muslim people and immigrants. They believed the United States to be a country that was meant to be reserved for and controlled by people like them—specifically, white people. These kids had an imagined sense of generally what Black people, Muslim people, and immigrants were like—and the ideas these kids held about these groups was not positive. That is, they identified "an abstract image of the subordinate racial group" on the basis not of individual experiences but of collective ideas "forged in the public arena."18 But their racist ideas about criminality, dangerousness, greediness, immorality, and so on came through in how they talked about *how they felt* about these groups. These children were explicit about differences between racial groups and why it was important to support politicians like Trump who would advocate for people like them. As such, while these kids' jokes and games were one way they expressed their thoughts and emotions, listening to their voices as they explain their ideas and emotions offers a window into some of the dynamics at play beneath the surface of their laughter and their claims that they do not care about race-related social issues. These children actually cared quite a bit about maintaining their group's position within a society organized hierarchically by socially constructed racial groups and were fearful of losing social power as a white person.19 And, as these kids made clear to me, one central messenger of the idea that white people were threatened as a social group—and what could be done about it—was Donald Trump himself.

"He Knows How to Handle, like, People Who Threaten Us and Stuff"

"I was happy that Trump won because I think he knows how to handle, like, people who threaten us and stuff," twelve-year-old Grace stated. She identified as a white, Christian, Republican southerner and viewed members of her own social group as other white people who fit into these same categories. In discussing her racial identity, Grace explained how she knew she was white: "I was born in America, and my skin is white, and my whole family's white. . . . And I came from Adam and Eve and Jesus, and they're white. And God, so, I guess, I'm white, so . . . [laughs]." Grace associated whiteness with her religion and suggested that part of being American to her includes being Christian and white. She also discussed aspects of living in the South, particularly with respect to ongoing debates (at the time these data were collected) about the Confederate emblem on the Mississippi state flag. She explained her perspective on this debate about changing the flag:

> I like [the flag] because it has the South sign, symbol, and it repre-sents the South. And but I get why people don't like it because of the slaves thing that happened, but, I mean [laughs], . . . I get—like, if—if I—well, if the white people were slaves and the Black people—and we still had that flag, then probably not—not a lot of people like—like, we wouldn't like it a lot because it obviously has the sign for, like, slavery and stuff. But, I mean, I get why they don't like it, but, I mean, it's still the flag of Mississippi, so . . . [laughs].

Although Grace indicated that she was able to see why the flag is understood to be racist by Black people, ultimately, she liked it, and that is what was ultimately most important to her. Her align-ment of racial politics with the South illustrates that even though she was "just a kid," she had produced clear understandings of larger racialized dynamics associated with place, as well as with the racial group to which she belongs. Perhaps most importantly, Grace believed that politicians like Trump were a good thing for the US because of their commitment to maintaining and protecting things that Grace cared about—like the Confederate emblem on the Mississippi flag—and protecting her from people who threaten "us."

Like Grace, Ned also had strong opinions about the Confederate flag remaining a symbol attached to the state flag of Mississippi:

> NED: I mean, like, some people might want [the Confederate emblem to stay on the flag], like, because it's, like, their heritage. Like, that's, like, the thing.

INTERVIEWER: Why do you think some people think it's not right?

NED: 'Cause they don't believe in slavery. But, like, it might not mean that. It mean—it might mean, like, somebody's heritage.

INTERVIEWER: Okay, so you think some people think it means slavery, but it might not mean that to other people?

NED: Mmhmm. I think that.

INTERVIEWER: What about the national anthem protests? Have you heard about that?

NED: Mhmm. I don't think it's right. Like, if they don't like America, why are they living here?

Ned said that just like he disapproved of the protests, he also wanted the Confederate flag to stay up because he identifies with the people who support it. Ned said that he viewed himself as part of a social group that should get to keep things the way they have always been in spite of calls from Black people to make societal changes to these symbols.

Grace's ideas about Trump protecting people like her from those who are threatening was particularly apparent when she talked about professional Black athletes' protests against racism and racist police violence. She explained, "Like, aren't [the athletes] kneeling to get, like—wait, I know. It's because of racism somehow. But, like, I don't know, like, how or something." Laughing, she continued, "I just know that I'm not gonna kneel!" When Grace was asked if she believed Black people were more likely to be mistreated by the police than white people were, she responded, "I really don't think so because, I mean, . . . like, if the Black people are—I'm not saying they are—but like *if* they are the normal people who usually do bad stuff, like, if white people did [bad stuff] too, then like . . . [the police] would try to do the same punishment." Although Grace guarded herself here against accusations that she believed Black people are "the normal people who usually do bad stuff," this is indeed what she seemed to believe. Her response illustrated that she did not believe Black people's claims of racist mistreatment by the police because to her, punishment is distributed based on who is doing the "bad stuff." The logical conclusion of her comment is, if Black people did not do bad stuff, they would not get punished. And since Black people are (potentially) the "normal people" who do bad stuff, then it makes sense that they would be punished more than white people are. In other words, if Black people are the criminals, then they are scary, and police are doing what they have to do to protect white people, like Grace, from them. To Grace, the "threats" that she thought Trump could protect people like her from included Black people demanding that the state flag she loved be changed, Black people doing "bad stuff," and Black people protesting racist violence inflicted on them by the state and ruining things she liked, such as football games. Underlying her laughter, thus, appeared to be a sense of fear.

Grace's responses are also sharp illustrations of how racialized emotions like fear are group-based and relational. How she felt emotionally about the flag and the protests was shaped by how she understood her membership in a particular social group that she viewed as in a binary opposition to another group: "us" versus "them." And these ideas, though not solely attributable to Trump, were certainly reinforced when she listened to him give speeches within the "public arena" of television.20 These speeches included rants against Black athletes like Colin Kaepernick or Women's National Basketball Association (WNBA) players protesting racism by kneeling during the national anthem before sporting events. Specifically, in September 2017, Trump stated the following in a widely publicized rally: "Wouldn't you love to see one of these NFL owners, when somebody disrespects our flag, to say, 'Get that son of a bitch off the field right now. Out. He's fired. He's fired!' You know, some owner is going to do that. He's going to say, 'That guy that disrespects our flag, he's fired.' And that owner, they don't know it. They don't know it. They'll be the most popular person, for a week. They'll be the most popular person in this country."21 As the sociologist Herbert Blumer explains, the public arena is where ideas and strong feelings about marginalized groups are often established or reinforced. As he writes, when a momentous public event occurs that "touches deep sentiments, that seems to raise fundamental questions about relations, and that awakens strong feelings of identification with one's racial group," this event shapes "the formation of the racial image," or how people think about a particular racial group.22 Although Trump did not say anything explicit in these comments about the players' racial group membership or even why these athletes were protesting in the first place, his words reinforced strong feelings among white people like Grace that contributed to how she formed ideas about Black people in the US.

Of course, Trump's comments in this moment were also accompanied by a range of other racist comments that sent even more explicitly racist messages about the subordinate racial group, such as when Trump referred to Mexicans as "rapists" or labeled Haiti a "shithole country" or when he frequently and relentlessly drew on long-standing racist stereotypes, like calling Congresswoman Maxine Waters an "extraordinarily low IQ person," calling Lebron James and Don Lemon "dumb," and using words like "lowlife," "not smart," and "dog" to refer to Omarosa Manigault Newman. From a sociological perspective, it is important to note here not just that Trump said these things but that in doing so, he spoke directly to and reinforced many of the fears that white people like Grace have related to losing power as a racial group as people of color make further advances in US society and seek justice in the face of racism. He also cultivated a sense of anger in people like Grace—anger at the audacity of people of color to demand equality. Many of these ideas articulated by Trump fit within well-established historical and present-day racist narratives, including the idea that Black people are scary criminals who "deserve" whatever punishments are inflicted by "good" white people. Kids like Grace interpreted these messages as they encountered them in various forms of media, listened to adults repeat these comments, and listened to the president speak.

Eleven-year-old Nathaniel, a moderate supporter of Trump growing up in Massachusetts, also shared his perspectives on the

Black Lives Matter movement and racial violence in the criminal justice system: "I feel like a couple times police have shot people just because of their race sometimes, but I'm pretty sure a couple times that that's happened, the police leader or manager was Black. So I don't feel like that they try to mention—they kind of just look over that and act like it doesn't happen." To Nathaniel, people getting shot was a universal problem and not one that had anything really to do with race. He even believed that athletes protesting at sporting events, such as Colin Kaepernick, were doing so to protest gun violence overall. "Kaepernick started that, and then he got released [from his team] for it, but I'm pretty sure it was because of gun violence. I think that's what he said about it." I asked Nathaniel what the thought about the gun violence he mentioned, and he immediately drew on a recent horrific school shooting in Florida at Stoneman Douglas High School: "I think [gun violence] definitely needs to be stopped, and we need to be taking a bigger look at it. But ever since that school shooting in Florida, people have started looking at it, but I think they're also trying to take away just every gun that people own, which could make it easier for people that are trying to, like, break into their house to protect themselves. It would make it harder for that, but I feel like they *should* have to go through more training to be able to own a gun legally." Threats in Nathaniel's mind took the form of his fear of people with guns, specifically people trying to break into people's houses. And Nathaniel believed that Trump could keep these threats at bay, which would reduce his own sense of fear of scary people with guns breaking into his house.

Simon, also a child in Massachusetts who felt frustrated being surrounded by so many liberal people, explained his perspective on the Black Lives Matter movement. "That's the dumbest thing I've ever heard," he told me dismissively. He went on to explain:

> They say "Black Lives Matter" because Black lives do matter, like *everyone's* lives matter. That's like walking up to a pit bull—which is the type of dog I like—and they're like, "They have a bad name because

some people train them to be mean." But, like, if you were then to say since they have a bad name, pit bulls' lives matter, they're the best thing ever, you should *only* get pit bulls because you want them to get rid of their bad rep because it's not their fault. But you shouldn't go out of your way to try to say they're the best.

Simon's analogy is striking for a number of reasons. First, of course, he misrepresented the demands of the Black Lives Matter movement: rather than claiming to be "the best," Black Lives Matter activists simply demand that Black lives be recognized as equal to white lives. But in misrepresenting Black Lives Matter, Simon demonstrated his inability to conceive of a world where Black people and white people are recognized as equals. For Simon, there could only be hierarchy, and if Black people were demanding to end white supremacy, then they must be trying to replace white racial dominance with Black racial dominance. Second, Simon's analogy works to undercut Black Lives Matter's demand for racial justice by dehumanizing Black people: he compared them to dogs and to pit bulls in particular. Even if pit bulls were Simon's favorite kind of dog, they are still dogs, and they are often thought of (fairly or not) as particularly aggressive and violent dogs at that. And third, Simon demonstrated his perception of racial groups like white or Black as discrete categories in opposition to one another ("people like me" versus "them").

Simon also attached particular kinds of emotions to these racial groups when he talked about how Black people "get mad" at the police while people like him experience feelings of "respect" for the police, again using an "us versus them" model for interpreting what he sees around him: "I've heard, like, people always saying, like, 'Police only shoot Black people' or 'Police are racist' and all that. But, like, police shoot anyone who's threatening them with a gun or about to shoot them. Like, everyone has the right to feel threatened, so, like, say there was a town, a big town, where there was more like Black people who were like in jail or something like that. . . . That doesn't mean the police officers are racist. That just means that that turned out that way." When asked to clarify what he meant by "turned out that way," he verified that he meant that more bad things happen in these "big towns" and if more Black people live in these places, then that is why there are a higher number of Black people in jail. In other words, Simon, in a roundabout way, argued that Black people in cities engage in more criminal behavior than white people in small towns do. For Simon, then, the violence against Black people is justified. Again, the association between Black people and criminality is articulated by yet another white child. And, like other kids in this chapter, Simon believed that violence was a reasonable response to a perceived threat. Overall, this group of children made it clear through what they said that they supported Trump because he protected people like them from people they feared, particularly Black people.

"You're Not Supposed to Be Here!"

As revealed in the games and jokes the kids described to me and as examined earlier in this chapter, another major "threat" that these kids identified were "Mexicans." Specifically, when the children used this label, they were using it to describe migrants crossing the border between the United States and Mexico. Their use of this term reflected their belief that the only people crossing the border were Mexican and suggested that to them, anyone in the United States who identified as Mexican (or who they thought looked like what they imagined a Mexican person looked like) was an undocumented person.

Thirteen-year-old Simon in Massachusetts, for example, immediately brought up the topic of immigration when I asked him if he thought about people saying Trump was racist:

> I mean, if you were to say he's racist, a lot of people have the same reason [for why they think] he's racist, [which is] because he's got white skin color. But now you're being racist saying he's racist! And

you're being racist like discriminating him because he has a white skin color and saying he's automatically racist. Like, he built a wall so Mexicans can't get in, not because they have that skin color [but] because [of] what they're doing. Like, I could've done the same thing, and I would have gone to jail, and if someone else did the same thing, they would have gone to jail.

Simon never really addressed the question of whether he thought Trump did or said racist things. Instead, he launched into a defense of the border wall. He also suggested that talking about racism is racist, and he was defensive about it, which points to an additional fear of being identified or labeled as racist. I asked him more about why he thought the wall was being built and what he thought about it. He replied, "I think [pauses] it's kinda fair because, like, if you're not a citizen of the country, then you're not supposed to be here! Like, if I just barged into someone's house, and I'm like, 'I live here now! I just live here now!' and they're like, 'No, get out!' [then], like, you should listen to them and not get all upset about it. Like, you're the one who came in here without permission." Simon viewed undocumented people as a threat in the same way that he viewed people breaking into someone's house as a threat.

Simon went on to share an interesting reflection with me when I asked him to compare President Obama to President Trump. He told me that he strongly believed that Trump was doing a better job "protecting America" from criminals and undocumented migrants compared to Obama and that Trump was better at "military stuff" and dealing with "other countries" compared to Obama. But he also shared the following: "I liked that Obama didn't like to separate races or anything. He liked to keep them together. Like, everyone's equal, because I believe that too. I feel like if you see a person of the different race, you shouldn't think anything different than if you were to see someone that looked exactly like you." In other words, the only thing that Obama was better at than Trump was not being racist. But, in the end, Simon preferred Trump.

"Just End Them"

Latinx immigrants and Black people were not the only groups that these white children perceived as threatening. For a handful of the boys interviewed, the biggest threat they felt was from "Middle Eastern countries." These boys talked a lot about the military and how Trump was better for the military than Obama had been. As eleven-year-old Bobby in Massachusetts put it, "Trump cares about protecting our country. I'm really happy he won." Similarly, ten-year-old Bryson in Mississippi told me, referencing his perceived threats from abroad, "I feel good. . . . I think he's gonna make the world a better place for the USA." And these boys explained that they thought kneeling for the national anthem in protest of racism was disrespectful specifically to people who serve or have served in the military. For some of these boys, they were interested in possibly being in the military in the future themselves, probably an expression of their masculine ideals.23

These boys also had strong opinions about their perception of the relationship between the United States and "other countries." They talked about the need for the United States to do more to stand up against other countries that "attack us" and how important it is not to let "our country" be "overruled by other countries," something these boys attributed to the presidency of Obama. And in these discussions about "other countries," these boys seemed focused on "Middle Eastern countries." While the group of white kids in chapter 3 were appalled by bans against immigrants from predominantly Muslim countries, some of the white boys described in this chapter celebrated the Muslim ban. Some even expressed their belief that Trump should take things a step further to prevent "Middle Eastern countries" from "hurting America."

For instance, Blake explained that he was fearful of international threats from countries in the Middle East and wanted Trump to protect him. Specifically, when I asked him if he thought Trump was doing a good job or a bad job as president, he answered, "It depends on if he protects us. If he is, then he's doing a good job. But if he keeps, like—if he keeps sending nukes and bombs when they're not needed, then he's doing a bad job." He continued by adding, "I would tell Trump to, like, try to end the war between the Middle East and us, 'cause you might not know: they might have a really good nuke that might blow us up. So . . . [shrugs]." Like other kids, Blake talked a lot about war and nuclear bombs and international conflict between the United States and other countries, specifically those in the Middle East. Like the children who believed Mexicans and Black people represented threats to their own personal safety but also that of the United States as a country, so too did these kids explain their perceptions that countries from the Middle East were threats that Trump needed to "deal with."

Other children agreed with Blake about the need for the United States to "protect itself" against the generalized perceived threat of "the Middle East." Ned introduced this topic on his own into the interview and expressed very strong emotions in the following exchange:

INTERVIEWER: Why do you think some people dislike Trump?
NED: They don't like his decisions. They probably don't like his decisions 'cause CNN is, like, up in New York, and they believe in different stuff than Republicans do.
INTERVIEWER: Okay, why do you think people in New York believe different things than Republicans?
NED: Well, like, some people in New York believe different things, but, like, Donald Trump is from New York, and he's Republican. But, like, [most of them] might believe in [being a Democrat] because of, like, different like, the lifestyle up there.
INTERVIEWER: Like, what kind of lifestyle?
NED: Like, it's not just, like, two races up there. It's like three— three gazillion, katrillion, so . . . There's, like, you know, Mexican, Black, white, Australian, British, um, Indian. There's, like, twenty races, but in the South, mostly it's just, like, three—three or four.

INTERVIEWER: Why do you think that having more races makes them have different opinions than Republicans?

NED: Like, 'cause they have more of a lifestyle. Like, they, like, come from, like, the Middle Eastern countries . . . and probably all the stuff that's going on in Iraq.

INTERVIEWER: What do you mean?

NED: I think it's silly that it's still going on, how, like, they've been fighting since 1999 and nobody's won and why they haven't dropped an atomic bomb on them.

INTERVIEWER: You think we should drop an atomic bomb on them?

NED: Mmmmhmm. It would just end them, so they wouldn't, like, come at us again.

Ned very quickly moved from "people in New York dislike Trump" to "we should drop an atomic bomb on the Middle East." In fact, it only took him two short steps to move from "there are lots of races" in New York to "everyone is a threat to us, and they should be wiped out." To Ned, regions of the country that he perceives of as more racially diverse than the Deep South are more likely to be politically liberal and more likely to pose a threat to people like him. They are also more likely to be where people from Middle Eastern countries live—countries that he perceives should be "ended." Ned's words powerfully demonstrate the interconnections he sees between various kinds of threats to his group position of dominance.

Overall, this group of white children explained, each in their own ways, their fear of immigrants crossing the southern border, Black people in general, and people from Middle Eastern countries. Clearly, the connections between these children's notions of which social groups represent a "threat" and those described by Trump as a "threat" were almost identical. This illustrates the powerful role that the political context of these children's childhoods played in shaping their ideas not only about government and certain politicians but also about racial groups and racist narratives about these groups more broadly. These children were very much aware of social groups being in conflict—and expressed racialized emotions connected to their status as a member of the dominant racial group. And this was true despite the claims otherwise that they did not care about racism or think much about it.

Racial Apathy as a Product of Racialized Emotions

At the end of Brayden's interview, he said, "I don't really know much about all that stuff," referring to interview questions about current events involving race. This is exactly the logic used by conservative parents, for example, when they argue against the teaching of the history of racism in schools: their child is "innocent" and does not know about this stuff, and it should stay that way. Based on what kids said initially about not knowing and not caring about racism, it might seem like this is true. It might seem on the surface that these white kids had no ideas about race and politics whatsoever or that, even if they did, it is not something they need to worry about. And yet, in talking with them and listening to what they said about *how they felt*, it was clear that these kids cared a lot about racism. Specifically, they demonstrated their anger toward and fear of Black people, immigrants and Latinx people generally, and Muslim or Middle Eastern people. Their fear was wrapped up in how they understood themselves as white children, how they made sense of their group position and perceived threats, and their desire to maintain their position of dominance. We cannot understand how they learn about race without accounting for their racialized emotions, since these emotions inform so much of what they then think ideologically.

Through childhood cultural routines such as playing games and engaging in racist humor, these kids constructed understandings of themselves as members of the dominant racial group in opposition to other groups of people within a society organized hierarchically by race and working to maintain these established group boundaries. Together, in concert with other children whom they viewed as similarly positioned to themselves, these kids interpretively reproduced ideas about racism in US society that shifted to fit the new conditions in which they experienced the social world—in this case, the Trump era. These kids made sense of their identity as a member of a social group through the games they played and the jokes they made—especially those in exclusively white settings. These games and jokes were not just about demonizing others or minimizing racism, though of course that was happening. But these games and jokes can also be understood as being a "meditation of the self" in which these white children's own fears and desires and their own sense of "us" versus "them" were revealed and shared with each other as a form of group identity formation.24

As these kids encountered their racialized social environment—a racial context of childhood shaped by many factors including the political landscape—they not only produced ideas and emotions about other groups of people but also produced understandings of themselves, their own group position, and where they fit in the racial order. Their sense of self as an individual white child was wrapped up their sense of group membership—a distinction that separates themselves from the "other." As the scholar Joel Kovol theorized decades ago, white fears of Blackness and Black bodies develop in white childhood as white kids learn to associate Black people with "dirt, danger, ignorance or the unknown."25 Just as kids of color are learning to "feel race" in childhood, as discussed in chapter 4, so too are white kids.26

Overall, I find that the ideological expression of racial apathy, of saying "I don't care" or "I don't know," is a product of racialized emotions. Although it may seem on the surface that racial apathy is a claim to feeling no emotion, beneath the surface, racial apathy is a lack of empathy with a whole lot of other emotions attached. For the kids described in this chapter, feeling superior, feeling powerful, and experiencing joy are all emotional experiences that these children like and want to continue to have. And the ideology of racial apathy serves to enable them to continue feeling those feel-ings. When white children play racist games at recess or tell racist jokes, they feel joy from laughing at people of color—and they like feeling that joy. Indeed, as these data show, they feel supported in experiencing that pleasure, here, by their white peers who laugh alongside them. These kids want to continue to experience the pleasure of feeling superior. And in order to do this without feeling bad or "racist" themselves, they believe that they do not care about racism. Racial apathy, then, emerges as an ideological position in response to a racialized emotion. In other words, it is the racialized emotion of pleasure, and the joy that comes with feeling dominant, that produces the claim that these children do not care. Of course, they do care and have a great deal of fear and anxiety about people of color. However, by believing that they do not care, they are able to maintain their pleasure of feeling superior—and continue to tell racist jokes and play racist games.

The pleasure, delight, fear, and anger expressed by this group of children in connection with the 2016 election led them to how they "understand a racial regime," or how they understand race and ra-cial hierarchy.27 It is for this reason, among others, that we must expand our theories of racial socialization and racial learning to include theories of racialized emotions. Not only recognizing that affective logic develops in childhood but also understanding how it functions overall is useful because it helps explain why, for in-stance, people might not vote in ways that align with their mate-rial interests. It explains how even if Trump's policies denied people like oneself access to good health care or education for one's kids, one still might support him.28 As Bonilla-Silva argues, Trump *made emotional sense* to his supporters when he talked about "draining the swamp" or getting rid of immigrants or banning Muslims or ridiculing Black Lives Matter protestors—that is, protecting them from "people who threaten [them]."29 Trump appealed to their rac-ism at the emotional level. What my research shows is that these emotions not only matter in adulthood but begin to develop long before people even reach the legal age to vote. And they play a foundational role in the production of racial ideas by kids. In this way, white kids, too, "feel race."

Race-making in childhood, then, or the social construction of race itself by kids as they try to make sense of the world in which they live, includes, at its core, the racialized emotions of kids. Racialized emotions are foundational to white racial socialization. And this is true even when kids claim to "not care" about race-related issues or when they express pleasure and delight at mocking entire racial groups of people.

As the words of the kids presented here illustrate in profound ways, these kids have many feelings and thoughts about race-related issues, even if they often disguise these behind claims of racial apathy or "joking around." Analyzing the "full range" of racialized emotions and how these emotions are expressed at early ages, as well as exploring how all of these emotions and ideas are shaped by the political landscape, offers insights into previously unexplored aspects of white racial learning processes.

6

"Hurry Up and Build That Wall!"

The Future of Dominant White Racial Ideology

CARTER: Trump is kind of racist, kind of not. He kind of is building a wall so other people won't come in. And that is kind of racist. . . .

INTERVIEWER: What would you say to President Trump if you met him?

CARTER: I would make a joke like, "Hurry up and build that wall!"

During the early 2010s, I conducted ethnographic research with a group of white families in order to explore how white kids learn about race and what their ideas constitute. One of the things I found then was that many of the kids embraced colorblind racism. They told me things like, "Racism was a problem in the olden days" or "Racism is not a problem anymore." These kids also defended themselves against accusations of racism and were cautious to say anything about race out of concern that it might come across as racist. Other kids believed that there were some bad, racist people in the world but that generally things were better than in the past. Still other kids in this previous study held racially progressive views and rejected colorblind ideology: they believed, for example, that racism is not just an individual-level or interpersonal phenomenon but rather is built into the laws, policies, and organization of US society. These kids talked about the racial wealth gap and residential segregation and policing practices that they thought were racially unjust. Despite the important variations in the ideological expressions of these white children in that Obama-era study, there was one thing they all shared: all of the kids agreed that racism was bad.

I was surprised, then, when I met white kids in this new research, like those featured in chapter 5, who were willing to state confidently that they were not bothered when people like Trump were overtly racist. I was surprised when instead of saying things like "there is no racism in America," they instead recognized that racism *is* present but not something that they think is especially problematic. I was surprised when kids, in describing racism, said, "It is what it is" or "It's fine." I was surprised not only that kids were tolerant of explicit forms of racism but that they participated in reproducing these overt forms of racist hate in their play and peer interactions.

While the children from the previous study still participated in the production and reproduction of racism—especially the "softer" colorblind version of racism—it is striking that only a few years later, similarly aged white kids in both Massachusetts and Mississippi were so unapologetically willing to embrace traditional, overt expressions of racism. In this theoretical chapter, I primarily explore the racial ideological positions of the kids who supported Trump during this new political era. I consider what we might learn from these white kids about the reproduction of dominant ideology, as well as the possibility for alternative racial ideologies to emerge, how racialized emotions and racial ideologies are connected, and what this could mean for the future.

Colorblind Ideology: Will It Remain Dominant?

Anti-Trump White Kids

The white kids described in chapter 3 offer convincing evidence that, at least for them, colorblind ideology is not going anywhere anytime soon, even with the explicit forms of racism on display during the era of Trump that horrified these children. It is true that a few of the white children said that growing up in the era of Trump fundamentally changed how they viewed the United States as a country, democracy, and racism—that they cannot unsee what has become visible and that they know they must do something productive with the anger they feel about the racially unequal reality surrounding them. These kids show that racialized emotions play a fundamental role in racial learning processes that lead kids to form ideological perspectives about what racism is, why it exists, and why it persists. But these kids were outliers in this research.

What most of the white kids disgusted by Trump believed instead was that if they waited long enough until Trump was out of office, things would "go back to normal." These children viewed racism as the result of the bad behavior of one individual—Donald Trump—which illustrated their continued commitment to the tenets of colorblind racism. These kids believed that it was not that the country is deeply racist; instead, it was that there was an individual in power who was racist—and convinced a lot of other people to be racist—but that once he was gone, things would be okay again and return to "normal." As many critics and race scholars have pointed out, however, the "normal politics" of the pre-Trump era were not void of racist policies and structures. Things were not "okay" when it came to racism in the US. Instead, forms of racism like colorblindness simply allowed for white people to "make non-racial claims about what are indeed racial disparities" and avoid taking any responsibility for the privileges of whiteness or the perpetuation of inequality.1 Returning to "normal," then, means little with regard to addressing ongoing racial inequality in the United States, even for kids who were horrified by Trump's explicitly racist public statements. In the case of most of the white kids who opposed Trump, then, it seems that colorblind racism is here to stay.

Further, as I argue in chapter 3, many of these children retreated back to colorblind thinking as a way to make themselves feel better, as a way to alleviate their feelings of shame, guilt, and anger. This illustrates how racialized emotions can drive the ideological views that children embrace or reject.

Pro-Trump White Kids

Something slightly more complicated than a straightforward reproduction of colorblind ideology appeared to be under way for the
children described in chapter 5. On the one hand, they offered evidence that colorblind ideology is likely to remain the dominant way
that Americans make sense of race. On the other hand, it is possible to characterize their words and emotions as fitting with a new,
alternative racial ideological framework.

One of the ways these kids reproduced colorblind racism was
through their expressions of racial apathy, an important extension of colorblind ideology. When these children told me they did
not know much about racism or care much about it, they disengaged from even having to think about the topic. And these kids
are not alone. Nationally representative data with high school students indicate not only that racial apathy is present but that it is on
the rise—that our current racial landscape increasingly includes
claims by young white people that they are unconcerned or do not
even know about racial issues altogether.2 And racial apathy has
powerful consequences. As Tyrone Forman explains, "If, in the
face of entrenched, systemic, and institutionalized racial inequality, most whites say that they have no negative feelings toward
racial minorities but feel no responsibility to do anything about
enduring racial and ethnic inequalities and in fact object to any
programmatic solutions to addressing those inequalities, is that
progress, or is it rather a new form of prejudice in its passive support for an unequal racial status quo?"3 Although expressions of
racial apathy may not directly disparage entire groups of people or
call for violence against them, the consequences of racial apathy
lead to a reproduction of the unequal racial status quo. Further,
as we have seen, expressions of racial apathy are a product of the
racialized emotions that kids experience, particularly that of pleasure. Saying "I don't know" or "I don't care" allows white youth to
carry on engaging in racist behavior that allows them to maintain

the pleasure and joy that they get from experiencing dominance without feeling bad about doing so.

Another way that these kids embraced colorblind ideology was in how they used racist humor. As recent scholars of racist humor have pointed out, racist jokes are often tied directly to colorblind ideology. Given the pressure people feel to go along with race-based jokes, these jokes "generate a normative response of silence, inaction or engagement with the joke," which reinforces colorblind ideology.4 When people deny that racist jokes are racist, this serves the social function of "deepening" racism in society.5 Building on these claims, Raúl Pérez argues that the logic used to defend the use of racist jokes "upholds the central frames of colorblind racism."6 In his words, "the strategic use and circulation of racist jokes during the post-civil-rights era, via equal opportunity offender rhetoric" (e.g., "I target everyone with my jokes! This isn't about racism!), "contributed to the articulation, reproduction, and acceptability of racist humor during the emergence of a 'colorblind' racial ideology."7 He argues, in fact, that racist jokes are an "everyday mechanism" that "contribute[s] to legitimizing, strengthening, and advancing 'common sense' notions of race and racism."8

Scholars who have studied the legacy of racist jokes in the United States have argued that these jokes reinforce notions of inferiority and superiority among racial groups. They show how making jokes "works to strengthen an ideology that maintains that racism is no longer a serious social issue" through trying to "minimize and normalize" racism as "unserious and far removed from 'racial hatred.'"9 In this sense, the jokes the children told and the games they played can be understood as attempts to minimize the real suffering of the targets of their joking, thereby reinforcing colorblind ideology.

And yet, when these jokes and games are taken into consideration alongside all the other racialized emotions that these children expressed, particularly their expressions of explicit racist hate, it could also be argued that these children are engaging in the work of producing an alternative racial ideology. For example, rather than joking around about immigrants to demonstrate that immigrants do not actually face racism, these kids joked around about immigrants because they believed that immigrants are not supposed to be here. Rather than distancing themselves from racist hate, these children appeared at times to celebrate it. In this sense, these children are embracing far-right ideologies that differ from the dominant racial ideology of colorblind racism.

White Rage, White Resentment, and Racial Ideologies

In order to even try to predict the future of dominant racial ideologies, my research shows that we should probably do more to account for racialized emotions—and how these emotions and ideologies inform each other as part of childhood racial learning processes. Examining the contours of ideology, the discursive strategies used during the Trump era, the inconsistencies in ideological expression, and how this relates to dominant ideology is certainly important. But so too is interrogating *how Trump's rhetoric made white people feel*—and how these feelings are deeply connected to how people, including kids, feel race. As explored in chapter 5, Trump made many of these kids feel safe from perceived threats. But he also made them feel angry that these threats existed in the first place or that others refused to recognize the threats for what they were.

The African American studies scholar Carol Anderson documents how Black advancement, whether it be in the form of voting rights or school desegregation or with respect to increases in Black economic and political power, has historically been and continues to be viewed as a threat to white dominance. The "white rage" that emerges from the expansion of equal rights to Black people is not about "visible violence" but instead "works its way through the courts, the legislatures, and a range of government bureaucracies," or, as Anderson describes, the "halls of power."[10] "The country's growing diversity, Obama's very existence in the White House, and the ever-increasing visibility of African Americans in college and corporations had fueled a sense that these gains were 'likely to reduce the influence of white Americans in society.' Trump's win exposed in frightening ways the 'ethnonationalist rage centered around a black president' and the fear that all the resources and wealth accumulated through centuries of public policy would be subjected to 'redistribution from older white America to its younger, more diverse' population."11 The idea that immigrants steal jobs, for instance, is connected to Anderson's concept of "white rage" as well as the notion of *white racial resentment*.12 This rage and resentment lead working-class white people to support policies that do not help them materially but that do appeal to them on an emotional level.

The medical sociologist Jonathan Metzl explores racial resentment across policies like education, gun control, and health care, and he finds that white people would literally rather die than support policies that would benefit people of color—even if those policies would also benefit themselves. As he writes, "When politics demands that people resist available health care, amass arsenals, cut funding for schools that their own kids attend, or make other decisions that might feel emotionally correct but are biologically perilous, these politics are literally asking people to die for their whiteness. Living in a state or a county or a nation dominated by the politics of racial resentment then becomes a diagnosable, quantifiable, and increasingly mortal preexisting condition."13 The children described in chapter 5 expressed versions of the "white anxieties" that Metzl found in his research with adults. They also expressed the racialized emotions that the sociologist Joe Feagin previously observed in white adults, like "racial hatred, racial arrogance, and a sense of racial superiority," as well as "a desire for dominance over others."14 Clearly, these children felt racialized emotions that led to particular ideological frameworks. At early ages, these kids learned to fear losing power and to fear their group's losing its dominant position. They learned to take pleasure and pride in the belief that they are superior to other groups and deserve this dominant position even as members of other groups suffer. These kids openly celebrated the dehumanization of entire racial and ethnic groups of people and called for more racist violence against these groups— and they did so with confidence and pride and an absolute sense of white racial dominance.

Indeed, Trump's rhetoric drew powerful racialized emotions out of white people, which in turn, shaped the ideas they produced about race. As Cameron Lippard and colleagues explore in a volume dedicated to understanding whiteness during the Trump era, this era witnessed a form of "whitelash," or "individual, institutional, and structural countermeasures against the dismantling of white supremacy or actions, real or imagined, that seek to remedy existing racial inequities" or, put plainly, "action and reaction against any progressive change that would call out racism."15 Importantly, they discuss how it is a "fear of change" that undergirds whitelash—a sense of fear that white people may lose their dominant group position.

What my own research shows is that these racialized emotions are not just reserved for white adults: they are developing in white children too, and they lead to the formation of kids' racial ideas— ideas we know are hard to change as kids reach late adolescence.

"New White Nationalism"

While white supremacy has always been part of US society, the Trump era ushered in a normalization of explicitly racist expressions and rhetoric that sociologists argue reinforced a "populist authoritarianism."16 As the sociologist Woody Doane theorizes, "What was considered beyond the pale or 'hate speech' has crept back into the mainstream, reminding us that distance was not as far as had been assumed. The white resistance we have seen in recent years is not new. . . . It is the latest manifestation of dominant group reaction to social changes and gains by oppressed groups that are seen as threatening to white supremacy."17 Doane argues that this new white nationalism includes elements of nationalism, external/internal threat, and an increased tolerance for racism. And he emphasizes that the emergence of this "new white nationalism" is a distinct racial ideology that presents an alternative to colorblind ideology. However, rather than colorblind ideology disappearing and being replaced by something new, Doane argues that a "new white nationalism" has emerged that "coexists and overlaps with both classical racism and colorblindness."18

My research supports Doane's theory. What is more, this framework helps explain why, for example, these kids expressed both racial apathy, an extension of colorblind ideology, at the same time that they also expressed ideas that correspond with new white nationalism—after all, ideologies are complex, inconsistent, and "in a constant state of flux, buffeted by the ever-changing political and social context."19 As such, even with this group of Trump-supporting white kids, it is inaccurate to conclude that they have outright rejected colorblind ideology or that colorblind ideology is no longer a dominant framework through which people understand race. "The political nature of racial ideologies requires that they be dynamic and flexible in order to maintain their utility in intergroup struggle."20 Instead, it is more accurate to view these kids as holding multiple racial ideological positions that are fluid and malleable and that overlap, at times even informing one another in complex ways.

What I have shown in this book is that children enact agency and participate in adapting dominant frameworks, like colorblind ideology, to fit new social conditions, such as a change in political leadership—and that racialized emotions seem to be a driving force behind the formation of racial ideas. Some of these children reject this dominant ideology. Others incorporate disruptions to colorblind ideology and rework colorblind ideology to fit these new conditions. And other kids seem to embrace both colorblind ideology and the new white nationalism. As Doane warns, "Analysts have tended to cordon off white supremacist ideology as limited to a small fringe of extremists. . . . In contrast, I contend that the new white nationalism has a much larger segment of the population that either share its view or, like Republican politicians, are willing to tolerate them in order to achieve conservative political objectives."21 In this sense, the new white nationalism, while not the dominant racial ideology of our day, has arguably become mainstream, available to be interpreted by both adults and kids alike.

The sociologist Cynthia Miller-Idriss, who serves as the director of the Polarization and Extremism Research and Innovation Lab at American University, studies the mainstreaming of far-right ideology and how youths become radicalized.22 She finds that young people are drawn into this growing, global far-right subculture through everyday encounters with "extremist messages and ideas in their ordinary lives—perhaps long before they have made an ideological commitment to the far right."23 She documents how interactions within everyday cultural spaces and scenes like schools, online spaces, soccer stadiums, fitness clubs, and even some evangelical churches, as well as consumption of commercialized products like music, clothing brands, and other products, provides youth access to far-right ideas. Unlike fringe groups of the past, she finds that young people encounter antisemitic, racist, and nationalist symbols and codes regularly in ordinary life as these messages have become widely available in mainstream society. To this point, in a guest essay she wrote in the *New York Times* on the one-year anniversary of the events of January 6, 2021, she stated, "Everyone is just a few clicks away from an ever-expanding series of rabbit holes that offer up whole worlds of disinformation and hate."24

Based on what I heard from the white kids in my study—not yet late adolescents or young adults but ten- to thirteen-year-old *children*—it seemed that at least some of them had the potential to be moving toward "the peripheries of far-right movements."25 When children expressed ideals of living in an exclusionary white ethnostate or when they engaged in behaviors that functioned to dehumanize groups of people or when they described an "existential threat to the dominant group" by claiming that there is a "need to defend or protect the country, the homeland, or the dominant people from immigration or demographic change," they articulated ideologies propagated by global far-right movements.26

Miller-Idriss also finds in her work that humor—like the jokes and costumes and games of the children described in chapter 5— also plays a powerful role in the radicalization of youth: "Jokes and funny memes create collective laughter and a sense of community among those who feel like insiders for getting the joke. They create plausible deniability and depict anyone who is offended as a triggered, liberal snowflake who doesn't get the joke. In this way, humor and satire shift the far right from a defensive to an offensive cultural position and help far right youth come across as counter-cultural and edgy, while simultaneously shifting public conversation to include more extreme ideologies."27 When children engage in violent and dehumanizing forms of play in which they trivialize human suffering and vilify entire racial or ethnic groups, they are doing the work of processing racialized emotions and desensitizing themselves to the many messages they have interpreted from interacting with the social world around them. So when Ned makes jokes about building walls, there is much more going on than simply a schoolyard game. The result of this play is the normalization of dehumanizing, racist, and potentially even far-right extremist ways of thinking.

Given what we know about how difficult it is to change the racial ideological perspectives of college students and young adults, the findings of kids moving toward the periphery of the far right is alarming.28 As Miller-Idriss convincingly writes, "It is my strongest belief that we need to understand as much as possible how young people are thinking in order to develop effective strategies to address this kind of hatred."29 I agree. My research suggests that in addition to understanding how kids are thinking, we also need to pay close attention to how they are feeling—and how what they are feeling is not just an individual-level emotion but a group-level one too. My research finds that racialized emotions shape the racial ideologies that are produced by kids in middle childhood, years before they reach adolescence. For these reasons, it is important to extend existing theories of childhood racial learning and incorporate more macro-level, sociological factors in these theories, such as the political context of one's childhood as well as racialized emotions.

In conclusion, it is unknown what the future of dominant racial ideology will be. The lead-up to the 2016 election of Trump and the four years that followed provided a unique case to study because this time period was one in which young people were exposed to conflicting, contradictory, and inconsistent messages about racism in the US. Evidence from listening to the kids in this research discuss how they interpreted these moments suggests that it is unlikely that colorblind ideology will disappear or even become less dominant. However, this research also provides empirical support for the theory that two alternatives to colorblind ideology have emerged, at least among the children interviewed in this research: one that rejects colorblindness in lieu of racially progressive ideas and another that explicitly embraces racist hate and white supremacy.

Conclusion

What Can We Do?

My son generally has the view that "hope is stupid," and I get it. The events of his life have supported that [view]. . . . He is angry and cynical that this is how the world is.

—ANITA, MOTHER OF THIRTEEN-YEAR-OLD SON

I began the new year of 2021 thinking that I had all the data I needed to write this book. President Trump's time in office was complete. I had interviewed the kids I planned to interview, I had analyzed my data for months, and I was ready to start writing. But then, January 6, 2021, happened. Like millions of others, I watched with horror as a mob of primarily white people, wearing Trump paraphernalia and waving Confederate flags, stormed the US Capitol building, chanting and shouting "USA! USA!," breaking down police barriers, and smashing windows open. They attacked and pushed past police officers, they shouted violent threats, and they looted the offices of members of Congress. Lawmakers were evacuated as members of this riotous mob worked their way through the building with the goal of disrupting Congress as it engaged in the democratic process of officially counting electoral votes and formally certifying that Joe Biden won the 2020 election. As I watched the events of the day unfold from my living room, I immediately wondered what American children were feeling and thinking as they saw these same images on their own television screens in their own living rooms. After listening to so many kids share their thoughts with me about what it was like to be a kid during the Trump era, I was genuinely curious about their ideas in this moment, at the dramatic end of Trump's term and in light of an attempted insurrection and Trump's refusal to concede election defeat.

In the days and weeks that followed, I talked with kids and parents in Mississippi and Massachusetts whenever and however I could about children's reactions to the attack on the Capitol.1 Perhaps unsurprisingly, however, much of what I heard from kids and parents paralleled what I had already found from conducting this research over the course of Trump's presidency. In fact, the most useful thing to come from these additional interviews was confirmation of much of what I had already observed: none of these children were shielded from or unaware of what happened on January 6, and the kids had many emotions about the attempted insurrection that related to how they made sense of racism in the US overall.

Like with my larger findings, the kids of color with whom I spoke or whose parents I interviewed were both demoralized and disgusted by what they saw on January 6, but they continued to express motivation for political organizing. These kids, and some of their white peers, drew explicit connections between the violence of that day and white violence in US society more broadly. This was particularly true for kids in Mississippi, who were more familiar with the meaning of the Confederate flag, which they saw on display in the Capitol rotunda that day. But other white kids believed that Trump rightfully won the election and thought it was appropriate for people like them to defend what had happened. I heard about the renewal of arguments and even fights on the school bus between kids about the attempted insurrection and relationships within families and among peers shifting even more than had already happened during the Trump years. But all the kids, no matter what position they took, continued to express racialized emotions.

In Massachusetts, for example, Anita and her two children, aged nine and thirteen, were working and going to school virtually due to the COVID-19 pandemic in January 2021. Suddenly, their afternoon was disrupted as Anita received notifications on her phone about the tension building in Washington, DC. She turned on her television to scenes of violence, and her children watched with her as the US Capitol was stormed. She shared with me her perception of her children's reactions: "Well, the nine-year-old was and is still processing what happened," she explained. "But to him, this was not particularly unusual. Trump's presidency is all he can really remember, so he thinks things like this are just how things are." She shared a bit more about her younger son's interests and personality. Then she turned her attention to her older son. "My thirteen-year-old son has a very cynical view of the world due to the pandemic, climate change, and especially Trump and all the terrible things he does." Anita told me that her son has grown more negative over the past four years: "When he talked about what happened at the Capitol, he basically just said that it all confirmed his outlook on the world. To him, no matter what happens, things are always going to get worse. And yesterday was just yet another example of that. . . . My son generally has the view that 'hope is stupid,' and I get it. The events of his life have supported that idea." Anita told me that she thought perhaps some of his cynicism was part of being an "ironic teenager" or maybe even part of his temperament; but, without a doubt, she also believed that something fundamental to her son's understandings of the world had shifted over the previous four years in response to the political and racial climate of his childhood. "He has witnessed an increase in chaos, death, and destruction during his formative years," she told me matter-of-factly. "He views the world as not a very happy or safe place. He does not trust that things will turn out okay, especially because he identifies as a South Asian person of color, and *he is angry* and cynical that this is how the world is" (emphasis added).

Like many of the kids of color described in this book, Anita also told me that it is her son's righteous anger that motivates him to pay attention to the news and to act in ways that will create change. "He feels like no one else is going to do anything about these terrible things, so if he doesn't try to do something, things will only get worse." Anita told me that she believed her children's perceptions of racism—among other topics—were powerfully influenced by the political and racial context that uniquely defined their childhood, that is, the Trump era. Evidence from interviews I conducted with kids certainly supports Anita's theory.

At the end of our interview, Anita confided in me. She said, "You know, I'm not really sure what I should do to help him." She shared ideas of things she was trying, like connecting her kids with existing groups organizing for racial and environmental justice in her community or talking with him at length about the political news of the day; but, ultimately, she seemed to be somewhat at a loss over what to do about her son's disappointment about the prevalence of racism in his country and his disillusionment with the US political system overall. She especially seemed to struggle with her son's notion that "hope is stupid," though she completely understood why he felt the way he did.

Anita's question is a version of the same question I have heard asked over and over by parents, school leaders, teachers, social workers, doctors, colleagues, and even close friends: What can we do? What can we do to positively influence racial learning processes in ways that help prepare young people to live in a multiracial democracy? What can we do to raise kids who reject racist thinking and actions? What can we as adults do to help kids feel empowered and hopeful rather than believing that "hope is stupid"? What can we do to help young people reject forms of racial apathy that allow for racial comfort in a deeply unequal racialized society? How can we challenge ideologies of hate and disinformation that are growing more prevalent and more mainstream, not just in the United States but across the globe? What can we do to help kids process the strong emotions they feel that are connected to their social location in hierarchies of power? What can we do to empower young people to work for a future that is more equitable, just, and ethical for all of us collectively, rather than just good for each of them as an individual? How can we help young people actively work to dismantle rather than reinforce racist systems?

Although I certainly do not have all the answers to these difficult questions, in this concluding chapter, I offer some concrete ideas of the kinds of interventions I believe we need. These ideas are based on the lessons I have taken away from the data in this study—that is, from listening to kids as they talk about their thoughts and feelings on racism and politics. Many of these interventions apply specifically to the kinds of things white people ought to do, as I believe white people must take account of our own culpability in the perpetuation of racism—and this includes white kids.

Reject Myths of White Childhood "Innocence"

The myth of the innocent white child is pervasive in US society and throughout history.2 This myth centers the feelings of white kids and operates to protect white children from experiencing negative racialized emotions related to their position in the racial hierarchy that brings them unearned advantages. However, kids of color are not afforded this assumption or privilege of "childhood innocence." How kids of color feel is often ignored, and instead they are disproportionately treated as if they are "bad" kids or even criminals.3

But the evidence is clear: white children are not "innocent" members of society who are unaware of racism, political debates, or current events. The white kids in this book talked about their desire to drop atomic bombs on entire regions of the globe. They talked about the racist jokes and games they played. Their white peers (and possibly even some of them) violently assaulted children of color, and they used racist language modeled after Trump's racist rhetoric. White kids laughed when asked about racism or made plans to stop worrying about racism once Trump was out of office. It was clear to me that children had formed feelings and ideas about the very topics that many adults claim kids "don't know about" or "can't learn about" because it will harm them or make them feel bad.

The first thing adults can do to achieve the previously stated goals is to reject the myth of white childhood "innocence."

Recognize How and Where Kids Learn Racism

Because I wrote a book called *White Kids: Growing Up with Privilege in a Racially Divided America*, I have been asked countless times by reporters, parents, and colleagues, *How should white parents talk to their kids about race?* Parenting magazines and advice columnists frequently write about this topic. Researchers increasingly seem interested in studying these white family conversations. And this question often emerges in moments like the "racial reckoning" of 2020 following the murders of Breonna Taylor and George Floyd, when suddenly more white parents expressed interest in talking about race with kids in color-conscious rather than colorblind ways.

This question, though, even if well intentioned, reflects another common misguided assumption about white children. To be clear, I absolutely think talking about race in family contexts is more productive than not talking about race. And I think it is good to see new researchers, particularly in child development, increasingly study these emerging conversations about race in white families after years of treating white families as if they did not "have race."4 But kids do not form their ideas about race exclusively on the basis of one conversation at the family dinner table or even a series of discussions about racism with parents. Kids do not only learn about race through conversations with their parents, no matter how popular this line of thinking is. As such, interventions cannot solely be offered at the level of parent-child conversations about race. Children learn about race through their own observations and interpretations of their social environment, or ideas and feelings they produce from living within a particular "*racial context of childhood*."5 A racial context includes local dynamics, such as patterns they observe in their communities and schools or interactions they have with family members or peers or what they notice at soccer practice, on television, in restaurants, in professional sports, or even on vacation or when volunteering. This means that decisions parents make about where to live or where to send kids to school or what media to consume matter in significant ways for the kind of social environments that surround their children.

What makes this even more complicated is that children are actors in this process: they interpret this context and the messages within it. As a result, the racial context that parents design for their children shapes kids' ideas about the social world, and the behaviors that parents model, even in subtle ways like locking car doors in Black neighborhoods, convey powerful racial messages to young people. Actions speak louder than words. And, as I show in *White Kids*, this remains true no matter what parents might say to their kids about being antiracist. We miss these important aspects of racial learning when we focus exclusively on family conversations about race.

I am not the only social scientist who has called for more complex theories of racial learning—theories that extend beyond the traditional racial socialization frameworks that focus exclusively on parent reports of their discussions with kids. The African American studies scholar Erin Winkler has shown how Black kids learn about race through a comprehensive process that includes aspects of where they physically live and spend their time. She shows, for example, how leaving a particular community to go to another one provides kids with powerful lessons about how race works in the United States.6 Scholars like Amanda Lewis, John Diamond, Karolyn Tyson, and Carla Shedd, among many others, have studied the messages that children receive about race and racism at school or on their way to school.7 Sociologists like Debra Van Ausdale and Joe Feagin have explored the messages that children interpret in early childhood day-care settings.8 Scholars have studied summer camps and kids' television.9 And Miller-Idriss points to social media spaces, memes, music, video games, food, fashion, mixed martial arts, educational spaces, and more as sites where young people are increasingly exposed to white supremacist and far-right propaganda.10

Racial learning happens *in addition to* family conversations about race. Thus, when it comes to what can be done to interrupt some aspects of what kids are learning about race, we first must take account of these many different messengers of racial knowledge. We must recognize that our interventions cannot not simply apply to what happens within families. We must account for the way racial learning works in its entirety, including, as I argue in this book, the political landscape of a kid's childhood as well as the racialized emotions that they produce as they begin to "feel race." Another thing adults can do to work against apathy, hate, and hopelessness with kids, then, is to embrace a more sophisticated understanding of how and where kids learn ideas about racism and develop interventions that extend beyond new conversations in white families.

Understand Racialized Emotions in Childhood

As I have shown in the book, it is not just *what* kids observe in their social and political environment that informs their racial learning but also *how they feel* race—and how these emotions are shared by others who are similarly positioned with the racial hierarchy. Though scholars have provided vivid ethnographic accounts depicting children's racialized emotions, this concept is rarely named in larger theories of racial socialization or racial learning. It is clear that racialized emotions play a foundational role in racial learning processes and guide children to various ideological positions. Often, these racialized emotions are connected to the events of the day in a child' life, whether it be racist actions of a peer at school or political rhetoric used during a presidential address. And as this book shows, these emotions inform the racial ideas children produce.

Given this, another thing we can do as adults to help prepare children to live in a multiracial democracy is to identify the powerful role that group-based racialized emotions play in US society and politics, recognize that racialized emotions form in childhood, and appreciate that racialized emotions are fluid and can change. With this knowledge, as Bonilla-Silva argues, we can develop an "effective affective politics" used to "challenge the racial order."11 Certainly, the anger and disgust of the kids of color in this book, as well as that of some of the white kids, contributed to a sense of group solidarity that led some of them to learn more about Black history, motivated them to stand up against racism when they felt it was safe to do so, and for some, pushed them to want to join with others in social organizing efforts to change the racial order. Fully supporting young people and their desires and youth-led efforts to do this work is yet another step we can take as adults. We can also work to build awareness about the kind of findings that Jonathan Metzl presents—that racism is literally killing white Americans and that living in a more equitable society can be good for all people.12

We can and must also work to develop strategies to decrease racial apathy. One common solution to apathy that is often cited is increasing empathy. And one environment that is often discussed is that of social emotional learning (SEL) curricula in school settings. While this sounds appealing and although this is certainly a strategic place to build a curriculum that resists racial apathy, scholars like Dena Simmons who study this topic warn of the potential negative outcomes of doing this. As she explains, when social emotional learning in school settings is not culturally responsive or attempts to be racially "neutral," much like antibullying programs discussed previously, it brings the risk of reinforcing white supremacy. As Simmons warns, "SEL that fails to address our sociopolitical reality and combat racial and social injustice will not prepare our young people for the world they will inherit." Instead, Simmons calls for schools to take responsibility for the harm they cause students of color and engage in practices of "collective healing."13

Despite these important considerations, for those white kids who say they do not care about racism, even though they know it exists, finding ways to cultivate empathy and other forms of social emotional learning that "fosters a political will to act" cannot be disregarded. Finding ways to encourage white kids to "feel *with* people of color" is also something we can work to do, drawing on expertise from critical, antiracist SEL scholars like Simmons in the process, such that we do not reinforce "white supremacy with a hug."14 This work probably includes helping white children develop more accurate understandings of the history of racial injustice in the US, as discussed later in this chapter. But this work also requires the challenging work of helping children make sense of and navigate their own white identity and what it means to be racialized as white in US society. This is important because "white identity is connected to privilege" as well as "a host of political and social behaviors."15 Lessons from kids like Zena, Peyton, and Zach in this book are useful examples, as we can see that it is possible for white kids to deeply care about the experiences of people of color and take action in their own life to work for racial justice, even though they cannot vote and are often told to stop talking about racism.

Think Sociologically about Kids' Racial and Political Learning

Sociologists like me are not the only social scientists to theorize how the political landscape of a person's childhood shapes social attitudes and behaviors. Political scientists have long been concerned with understanding the voting behaviors of people and why people develop the partisan identities that they do. One classical theory that comes from this field is Karl Mannheim's concept of *generational imprinting*, which "implies that the present foreshadows the future: events and personalities that shape the political attitudes prevalent among younger cohorts when they enter political life will continue to register in future years."16 In other words, the political moment in which one comes of age and first learns about politics has been shown to shape the political attitudes and behaviors of people, not only in adolescence but for years to come.17

Though this theory is focused on the formation of partisan identity specifically, this research is also useful in thinking about ways to expand our understandings of racial learning among children.

Overall, kids' racial learning processes and outcomes can be more fully understood—and can be more strategically influenced—when we think sociologically about them. Another thing we as adults can do to address racial apathy, hate, and hopelessness, then, is to *think sociologically about how kids learn about race and racism.* This means that we need to work to better understand "the interplay of [individuals] and society, of biography and history, of self and world," and when we do, we can "achieve lucid summations of what is going on in the world."[18] Despite popular assumptions that kids are somehow removed from the political realm, children's racialized emotions and ideological perspectives on race are, in part, informed by the political landscape of their childhood.

Counter Explicit Racist Rhetoric and White Kids' Hateful Actions

By appreciating more fully how and where kids encounter messages about race, both within and outside of the family, adults working with kids in a wide range of realms can develop proactive and early interventions at countering racist rhetoric and white kids' racist behaviors. As Miller-Idriss recommends, countering far-right hate, especially with young people, requires more than just "government monitoring of extremists."[19] Drawing on what Germany has embraced following the Nazi era, she suggests that we need increased media literacy skills and awareness efforts about "extremist propaganda and disinformation campaigns that work to destabilize the public's trust in government by claiming elections were illegitimate, news is fake, or all politicians are corrupt."[20] Given what she has learned about where these messages are propagated, we need everyone, from martial arts teachers to summer camp counselors to school leaders to parents to nonparents, to increase their awareness of extremist rhetoric and improve their ability to identify it when they see it. Miller-Idriss also points out that law enforcement monitors extremist activity that has escalated to the level of criminal violence but that "radicalization pathways begin at the peripheries."[21]

When we think about the kids described in chapter 5 of this book, what interventions are being made to address their engagement with far-right ideas? After all, these kinds of ideas played a powerful role not just in the January 6 attack but also in what the sociologist Victor Ray refers to as the "institutionalized erosion of American democracy" more generally, evidenced by new voter-suppression tactics, new laws banning the teaching of "critical race theory," and so on.[22] This is work that needs to be taken on not just by those adults who have children or who work directly with kids but by all of us, working together collectively to challenge and disrupt white supremacist propaganda, thinking, and actions. And part of this includes developing a better awareness of the prevalence of these messages in everyday life and the development of skills to intervene and counter these messages, especially with children.

Countering explicitly racist behavior of white children also must be addressed, particularly by school leaders. Evidence of the "Trump effect" illustrates just how prevalent racist behavior at schools was and perhaps still is. Schools need proactive plans to counter this kind of behavior that extend beyond traditional models of antibullying. Lumping all "bad" behavior of kids at school into one large generic category of "bullying" does little to address racism in the lives of kids—both why kids are engaging in this behavior and what effect this behavior has on kids of color. And increasing awareness about racism is only part of these efforts. Many schools I have visited did not have plans for what happens when kids share racist memes on Snapchat or TikTok, for example, even though this kind of behavior happens regularly. These interventions must also be employed at predominantly white schools in addition to racially diverse schools, particularly given what my research demonstrates about the racist behavior of white kids in white environments—especially kids who may be at the periphery of the far right.

Challenge Colorblind Racism

It is important to take stock of the violence against US democracy that took place on January 6, 2021, and to increase adult and child awareness about the mainstreaming of far-right propaganda and disinformation. But US racism and the harm that comes to people as a result does not depend on far-right extremists alone, nor did it depend on Trump being president, nor is it isolated to the years that Trump was in office. After all, Obama was known to many people as the "Deporter-in-Chief"; the second Bush administration oversaw the passing of the PATRIOT Act, which contributed to widespread Islamophobia; the Clinton administration has a role in advancing mass incarceration and reforming welfare, policies that both created great harm for Black families; and so on.23 Racism is perpetuated in US society by systems, institutional practices and policies with historical legacies and roots, by leaders in power, and by everyday people, often including those who do not intend to do so.24 And this includes kids.

As chapter 3 explored in detail, despite the ways that the Trump era disrupted some white children's understandings of racism in the United States, only a handful of the kids in this study who were confronted with this new perspective on US society fundamentally shifted their racial ideological viewpoints. Instead, the majority of these kids found ways to convince themselves that the country really was not as racist as it appeared, many believing that once Trump was out of office, everything would "go back to normal." These children missed the emotional well-being that comes with the willful ignorance offered by colorblind logic. In this sense, the Trump era did not fundamentally seem to shift the ideological positions of this group of white kids or threaten the dominance of colorblind racial logic. Although some kids were shocked by Trump's explicit expressions of racism, they also reasoned that this was temporary, or they drew boundaries between themselves as "good white kids" versus racist white kids, resulting in them absolving themselves and distancing themselves from having anything to do with racism or the many ways they benefit from it. So, while these kids were not saying, "Racism exists and it is fine with me," like the children in chapter 5, they did say, "Racism was over until Trump was elected." I think these two statements are different in meaningful ways and should not be equated; but these statements are also not entirely disconnected from each other, particularly when we think about the similar outcomes that emerge from both lines of thinking. Whether we accept the existence of racism but say we do not care or whether we ignore and minimize it, either way, racism and the harm it causes to individuals as well as democracy persists. What we can certainly see, though, is that children participate in the construction of their racial ideological views and that the Trump era interrupted colorblindness in this group of kids, at least for a period of time, which required them to be flexible in how they thought ideologically. And, for a few of them, this led to fundamental shifts in their racial ideological perspectives and an increased awareness of the realities of racism in US society and the need to do something to work for social change. This theoretically demonstrates the role that kids play in reworking dominant ideologies, at the same time that it shows the staying power of colorblind ideology.

Another thing that adults can do is to provide kids with opportunities to develop critical analysis and critical literacy skills that help them interpret the world around them. This is not difficult work to do because many kids are well aware that race matters in US life. Some ways this work can be embraced include giving children the chance to learn about racism in the United States, to read literature written by people who experience the world differently from the way they do, to explore sociological data and decide for themselves what to make of it, to become familiar with examples of other people similarly positioned to themselves advocating for the advancement of rights of all, to encounter opportunities to develop genuine care and concern about people who are positioned differently in social hierarchies, and to learn to respond productively when their assumptions are challenged and to situations in which they have to rethink taken-for-granted ideas about how things work.

Teach History of Racism

One excellent strategy for countering racism is teaching kids about the history of racism in the United States. White kids who have a clear sense of the history of racism in the US are better equipped to make sense of contemporary patterns of racial inequality and to engage productively as members of a multiracial democracy.25 Kids of color who have learned the history of racism or even the history of groups aside from white people have been shown to have better educational outcomes and to build more positive ideas about their own racial group.26 In order to confront the problems of the present, we must understand how we arrived where we are—and denying children access to this historical knowledge hinders their ability to think critically and think through solutions to our current problems and, ultimately, violates their human right to education.

Debates about what ideas children should learn about have long persisted in US society because no matter what proponents of "traditional," white-centered education may say, all education is political.27 In recent years, these debates have taken center stage due to the racial politics associated with them. Much has been written about the debate over kids learning "critical race theory" in K–12 schools. School boards have banned books that discuss racism. White parents have thrown angry fits at school board meetings, new legislation banning the teaching of this material has been passed in various states, and the work of public intellectuals like Nikole Hannah Jones has been disparaged, primarily by white people who do not want their children learning about the history of slavery and racism in the US. Instead, these parents want their children presented with a version of US history that "helps to maintain the mythology of racial progress that so many Americans find so deeply attractive" and that does not threaten their group position of dominance.28 As the political scientist Hakeem Jefferson and the sociologist Victor Ray explain, debates on kids learning about racial inequality in school is part of "the racial reckoning of this moment—one characterized by white backlash to a perceived loss of power and status."29 Certainly, this perceived sense of threat is on display when parents decry their children learning about racial inequality—or when they do not want their high school kid reading Toni Morrison's *Beloved* or Kiese Laymon's *Heavy*.30

When white parents tell me that their white children have "no ideas about race" and that they "don't even notice race," it only takes a few minutes of actually listening to their kids to realize that these kids have *all kinds of ideas* about race. The same can be said for white parents' suggestions of their white children's so-called innocence and claims that their children do not know anything about the history of slavery. As the kids in this book illustrate, they already have all kinds of ideas about slavery, much like they have all kinds of ideas about politics, race, current events, and more. They might not have ideas that accurately reflect the historical record, and they might not have ideas that are entirely worked out; but when white children like Ned see their own identity as a white southern Republican as somehow tied to the history of Mississippi and the institution of slavery or when white kids identify racism as only existing during the times of legal enslavement, it is clear that they are not entirely ignorant of the racially unjust past. And certainly, when white kids inflict racist violence on their peers of color at school, these white kids are not "innocent" or "naïve" or incapable of understanding how power dynamics work.

Indeed, many kids I spoke to while conducting this research—and many students I teach in Mississippi—*want* to learn more about this history and are frustrated that they did not learn about it earlier in their lives. The middle-school-aged kids in this research told me that they wished their teachers and parents would talk more about the facts of political debates, share multiple perspectives on a particular issue, explain why people have different positions on a particular issue, and let kids share their viewpoints rather than just avoiding it altogether. I found this pattern to be true across kids of different political viewpoints in this research. These kids were asking not only to be taught about the history of racism but also to be treated as political participants. Likewise, my college students tell me that they feel woefully unprepared for the world because they learned so little about this history of racism before they got to college.

Treat Kids as Political Participants

The day after Trump was elected, Peyton told me he boarded his school bus as he normally would. However, before the bus even started moving, he was bombarded with kids arguing with each other and throwing insults back and forth. Peyton reenacted the arguments for me:

I like Hillary Clinton.
I like Donald Trump.
I hate him!
You're a loser!

Hey. Do you like Donald Trump?
No, I like Hillary Clinton.
You're stupid!
No, you're stupid!

Peyton noticed that the kids were insulting each other, but he also noticed that they were talking about politics—they were engaged in what was happening in the United States, even if it took the form of school-bus taunts. "They were really into it! Some kids were mad, but others were really excited." The political banter had been going on in the weeks leading up to the election, according to Peyton, but that particular bus ride to school was especially dramatic. In fact, the arguing was so intense and became so emotionally heated that the bus driver reported the children's behaviors to the school officials. A school assembly was held later that day during which the principal told the kids that, in Peyton's words, "these conversations are inappropriate for school." Peyton and his friends interpreted this to mean that they were "not allowed to discuss politics at school or even on the bus" ride to school. "You can't do that anymore," Peyton said with a tone of astonishment and disgust. "We should be able to disagree about politics and talk about our ideas. Come on."

Peyton told me that this decision by his school officials made him "very mad" because he is "from a very political family" and thinks of himself as a "political person." He went on to say that he thinks the voting age "should be lowered down to like nine and eight. Those are actually fairly good ages [for people to vote] instead of like sixty. Nobody's ever even been that old!" Peyton suggested that older people are out of touch with the real issues that face Americans. Peyton also believed that kids should have a say about the political future of the United States since they are the people who will live in that future—and are living in the present right now as members of society. He mentioned not only ongoing debates about human rights but also environmental issues including climate change and endangered species, social problems that he believed would indeed impact his generation more than anyone older than him.

Peyton was angry the day after the election because he did not want Trump to win the election. But he seemed even angrier that he was not allowed to participate in the democratic process of voting as a kid—and that he was not even allowed to express his political views at school or with his peers. "I can't vote, and apparently I can't even talk about who I would vote for if I could!" he exclaimed with a tone of frustration. Peyton shared these opinions with me loudly as he stood up and gathered his belongings so that he could leave the interview and go to basketball practice. "And now look! We are stuck with Trump!" he yelled passionately as he waved his arms around him. He started to share his strong views about problems with the Electoral College as his mother quietly validated him but also assertively ushered him out of the room so that he could move on with his afternoon.

Peyton was not the only kid who was frustrated with adults' placing boundaries on the political expressions of young people. Specifically, kids like Maya said that teachers in Mississippi told children "not to talk about" the election, while kids like Rebecca in Massachusetts shared that teachers "avoided" the subject altogether. And, according to the children and parents I interviewed after the storming of the Capitol in 2021, the general sentiment seemed to be that school leaders "did not know what to do" and avoided the topic altogether to prevent conflict.

Adults did not just refuse to treat kids like political participants at school. Kids were treated the same way in other parts of their lives too. Zena shared her experience:

Last summer, I went to Georgia with my Girl Scout troop. And like three of us were watching news in this restaurant. We were sitting there, and there was a TV right beside us. The news [was on, and] we were watching it. And there was something about a white cop that was shooting an African American person, and the white cop clearly had no reasoning to shoot him. And, I mean, it was a very bad thing. And our Girl Scout leader yelled at us for watching the TV. She was like, "Why are you watching that? No. Turn around." We all kind of turned around, and for a few minutes, we're all talking. But slowly, we just drifted back to the TV. And then she's just yelling at us again! Like, "Don't watch that! You're too young to watch that!" And, I mean, [it is] this kind of thing [that] is definitely, like, the reason I think I'm more educated on topics than my peers. Because some [kids'] parents are thinking, "I need to shield my child as long as I can," and not really realizing, like, you know, when you purposefully put your white child out to the world at eighteen and they still think it's all bubble gum and rainbows, you know, it's a problem.

As Zena explained, her Girl Scout leader did not want her or her friends paying attention to the news story. But no matter how much reprimanding the girls received from their Girl Scout leader, the girls still engaged with that content and formed ideas as a result. Throughout this research, kids talked with me about how adults in their lives either encouraged or discouraged them from talking about racism in US society as well as politics writ large and tried to control their behavior.

Though kids in my research cannot yet vote and are often not taken seriously as political participants despite living in a democracy, the political realm nevertheless shapes kids' individual-level lived experiences and the ideas and feelings they form about racism. Given these findings, we cannot discount the lessons kids learn about racism from their engagement with their families and aspects of their local communities, as well as the current political events, campaigns, ideas, and public discourse of their childhood.

Address Structural Drivers of Racism

Children learn about race as a direct result of the racialized society in which they live. Therefore, reworking how young people learn race requires a fundamental reshaping of how our society is organized structurally. This work could include local-level efforts to reject school discipline policies and tracking practices in schools that are shown to exacerbate racial inequality. This work could also include efforts to create policies that resist the practices of powerful parents as they attempt to hoard opportunities for their own kids or use their various forms of social capital, including their whiteness, to access advantages for their children at the expense of other kids. This work could include efforts on the behalf of white parents to avoid dominating spaces like the parent-teacher association (PTA) and to prioritize the interests of all children in one's community rather than just one's own.31 But this work of challenging how our society is organized in racist ways also means supporting policies, practices, and laws designed to create broad changes in society that extend rights to more groups of people. This includes voting for politicians who support redistributing material resources in society, including in realms such as public-school funding, affordable child care, and quality health care. Supporting politicians who enact new laws protecting voting rights, civil rights, fair housing protections, environmental justice, criminal justice reform, and economic policies targeting the racial wealth gap can help restructure US society in ways that make life better for more people, especially people who are members of groups that have faced historical and contemporary marginalization and dehumanization.

Material changes would also redefine children's social environments, which in turn would probably shape how they feel race and think about race ideologically. The material conditions of childhood shape the ideas that kids produce about race. Therefore, another thing we can do to influence racial learning processes is to structure our society differently or at least work toward that goal. And while I personally believe that this would ultimately improve the lives of all Americans, not everyone sees things this way, and they actively work against these kinds of structural changes. Indeed, this would probably lead to even further white resistance—the kind of white backlash rooted in racialized emotions that makes racial progress difficult in the first place.

Prepare Kids to Live in a Multiracial Democracy

Public debates about race, politics, and LGBTQ+ rights have only grown more contentious since I conducted the interviews in this book, at least in the context of public schools. In 2022, for instance, a nationally representative survey of 682 public high school principals and follow-up interviews with a selection of principals was conducted by researchers at UCLA and UC-Riverside. This survey found that nearly 70 percent of the principals surveyed reported "substantial political conflict" with parents and other members of their community related to "teaching about issues of race and racism, policies and practices related to LGBTQ+ student rights, social emotional learning, [and] access to books in the school library."32 Nearly 70 percent of the principals also reported that "students have made demeaning or hateful remarks towards classmates for expressing either liberal or conservative views." Based on their findings, the authors of this report, *Educating for a Diverse Democracy*, write, "Schools also are impacted by political conflict tied to the growing partisan divides in our society. These political conflicts have created a broad chilling effect that has limited opportunities for students to practice respectful dialogue on controversial topics and made it harder to address rampant misinformation. The chilling effect also has led to marked declines in general support for teaching about race, racism, and racial and ethnic diversity."33 I am not surprised by these empirical findings because of my conversations with school leaders around the nation over the past few years. I am also not surprised after conducting this research and listening to kids share their feelings and thoughts with me. But I am disappointed to hear about the "chilling effect" that this moment seems to be having in school contexts. This is the opposite of what we need for the health of our multiracial democracy.

If we as adults do not act urgently to address how kids feel race, if we refuse to take seriously racial learning processes that involve dynamics outside the home, like those associated with the political landscape, and if we ignore the impact that the mainstreaming of hate is having on youth, we will probably see more future adults approach racism with apathy, disempowerment, hopelessness, and perhaps even violence like that of January 6. If we continue to promote narratives that suggest that white kids are too innocent to learn the history of racism or that they are clueless about race or current political events, we are not serving the best interests of kids and certainly not preparing them for the realities of living in a multiracial democracy. This is bad for kids, but it is bad for our democracy too.

From the early days of the Trump campaign through to the "culture wars" playing out in communities and schools across the nation right now, the social and political particularities of the post-Obama era provide an opportunity to explore sociologically how macro-level political dynamics inform children's racial learning. Through listening to kids experiencing childhood during a moment they understand to be deeply divided and, for some, even a moment of crisis, how kids *feel race* is central to how kids form racial ideas. Based on the intense and at times disturbing words of kids and the racialized emotions they express, my hope is that this book delivers a warning to us all about the pressing need to do more—not less—to help prepare young people to live in a multiracial democracy now and in the future.

ACKNOWLEDGMENTS

Writing a book about racism, kids, and politics during a tumultuous political moment and a traumatic global pandemic did not always leave me feeling particularly hopeful or inspired about the future. Thank you to my family, friends, and community for bringing me much-needed encouragement, connection, and joy amid everything else going on in the world.

Eric, thank you for helping me write this book. I appreciate your scholarly expertise as I tried to make sense of theories of satire/humor and how these ideas related to the children's "jokes." Thank you for suggesting articles and books for me to read about politics (whether or not I actually read all of them). And thank you for putting your English-professor eyes on this manuscript more than once. From those early book-proposal writing days when we couldn't leave our house in 2020 to the days leading up to Charlie's birth when I was desperate to finish a full draft of this book, you have always encouraged me and supported me in every imaginable way. You're an incredible husband, father, friend, and colleague, and I love you more than ever.

Charlie, I never expected you to bring so much joy into my life. I can't wait to hear your ideas about the social world once you figure them out.

Thank you to Mikyla Smith for being such a consistent source of support in my life despite the ocean between us. Thank you for listening to me talk about this research over a long period of time and for offering your feedback—I always appreciate your perspective.

Thank you to my mom and dad, Jean Maloney Hagerman and Douglas Hagerman, for housing and feeding me while conducting interviews in Massachusetts, for helpful insights about the context, and for helping me make some key connections. I am fortunate to have parents who care about young people and who take seriously the social problems that uniquely impact children and youth. Thank you for supporting me—and other people's kids too!

Thank you to James Hagerman and Kayla Ormandy for their interest in this work. I am also very grateful for the lively McKay Family Tuesday Night Happy Hour Zoom calls during 2020–21 with Gail and David McKay; Melissa McKay and Michael Sondel; Dave McKay; and Laura, Matt, Nolan and Callie Vaughn. Connecting during that time kept us all going and reminded me what is actually important.

Thank you to Heather Beth Johnson, my first sociology professor and longtime friend, for inspiring me, for continually inviting me to talk about my research with her current Lehigh University students, for supporting me both personally and professionally at every phase of my life, and for reminding us all that we can choose joy.

Thank you to my Mississippi friends who sat ten feet apart from me outside in backyards after a long day of coding or writing during the especially bleak days of the pandemic. In particular, I appreciate the comradery and friendship of Arialle Crabtree, Braden Leap, Robby Lozano, Kerri Mathews, Shane Miller, Nicole and Cody Rader, Tara Sutton, and Ashley Vancil-Leap. Thank you especially to Gabe Miller for constantly making me laugh with many ridiculous antics, for always having such a critical perspective, for helping me track down demographic data, and for encouraging me to move ahead with this book idea—I am so grateful for all the support you have given me and even more so for our friendship.

Thank you to Lizzie Botfield, Julia Dauer, Georgiann Davis, Jessica De Pinto, Devin Garofalo, Vicky Gately, Jen McCarthy, Hassan Pasha, Ranita Ray, Mike Roach, and Danielle Wylie, who have each supported this work in their own unique way.

This research would not be possible without the contributions of outstanding graduate and undergraduate students at Mississippi State University who worked as research assistants at various stages of this project. Courtney Heath and Kimberly Mason were crucial to generating the Mississippi data for this project. Thank you for your time, energy, thoughtfulness, and interest in listening to kids share their ideas about the social world. You have incredible child-centered interviewing skills, among other things, and I cannot wait to see what the future holds for each of you. Thank you to Emily Tingle for her careful transcription work. And thanks to Anne Elizabeth Harrington for her assistance with reading drafts of early chapters and assisting with the literature review.

This work would also not be possible without a semester-long research sabbatical from Mississippi State University and the Department of Sociology and without funding from the MSU College of Arts and Sciences Strategic Research Initiative. Thank you to Giselle Thibaudeau Munn for her enthusiasm and support for new research projects in the college, including this one, as well as for her support for research on race and racism specifically. Thank you to Rick Travis for publicly supporting my research on racism and whiteness, even in the current political climate. Thank you to Karyn Brown for helping me share my work with larger audiences. And thank you to Tommy Anderson for always cheering me on.

I love working in a department surrounded by so many brilliant and generous people doing meaningful work, especially here in Mississippi. Thank you to Nicole Rader for supporting my professional and personal goals and helping me accomplish them. I am grateful to Diego Thompson for talking with me about his important research on the impact of Mississippi immigration raids on children. Thank you to Paula Jones for assistance with research funds, managing research assistantships, and being the best Gigi! I also really appreciate Tara Sutton for providing helpful citations on youth violence and for always being open to talking through the ideas in this book. Thank you to Braden Leap for conversations about rural sociology and political dynamics in Mississippi. And I am grateful to Kimberly Kelly for helping me think through the way the political landscape impacts all of us, including kids. Thank you to Sanna King for always being supportive of my research on kids and racism. And thank you to Raymond Barranco for being a good, consistent friend. I also would like to acknowledge my (now graduated!) PhD students Kelli Russell and Izzy Thornton, who helped me understand aspects of growing up in Mississippi. I also appreciate the ongoing conversations about this work with my current PhD students, Lisa Gooden-Hunley, Courtney Heath, Ashley Melcherts, and Bria Young.

Chris Snyder, a great friend and colleague, helped me gain access to the Bodleian Library at the University of Oxford for a few weeks during the summer of 2021 so I could read as much as I could in a short period of time. I am very grateful for this time in the library, which made all the difference for this project and provided me space to think. Thank you also to Brian Shoup for sending me a list of important research to read about political socialization.

I would like to acknowledge members of the Race and Racism Working Group here at Mississippi State University. Thank you to Gabe Miller and Leigh Soares in particular for working so hard to create this space to support scholarship on race and racism. Thank you to Donald Shaffer for his support of this group. And thank you to the members of the group for listening to me talk about this project over the past two years.

Tiffany Pogue and Qiana Cutts offered key insights during a panel discussion at Mississippi State University in February 2020 about the importance of teaching Black history, particularly to young people and particularly right now, which informed my thinking about elements of this research. I am very appreciative of you both and the important work you do.

Thank you to my intellectual mentors, Amanda Lewis and Tyrone Forman, for reading early drafts of book materials, for offering ideas and suggestions, and for helping me at every stage of my career. I am very lucky to have you both in my life, even if I don't get to see you nearly enough.

Thank you also to Irene Browne, Helen Marrow, Yami Rodriguez, and Natasha Warikoo for incredibly useful feedback on some of the chapters of this book as part of our Virtual Writing Group. Thank you to Cynthia Miller-Idriss for sharing helpful insights as well as advice about navigating the consequences that come when writing about this topic. Thank you to Eleanor Seaton for our fun and meaningful conversations about kids, racism, and politics—I learn so much from you. And thank you to Megan Underhill and Erin Winkler for their encouragement and their own research that deeply informs my own.

Thank you to my editor, Ilene Kalish, for her thoughtful feedback and ongoing support of my research. Ilene, I truly value your advice, and I am so grateful to have had the opportunity to work with you and New York University Press a second time. Thank you also to the other staff at NYU Press for helping me bring this book to fruition, especially Andrew Katz. My sincere gratitude also goes to the anonymous reviewers who offered particularly useful feedback and ideas for improvement—thank you!

Thank you to all the parents who scheduled interviews for their children, provided their kids with transportation to interviews, and encouraged their kids to share their ideas in the first place. Thank you as well to the teachers at the after-school program in Massachusetts for facilitating interviews and providing a space for the interviews to happen.

Most importantly, thank you to the children in this book who were willing to take time away from friends, sports, and other activities to share their honest views on race and politics. I am grateful for all that you taught me.

APPENDIX A

Tables of Participants

TABLE A.1. Mississippi Participants

Name	Race/ethnicity (as defined by kids)	Age	Gender
Amy	white	10	girl
Ashley	Black	11	girl
Brit	Black	12	girl
Bryson	white	10	boy
Carter	white	11	boy
Crystal	African American and mixed	10	girl
Elsa	white	12	girl
Grace	white	12	girl
Ian	white	10	boy
Jackson	white	12	boy
Joshua	white	12	boy
Katie	white	12	girl
Kenny	Black and African American	10	boy
Keshunna	Black	12	girl
Marcus	Black	12	boy
Marybeth	white	12	girl
Maya	Black	12	girl
Ned	white	12	boy
Paige	white	12	girl
Peyton	white	10	boy
Ria	Black	11	girl
Sarah	white	12	girl
Stephanie	white	12	girl
Zach	white	12	boy
Zena	white	12	girl

TABLE A.2. Massachusetts Participants

Name	Race/ethnicity (as defined by the kids)	Age	Gender
Aiden	white	10	boy
Alexis	biracial or mixed	13	girl
Blake	white	10	boy
Bobby	Latino	11	boy
Brayden	white	13	boy
Cammie	white	11	girl
David	white/biracial/mixed	12	boy
Devion	Black	11	boy
Dominick	Black + Cape Verdean	11	boy
Hazel	white	11	girl
Juliana	Black	10	girl
Lucy	white + Cape Verdean	13	girl
Mariana	Mexican American + biracial	10	girl
Monique	Black	12	girl
Nathaniel	white	11	boy
Nora	White + Portuguese	12	girl
Sam	biracial	11	boy
Simon	white	13	boy
Sofia	Hispanic	11	girl
Suzanna	Cape Verdean + Italian	10	girl

APPENDIX B

Methodological Considerations

When I started this research, I did not intend for it to turn into a book and certainly not one about kids' racialized emotions. This was an exploratory project, and more than anything, I wanted to see where the data took me. I expected perhaps to write a few journal articles at most. In March 2020, though, as I was coding the data and planning to begin a new ethnographic study, the COVID-19 pandemic hit. Given the challenges of conducting in-person fieldwork during a pandemic, I decided to rework my plans. I gave it some thought, looked more carefully at the data I had already collected, and ultimately decided that these interviews told a pretty compelling story—and that they might even tell one that would be worthy of a book.

Even after I decided to write this book, I expected that more of this story would be about geography and how kids in different parts of the country learned about racism during the Trump years differently. But, after writing research memos and looking at my coding analysis and thinking through things carefully, I found that while there were some regional variations, the data I gathered instead, more than anything, demonstrated the broadly American project of racism—that the patterns between different groups of kids as they learned about it did not correlate with geography but instead with racial and political identities.

Finally, I did not anticipate exploring kids' racialized emotions. I only focused on this area of inquiry after the kids in the research continually brought such intense emotions to the interviews—and in ways that were clearly patterned. Child-centered research is powerful in that it allows us as researchers to learn from kids themselves about how they experience and make sense of the social world. This study reinforced for me the importance of adult researchers creating research environments in which kid participants can lead the research in new directions, including those that the researcher never expected.

Overall, this project took a number of unanticipated turns. But this experience has shown me how important it is to be flexible when it comes to inductive, qualitative research. Despite all these unexpected directions, however, it is important to state clearly how this research was designed.

Methodological Approach

In order to examine my initial research questions about the way the political landscape shapes children's racial learning processes, as well as my interest in examining different regions of the country, I selected two very different places from which to sample: Massachusetts and Mississippi. These two states consistently rank as one of the highest and one of the lowest scoring states on a range of child well-being outcomes, respectively.[1] These states are remarkably different when it comes to their politics, geographic region, population size, urbanity/rurality, and income/wealth. Given these important contextual differences, I selected two towns and recruited participants from each place. The towns selected shared similar class and population size demographics at the local level despite being embedded within state contexts with tremendous differences. With regard to racial demographics, while the racial groups varied due to regional demographic differences, both places had a similar percentage of white people compared to people of color. In Mississippi, most of the kids of color were Black or mixed race. In Massachusetts, there was more racial diversity among the groups of kids of color. These two towns also had different levels of access and availability to opportunities, different kinds of social safety nets, and very different public policies that impact the lived experiences of children. I also had connections in both communities that allowed me to build relationships with local parents and after-school programs for purposes of recruitment. Through building these adult relationships, I was then able to access and recruit the child participants.

TABLE A.3. State Demographics

Aspects of place	Massachusetts	Mississippi
2016 presidential election results[a]	65.88% voted for Clinton and 32.28% for Trump	41.06% voted for Clinton and 57.60% for Trump
Location	Northeast	Southeast
Total population[b]	7,029,917	2,961,279
Size of land area[c]	7,800 square miles	46,923 square miles
% residents in rural areas[d]	8%	50.5%
Racial and ethnic demographics[e]	% Asian alone: 7.2%	% Asian alone: 1.1%
	% Black alone: 7.0%	% Black alone: 36.6%
	% Hispanic or Latino origin: 12.6%	% Hispanic or Latino origin: 3.6%
	% white alone: 69.9%	% white alone: 56.0%
	% two or more races: 8.7%	% two or more races: 3.7%
Median household income[f]	$89,645	$48,716
Median home value[g]	$487,600	$177,700

a US National Archives and Records Administration 2020.
b US Census Bureau 2021c, 2021d.
c US Census Bureau 2010.
d US Census Bureau 2020.
e US Census Bureau 2021c, 2021d.
f US Census Bureau 2021b.
g US Census Bureau 2021a.

Child participants were recruited using a theoretical snowball sample, beginning with multiple nodes, such that data from different parts of each community were generated. Like similar research in the field of ethnography, theoretical sampling techniques allowed me to recruit in ways that crossed both race and class lines, as well as across other social divisions that were relevant, such as private/public schooling, religion, gender, and so forth. I also gained access to an after-school program in each community, which also helped me recruit participants. Some of the parents in each community learned of my research through word-of-mouth. Because I knew parents in both places, they helped me connect with parents in their networks, which then led me to more contacts.

Children interviewed were all between the ages of ten and thirteen, which is a developmental period in which kids begin to think more about the world around them.2 Following parental permission and child assent processes, as well as gaining permission from an after-school program in each location, my research assistants and I then conducted child-centered interviews. These interviews took place at the after-school programs, in my university office, or at children's homes or my home, depending on the preference of the parents and their children. Overall, twenty-five children were interviewed in Mississippi, and twenty children were interviewed in Massachusetts. See appendix A for more information about the children's demographics.

Interview questions were designed to ask children about their schools and families, current events, politics, and anything else they wanted to discuss that they believed we should know. There were many opportunities built in for the kids to take the interview in the direction of their choosing, and we saved the most controversial or difficult questions for the end of the interview, such as about gun violence and controversial current events, unless kids otherwise introduced these topics on their own. These interview guides were piloted with kids who were not included in the study. Data collection for this study began in 2017. The bulk of the interviews were conducted between 2017 and 2019. Given when specific interviews were conducted, the kids were attentive to particular topics that were of national interest during this time, such as professional athletes protesting racism at sporting events during the playing of the national anthem, international relations with North Korea, and ongoing headlines about immigration policy, particularly surrounding the construction of a border wall between the US and Mexico.

Following data collection, interviews were transcribed and coded in multiple different ways. First, I coded the data using initial coding. Then, I went back and coded again using thematic coding. I then analyzed patterns in the data, which are presented here.

Unlike previous ethnographic research in which I spent significantly more time with children, this study was limited in that I only met some of these kids one or maybe two times. Research with children is stronger in my view when interviews are conducted as part of a larger child-centered ethnography.3 Ethnography allows researchers to more fully make sense of what kids feel and think, helps the adult researcher and child participant build better rapport, and helps kids build trust and feel more comfortable sharing their ideas with a researcher. Certainly, there are moments in this book when the quotes are unclear or nonsensical to the adult eye or when more contextual information would have helped me make better sense of what was going on in the moment for the child. If these interviews had been part of a larger ethnography, the data would probably have been richer and more complete. Nevertheless, interviews with children are still useful and certainly are easier to conduct from a logistical standpoint than a full-fledged ethnography, but the interview genre as a whole is less ideal for research with kids. Nevertheless, many of the children in this study opened up to me and my team, shared their beliefs even when they knew their ideas were controversial, and engaged seriously with the study. I did my best to make sense of what they shared and did what I could to understand their references and dynamics in their communities.

In 2021, following the attack on the US Capitol, I conducted additional interviews, primarily by phone, with six parents and five children in Massachusetts and Mississippi. These were not the same children from the primary data collection for this project. I saw very quickly the same patterns emerging in these interviews as I did earlier in the study, and therefore, I did not continue collecting data at this time.

Limitations

One primary limitation and a challenge I faced in this research is related to conducting interviews at an after-school program location. First, the volume levels at these programs were high, which meant that even in a separate classroom with the door closed, the environment was still noisy, which seemed to make it difficult at times for the children to concentrate and difficult for transcription later. I frequently had to redirect the child back to the interview due to a distraction outside the classroom door. However, kids also felt comfortable in this environment, and we laughed together at the funny noises that their peers made in the big gymnasium nearby.

Second, the children talked to each other about being interviewed after they were done. In some ways, this encouraged additional kids to want to participate so they could tell me what they thought. In other ways, this was not ideal, because some children did not have signed parental consent forms and could not participate when they wanted to. Ideally, I would have loved to listen to the conversations between the children about their experience being interviewed, a possible area for future research. On the basis of reports from the staff at this program who overheard these conversations though, the children enjoyed participating and found the experience meaningful and "fun." Some of the kids I interviewed once saw me a few days later and asked to be interviewed again. However, research in spaces like these really poses unique challenges and limitations, especially when it comes to transcribing audio recordings.

Third, this study does not explore in-depth the role that class, sexuality, religion, or gender play in racial learning processes. Although I point to moments when I see evidence of some of these factors shaping racial and political learning processes, these are not the focus of the study. Future work could interrogate these topics more carefully in the context of how kids learn about race and racism.

Finally, as discussed earlier, the research design for this project would have ideally been an ethnography. However, due to limitations of time and resources, as well as my desire to conduct research in two distinct regions of the country, it was not feasible for me to conduct an ethnography at this time.

Researcher Positionality and Strategies for Interviewing Children about Race and Politics

Interviewing children always involves a unique set of methodological challenges. One important consideration that has received less attention by sociologists is how kids' perceptions of the politics of the interviewer and/or the kids' notions of "where you are from" shape how open the kids are in their responses. We know that the race of interviewer matters, and many times, childhood sociologists talk about how their own age matters in particular ways as they seek to build rapport with child participants. But it was not until this research that I noticed just how much kids' perceptions of an adult interviewer's own politics and geographic place of origin seemed to matter in building rapport and trust with the kids. I found that it was important to be attentive to these dynamics in order to produce rich data. And I noticed that this seemed especially important given the divisive and highly controversial political context during which this study was conducted and given the topics we covered in the interviews.

I was fortunate for the assistance of two outstanding graduate-student research assistants at Mississippi State University, Courtney Heath and Kimberly Mason, who helped me in tremendous ways with this study. While they assisted with various research-related tasks, most significantly, these two students also helped with data collection. Their knowledge of the local context, as well as their understandings of typical adult-child interactions and power dynamics common in the Deep South (such as general deferential behavior toward adults), provided a significant advantage in helping kids feel comfortable expressing their thoughts and feelings.

Courtney Heath, a white graduate student from Mississippi, was easily able to build rapport with white kids who were also from

Mississippi. The kids saw her as similar to them: they shared the same accent with her, and they saw her as someone who would relate to their experiences and someone who they believed would probably be supportive of their politics. Ultimately, she was someone they believed they could share their ideas with freely. And, certainly, they did. Courtney also was familiar with the local school and religious references that these kids made, which were at times lost on me, and she was able to offer helpful interpretations of the data along the way.

Kimberly Mason, a Black graduate student and licensed professional counselor from the Deep South, was also easily able to build rapport with kids in this study and, in particular, the Black children interviewed. I wanted to be especially cautious in this study not to put Black children in an uncomfortable position in which a white adult asked them to talk about topics that, as some of the children in Mississippi even stated, their parents told them not to discuss with white teachers or strangers as a way to protect themselves. For the Black kids in Mississippi, Kimberly was able to put them at ease and create an environment in which they felt safe sharing their experiences, thoughts, and emotions related to racism. Her background in counseling psychology was also a tremendous asset, as she had experience talking with kids about emotional topics and was able to navigate these interactions confidently.

I am white, and I am not from Mississippi. Most of the white kids I interviewed in the South were children whose parents were not raised there. This mattered in meaningful ways as well. These kids assumed that I knew very little about Mississippi and felt empowered to offer critical explanations of various dynamics—they were not afraid to tell me about the problems they noticed and how they felt about growing up in this place. These white kids were quite forthcoming in their critiques of the state's social problems and political leaders, and they were very open with me about their emotions and thoughts. I am not sure if they would have expressed their positions so confidently or emphatically if Courtney, for instance, or someone they identified as "from here" had interviewed them. Some of the mixed-race and Black children in Mississippi requested that I interview them because they knew their parents knew me, which brought them some degree of comfort. One of these children, whom I interviewed in my office at work, spent the first few minutes of the interview looking around my office, inspecting some of the books on my shelf and paying particular attention to some photographs I have on my wall of iconic moments from the civil rights movement. The physical environment of my office appeared to convey a set of messages to him about how honest he could be in his interview. This observation really made me think about the range of power dynamics involved in child-centered research about race and politics.

Due to limitations in resources and logistics, I conducted all the interviews with the children in Massachusetts. I grew up in this part of the country, and the kids thought it was "cool" that I grew up in the Northeast but I now lived far away in Mississippi. Of course, I still had the same concerns about power dynamics and race when interviewing the kids of color in Massachusetts. I tried to address this power imbalance in race as well as age by encouraging children only to share what they felt comfortable sharing. I emphasized that there were no "right or wrong" answers and that I just wanted to know what they thought about all these things. I strategically moved interviews away from certain topics if the kids were noticeably upset (e.g., if they started crying or looked tearful, if they said they were feeling upset, or if their body language conveyed discomfort), and I did check-ins with them throughout the interview to make sure they felt okay. I did this by asking questions like, "Is this going okay? Are you comfortable continuing? Do you want to keep answering more questions?" and so forth. A few times, kids explicitly told me that they did not want to talk about certain topics, and when that happened, I followed the children's instructions and did not push them to share more about the subject. Interestingly, in these cases, usually the kids returned to the topic later in the interview and shared more about what they had been thinking.

I think it is important to take account of how kids can both feel empowered to share their political beliefs and be heard by adult researchers, as well as how these kinds of interviews can also bring about feelings of stress or unease in children. One methodological consideration with regard to data production that is worth prioritizing is for researchers to collaborate with colleagues who experience the social world in different ways due to their own positions in various social hierarchies. Another strategy is to constantly assess how the child seems to be feeling as the interview progresses and to periodically check in on them in a way that gives them an easy "out" if they do not wish to continue.

Overall, in addition to learning important lessons about how to scrap research plans and move in a different direction, I also was reminded over and over in this study how important it is for those who embrace child-centered methods to truly let children speak and lead the way in interview contexts. As I mentioned at various points throughout this book, I never would have even considered focusing on racialized emotions if not for the insistence by the kids that how they felt race was important to talk about and for me to acknowledge. We have so much to learn from kids if we let them take the lead.

NOTES

Introduction

1 Jacobo 2016.
2 Lewis 2003, 32.
3 Bonilla-Silva 2018; Bonilla-Silva and Forman 2000; Carr 1997; Crenshaw 1997; Forman 2004; Gallagher 2003.
4 Lewis and Hagerman 2016, 158.
5 Bonilla-Silva 2019b, 21, quoting Thompson 1984, 132, and citing Jackman 1996.
6 C. Wright Mills 2000.
7 Bonilla-Silva 2019a.
8 Green 2013, 961.
9 Bonilla-Silva 2019a, 3, citing Emirbayer and Goldberg 2005, 471.

Chapter 1. The "Trump Effect"

1 Wells 2017.
2 Mathis-Lilley 2017.
3 Garcia and Dutro 2018; Huang and Cornell 2019; Patel 2018; Southern Poverty Law Center 2016; Wray-Lake et al. 2018.
4 *New York Times* 2016; Costello 2016; Southern Poverty Law Center 2016.
5 Costello 2016; Darragh and Petrie 2019; Garcia and Dutro 2018; Sondel, Baggett, and Dunn 2018; Justice and Stanley 2016; Kohli, Pizarro, and Nevárez 2017; Matias and Newlove 2017; Nguyen and Kebede 2017; Rogers et al. 2017; Wray-Lake et al. 2018.
6 Center for American Progress 2000; Rosenbaum and Neuberger 2020.
7 Alker and Corcoran 2020.
8 Pirtle 2020.
9 Cheah et al. 2020, 4.
10 Cheah et al. 2020.
11 Gaitán 2019.
12 Rice, Schmit, and Matthews 2019.
13 Flaccus 2017.
14 Evans 2017.
15 Smith 2020.
16 Reid 2020, 1.
17 Paris 2019.

18 Costello 2016; Jones et al. 2020; Wells 2017.

19 In 2018, Trump reportedly said, "Why are we having all these people from shithole countries come here?" in reference to African nations, Haiti, and El Salvador.

20 Meckler 2018; K. Johnson 2017; R. Reilly 2017.

21 Heath 2015.

22 Levy and Ailworth 2021.

23 Gershon 2020.

24 Costello 2016, 8.

25 Grabar 2019.

26 CNN Wire 2019.

27 BBC News 2018.

28 Long 2019.

29 Briggs 2020; D. Roberts 2002.

30 Cervantes, Ullrich, and Matthews 2018, 11.

31 Zayas and Heffron 2016.

32 Cervantes, Ullrich, and Matthews 2018, 8.

33 Cervantes, Ullrich, and Matthews 2018.

34 Cervantes, Ullrich, and Matthews 2018, 8.

35 Cervantes, Ullrich, and Matthews 2018; Shonkoff and Garner 2012.

36 Dreby 2015.

37 Cervantes, Ullrich, and Matthews 2018; Zayas and Heffron 2016.

38 Artiga and Ubri 2017; Gonzales and Vargas 2015; Patler et al. 2019.

39 K. Reilly 2016.

40 Wray-Lake et al. 2018.

41 Rodriguez and Ybarra 2020.

42 Rodriguez and Ybarra 2020, 933.

43 Morales, Abrica, and Herrera 2019, 11.

44 Huang and Cornell 2019.

45 Khoo 2017.

46 Research conducted during this time period demonstrated the serious violence, violation of rights, and discrimination that Arab American and Muslim American families and young people experienced at the hands of individuals as well as the state (Abu El-Haj 2010).

47 Yoder 2020, 350.

48 This research also found that Muslim children are often incorrectly labeled by their peers. For example, a child explained to the researcher how her non-Muslim peers frequently labeled her as Arab, Pakistani, or Iranian based on her hijab, and when she told them that her family was from India, they told her that she must be Hindu (Merchant 2016).

49 Yoder 2020.

50 Desmond-Harris 2017.

51 Artiga and Ubri 2017.

52 Artiga and Ubri 2017.

53 Miller-Idriss 2020, 1–2.

54 Cypers 2020; Miller-Idriss 2020, 20.

55 Miller-Idriss 2020, 19.

56 Lavoie 2021.

57 Miller-Idriss 2020, 12.

58 Arango, Bogel-Burroughs, and Benner 2019.

59 National Public Radio 2021.

60 Diaz and Treisman 2021.

61 Miller-Idriss 2020.

62 Miller-Idriss 2020.

63 Cox 2018. See also Daniels 2018; Noble 2018; Weimann and Masri 2020.

64 For more on this subject, see Finley and Johnson 2018.

65 Zraick 2016.

66 As discussed in the introduction, colorblind ideology is a commonly accepted way of seeing the world that claims that racial discrimination is a thing of the past, that segregation is due to people's "natural" desire to live near people who are the same race as they are, and that the United States is a place of equal opportunity for all. This ideology supports the idea that policy interventions aimed at addressing racial inequity are unnecessary.

67 Hagerman 2018b, 1.

68 Alwin and Krosnick 1991; Jennings and Niemi 1981.

69 Huang and Cornell 2019.

70 McDevitt and Chaffee 2002, 283; Niemi and Hepburn 1995.

71 Ojeda and Hatemi 2015.

72 Ojeda and Hatemi 2015, 1169.

73 Bonilla-Silva 2019a, 1.

74 Bonilla-Silva 2019a, 12.

75 Mercer 2014, 530.

76 Bonilla-Silva 2019a, 14.

77 Yoder 2020, 347.

78 Wray-Lake et al. 2018, 202.

79 Jacobson 2016; Byrd 2017; Hagerman 2020; Mueller 2017; Warikoo and de Novais 2015.

80 Jacobson 2016.

Chapter 2. "Feeling Race"

1 Emirbayer and Goldberg 2005.

2 Thoits 1989, 319.

3 Bonilla-Silva 2019a; Smith and Mackie 2015.

4 As Jonathan Mercer writes, "Emotion goes with identity: group-level emotion can be stronger than, and different from, emotion experienced as an individual; group members share, validate, and police each other's feelings; and these feelings structure relations within and between groups" (2014, 530).

5 Bonilla-Silva 2019a, 1.

6 Bonilla-Silva 2019a, 2; Green 2013, 961.

7 Bonilla-Silva 2019a, 2.

8 Bonilla-Silva 2019a, 3; Smith and Mackie 2015.

9 Bonilla-Silva 2019a, 4, citing Rosino 2017.

10 Bonilla-Silva 2019a, 10, citing Rafanell and Gorringe 2010, 615.

11 Albertson and Gadarian 2015.

12 Bonilla-Silva 2019a, 3.

13 Miller et al. 2021.

14 Bonilla-Silva 2019a, 2. See also work by authors like James Baldwin, Audre Lorde, and Kiese Laymon, as well as fiction by authors like Zora Neale Hurston and Toni Morrison.

15 Marable 2000, 9, cited by Bonilla-Silva 2019a, 9.

16 Mercer 2014, 530.

17 As the sociologists Kerry Ann Rockquemore, David L. Brunsma, and Daniel J. Delgado explain, "the parameters of racial identity formation are socially, culturally, and politically constructed" (2009, 22).

18 Bonilla-Silva 2019a, 7, citing Charles W. Mills 2003.

19 Thoits 1989, 319.

Chapter 3. "I Had No Idea the Country Was So Racist!"

1 Given when these data were collected, the children I am referencing were born between 2003 and 2005.

2 Hagerman 2018b; Ladner 2020; Lewis 2001; Wills 2019.

3 Dubrofsky 2013; Nilsen and Turner 2014.

4 E. Alexander 2017; Bonilla-Silva 2018; Carr 1997; Crenshaw 1997; Gallagher 2003; Krysan and Lewis 2006.

5 Hagerman 2018b, 106.

6 Joyce Bell and Douglas Hartmann (2007) discuss "happy talk," in which people talk about diversity but do not discuss power or inequality. Research documenting the use of "happy talk" in white families includes the work of Hagerman 2018b; Halley, Eshleman, and Vijaya 2011; Underhill 2018; Vittrup 2018.

7 Hagerman 2016.

8 Healy and Peters 2016.

9 *Guardian* 2019.

10 Dunlap 2015.

11 Lopez 2020.

12 Hughey 2012; Miller-Idriss 2020.

13 Hagerman 2018a.

14 Hagerman 2018b, 20.

15 Forman 2004, 43.

16 Schuman et al. 1998.

17 Doane, Bonilla-Silva, and Johnson 2003; H. Johnson 2014; Shapiro and Johnson 2005.

18 Bonilla-Silva 2018, 11.

19 Bonilla-Silva 1997.

20 Hagerman 2016.

21 Blumer 1958; Pettigrew and Meertens 1995.

22 Bobo, Klugel, and Smith 1997. As the sociologist Tony Brown and his colleagues write, "the field has moved away from reliance on blatant indicators of white racial prejudice toward reliance on subtle and colorblind indicators" (2019, 1).

23 Bonilla-Silva 2018; Crenshaw 1997; Gallagher 2003.

24 Bobo, Klugel, and Smith 1997; Bonilla-Silva 2018; D. Roberts 2011; Takaki 1998.

25 Mueller 2017, 221; Bonilla-Silva 2018; Gallagher 2003.

26 Colorblind ideology "fosters a view that existing racial inequality must be the result of personal choices, not blocked opportunity" (Forman 2004, 46).

27 Krysan and Crowder 2017; Massey and Denton 1993; Oliver and Shapiro 2006.

28 Forman 2004, 46.

29 Bonilla-Silva 1997.

30 D. Roberts 2011, 4.

31 Thomas and Thomas 1928.

32 Omi and Winant 1994; Takaki 2008.

33 Blumer 1958; Lewis 2004; Sewell 1992.

34 Gallagher 2003; Halley, Eshleman, and Vijaya 2011; McIntosh 1989; Du Bois 1998; Roediger 2007.

35 Bonilla-Silva 2018; Feagin 2013; Lewis 2003; Noble 2018; Omi and Winant 1994; V. Ray 2019; D. Roberts 2011. Given the dominance of colorblind ideology, people of color also adopt this framework.

36 For more on this discussion and for evidence that, if anything, Black parents have been shown to support education more than white parents, see Lewis and Diamond 2015.

37 As Mueller writes, "racial ideologies are . . . grounded in socio-cognitive processes that distort and suppress whites' capacity for 'knowing' about matters of racial and white supremacy—what critical race philosopher Charles Mills . . . refers to as epistemologies of ignorance. Mills argues learning to abide by an epistemology of ignorance is common to most whites' socialization, *enabling a more comfortable complicity with white supremacy*" (2017, 222; emphasis added, citations omitted).

38 Bonilla-Silva 2019a, 7, citing Charles W. Mills 2003.

39 Existing theories about racialized emotions suggests that "because [white] racial actors derive emotional well-being from racial domination . . . , they develop affective interests in keeping their standing vis-à-vis racial Others" (Bonilla-Silva 2019a, 7).

40 Gould 2009; N. Kim 2021.

41 Forman 2004.

42 Bonilla-Silva 2019a, 4.

43 Williams 1978.

Chapter 4. "He Likes the People with the Lighter Skin Better . . . and That's Not Me"

1 See chapter 1.

2 See chapter 1.

3 Throughout this chapter, I use the racial categories used by the children themselves to describe their identity. While much discussion exists about terminology, I center the perspectives of the children and use the words they told me they liked best to describe themselves.

4 hooks 1995, 20, quoted, in Bonilla-Silva 2019a, 15.

5 Bonilla-Silva 2019a, 6.

6 Waxman 2021.

7 Constantine and Blackmon 2002; Hughes and Chen 1999; Hughes et al. 2006; Thomas and Blackmon 2015; Winkler 2012; Gartner, Kiang, and Supple 2014.

8 Dow 2019, 52 (emphasis added).

9 Ewing 2018, 10.

10 Ewing 2018, 127.

11 Ewing 2018, 13.

12 Ewing 2018. In explaining the reason why communities like that of Bronzeville fight so hard to keep "failing" schools open, Ewing provides extensive evidence of the collective grief and sorrow, as well as the institutional mourning, experienced by the African American community as a result of these school closures. These racialized emotions of grief and sorrow are also linked to a sense of group solidarity and agency or, as she puts it, a sense that "we are all in this together" (130). As she writes, "After you're gone, they'd prefer you be forgotten. Mourning, then, is how we refute that erasure. It's a way to insist that we matter. It's a way to remember" (156).

13 Lewis 2003, 82.

14 Bettie 2014; Perry 2002; M. Fine 1991; Tyson 2011; Ray 2017; Lewis-McCoy 2014; Lewis and Diamond 2015.

15 During the time that many of these interviews were conducted, relations between Trump and Kim Jong Un were widely discussed in the media.

16 Gershon et al. 2019.

17 Dreby 2015; Gonzales and Vargas 2015.
18 Shelton 2019; Tatum and Osborne 2019.
19 Flores-González 2017.
20 See Goyal et al. 2015; Bernstein 2011; D. Roberts 2002; Gilliam and Shahar 2006; Skiba et al. 2011; Oakes 2005; among many others.
21 Bonilla-Silva 2019a.
22 Baldwin 1963, 26, quoted in Bonilla-Silva 2019a, 2.
23 Pascoe 2014.
24 Rogers and Ishimoto 2021, 50.
25 Rogers and Ishimoto 2021, 52.
26 Pascoe 2014.
27 Gershon et al. 2019.
28 Bonilla-Silva 2019a, 15, quoting Hattam and Zembylas 2010, 24, who in turn quote Lyman 2004, 134.
29 Kessler and Hollbach 2005, quoted in Bonilla-Silva 2019a, 15.
30 Ahmed 2015, 174, quoted in Bonilla-Silva 2019a, 15.
31 Bonilla-Silva 2019a, 15.
32 Halberstadt et al. 2020.
33 Dawson 1995; Gershon et al. 2019.
34 This finding connects in general terms with the important work of developmental psychologists like Adriana J. Umaña-Taylor, Deborah Rivas-Drake, and Eleanor Seaton who have examined racial identity formation in youth of color from a psychological developmental perspective. These scholars, and others, have explored the complexities of what they refer to as the "positive affect that individuals feel toward their ethnic-racial group" from a psychological perspective and have considered the role that discrimination plays in shaping racial identity overall. Umaña-Taylor et al. 2014, 27; see also Umaña-Taylor and Hill 2020; Rivas-Drake et al. 2014; Seaton et al. 2014.
35 Kozol 2012, 35.
36 Bonilla-Silva 2019a, 2.
37 Bonilla-Silva 2019a, 2, quoting Jensen 2005 and Robinson 2008.
38 Bonilla-Silva 2019a, 2.

Chapter 5. "Racism Is Fine"

1 Forman 2004, 44.
2 Forman and Lewis 2015, 1397.
3 Bracey 2017; Mueller 2017, 230.
4 As Jennifer Mueller finds in her work with college students as they confront their own family's connection to racism and the intergenerational transmission of wealth, "developing tautological explanations specifically emboldened students to reify structure as solely responsible for reproducing white supremacy, while whites appeared most unwitting and involuntary

participators." Mueller further explains that this is "a move that preserves white virtue while minimizing agency and motive" (2017, 230).

5 Bartky 2002, 147.

6 Bonilla-Silva 2019a, 7.

7 This is similar to findings from Nolan Cabrera's study of white male college students who engage in racist joking in "racially homogenous, white environments" (2014, 9).

8 Corsaro 2011, 21.

9 Corsaro 2011, 20.

10 Corsaro 2011, 20.

11 Natanson 2021.

12 Bonilla-Silva 2019a, 8.

13 Boskin 1997; Weaver 2011, cited in Pérez 2017, 958.

14 Pérez, 2017, 958, citing G. Fine 1976; Meyer 2000.

15 Picca and Feagin 2007, 69.

16 Pérez 2017, 962.

17 Bonilla-Silva 2019a, 8.

18 Blumer 1958, 6.

19 Blumer 1958.

20 Blumer 1958.

21 Jenkins 2017.

22 Blumer 1958, 6.

23 Vandello et al. 2008.

24 In *Playing in the Dark*, the author and literary critic Toni Morrison analyzes how and why white authors have included Africans or African Americans in their works of fiction: "I began to see how the literature I revered, the literature I loathed, behaved in its encounter with racial ideology. American literature could not help being shaped by that encounter. . . . I came to realize the obvious: the subject of the dream is the dreamer. The fabrication of an Africanist persona is reflexive; an extraordinary *meditation on the self*; a powerful exploration of the *fears and desires* that reside in the writerly conscious. It is an astonishing revelation of longing, of terror, of perplexity, of shame, of magnanimity. It requires hard work not to see this" (1992, 17). Though Morrison writes about these elements of whiteness in the literary imagination, her point speaks directly to the racial imaginations of the children described in this chapter.

25 Feagin 2009, 110; Kovel 1984.

26 Kovel 1984.

27 Bonilla-Silva 2019a, 7.

28 Metzl 2019.

29 Bonilla-Silva 2019a, 8.

Chapter 6. "Hurry Up and Build That Wall!"

1 Mueller 2017, 221.
2 Forman and Lewis 2006, 179. Tony Brown et al. also write, "The current sociopolitical climate and growing intergroup antagonism in the United States mandate future studies of racial apathy" (2019, 9).
3 Forman 2004, 59.
4 Sue and Golash-Boza 2013, 1595.
5 Jung 2015.
6 Pérez 2017, 964–65.
7 Pérez 2017, 965.
8 Mueller 2017, 219; Pérez 2017, 970.
9 Pérez 2017, 970.
10 Anderson 2016, 3.
11 Anderson 2016, 170, citing Woodiwiss 2016; Thrasher 2014; Chait 2016.
12 Kinder and Sanders 1996.
13 Metzl 2019, 18.
14 Feagin 2009, 14.
15 Lippard et al. 2020, 8.
16 Bonilla-Silva 2020, xi.
17 Doane 2020, 37.
18 Doane 2020, 33, 38.
19 Doane 2020, 33.
20 Doane 2020, 38.
21 Doane 2020, 38.
22 Such youths adopt beliefs and ideals that "run fundamentally counter to the norms, values, and beliefs that underpin democratic practice across the globe," which include practices like "threatening hallmarks like free and fair elections; systems of checks and balances; the protection of individual freedom; the rule of law; and freedoms of the press, religion, speech, and assembly" (Miller-Idriss 2020, 4).
23 Miller-Idriss 2020, 4.
24 Miller-Idriss 2022.
25 Miller-Idriss 2020, 163.
26 Miller-Idriss 2020, 9.
27 Miller-Idriss 2020, 65.
28 Hagerman 2020; Mueller 2017; Warikoo and de Novais 2015.
29 Miller-Idriss 2020, xv.

Conclusion

1 For more on methods, see appendix B.
2 Bernstein 2011.
3 Bernstein 2011; Ferguson 2001; Gilliam and Shahar 2006.

4 Burton et al. 2010, 453.

5 Hagerman 2018b, 20.

6 Winkler 2012.

7 Lewis 2003; Lewis and Diamond 2015; Shedd 2015; Tyson 2011.

8 Van Ausdale and Feagin 2001.

9 Moore 2002; Berry 1998; Dubrofsky 2013; Guidotti-Hernández 2007; Nilsen and Turner 2014; E. Roberts 2004.

10 Miller-Idriss 2020.

11 Bonilla-Silva 2019a, 1.

12 Metzl 2019.

13 Simmons 2021.

14 Bonilla-Silva 2019a, 14, citing J. Kim 2016, 500. As Simmons (2021) writes, "In mostly Black, indigenous, and people of color (BIPOC) school districts, SEL is often about compliance and control. SEL then becomes another way to penalize and police BIPOC youth for their non-whiteness and to justify their supposed inferiority for lacking 'these necessary skills.' . . . What is even more perverse is the implicit belief that SEL skills are exactly what BIPOC students need to function in underresourced classrooms and to smile through the pain of racism. On the other hand, for white, privileged students, SEL is about supporting college and career readiness. These opposing mindsets lead to different practices and outcomes, which ultimately perpetuate a racial hierarchy that positions white students on top" (citations omitted).

15 McDermott 2020.

16 Jacobson 2016, 73, citing Mannheim (1928) 1972. As people get older, their political attitudes and behaviors "are likely more 'crystalized' and thus resistant to alteration," which why it is important to study what happens during the time of the life course in which these ideas and identities are first formed (Jacobson 2016, 73).

17 Green, Palmquist, and Schickler 2004, 108. See also Campbell and Wolbrecht 2020, in which the authors draw parallels to the "protest cohort" of the 1960s, when young people experienced a set of political events during formative years that powerfully shaped their political activity into the future (Jennings 1987).

18 C. Wright Mills 2000, 5.

19 Miller-Idriss 2020, 173.

20 Miller-Idriss 2020, 169.

21 Miller-Idriss 2020, 164.

22 Ray 2022.

23 Golash-Boza 2018; Cainkar 2011; M. Alexander 2010; Quadagno 1996; D. Roberts 2002.

24 For example, research shows how many liberal white people, even those who view themselves as "not racist," participate in everyday forms of racial

domination, exhibited through the hoarding of resources and wealth for their children, despite claims of wanting all kids in the US to have an equal opportunities. Decades of research documents the dominance of colorblind ideology, as discussed earlier in this book. See Calarco 2018; Hagerman 2018b; Lewis and Diamond 2015; Roda and Wells 2013; Tilly 1999.

25 See Hagerman 2018b as well as evidence presented in this book.
26 Cabrera et al. 2014; Chapman-Hilliard and Adams-Bass 2015.
27 Cabrera et al. 2014; Saltman 2018.
28 Jefferson and Ray 2022.
29 Jefferson and Ray 2022.
30 Schaub 2022.
31 Posey-Maddox 2013.
32 Turner 2022.
33 Rogers et al., 2022.

Appendix B

1 Annie E. Casey Foundation 2017.
2 Hughes 2001; Meece 2002.
3 Hagerman 2017.

REFERENCES

Abu El-Haj, Thea Renda. 2010. "'The Beauty of America': Nationalism, Education, and the War on Terror." *Harvard Educational Review* 80 (2): 242–74.

Ahmed, Sara. 2015. *The Cultural Politics of Emotion*. New York: Routledge.

Albertson, Bethany, and Shana Kushner Gadarian. 2015. *Anxious Politics: Democratic Citizenship in a Threatening World*. Cambridge: Cambridge University Press.

Alexander, Elizabeth C. 2017. "Don't Know or Won't Say? Exploring How Colorblind Norms Shape Item Nonresponse in Social Surveys." *Sociology of Race and Ethnicity* 4 (3): 400–416.

Alexander, Michelle. 2010. *The New Jim Crow: Mass Incarceration in the Age of Colorblindness*. New York: New Press.

Alker, Joan, and Alexandra Corcoran. 2020. "Children's Uninsured Rate Rises by Largest Annual Jump in More than a Decade." Georgetown University's Health Policy Institute, October 8, 2020. www.ccf.goergetown.edu.

Alwin, Duane F., and Jon A. Krosnick. 1991. "Aging Cohorts and the Stability of Sociopolitical Orientations over the Life Span." *American Journal of Sociology* 97 (1): 169–95.

Anderson, Carol. 2016. *White Rage: The Unspoken Truth of Our Racial Divide*. New York: Bloomsbury.

Annie E. Casey Foundation. 2017. "2017 Race for Results." October 31, 2017. www.aecf.org.

Arango, Tim, Nicholas Bogel-Burroughs, and Katie Benner. 2019. "Minutes before El Paso Killing, Hate-Filled Manifesto Appears Online." *New York Times*, August 3, 2019. www.nytimes.com.

Artiga, Samantha, and Petry Ubri. 2017. "Living in an Immigrant Family in America: How Fear and Toxic Stress Are Affecting Daily Life, Well-Being, & Health." Issue Brief, Immigrant Learning Center, December 2017.

Baldwin, James. 1963. *The Fire Next Time.* New York: Dial.

Bartky, Sandra Lee. 2002. *Sympathy and Solidarity: And Other Essays.* Lanham, MD: Rowman and Littlefield.

BBC News. 2018. "Trump Migrant Separation Policy: Children 'in Cages' in Texas." June 18, 2018. www.bbc.com.

Bell, Joyce M., and Douglas Hartmann. 2007. "Diversity in Everyday Discourse: The Cultural Ambiguities and Consequences of 'Happy Talk.'" *American Sociological Review* 72 (6): 895–914.

Bernstein, Robin. 2011. *Racial Innocence: Performing American Childhood from Slavery to Civil Rights.* New York: New York University Press.

Berry, Gordon L. 1998. "Black Family Life on Television and the Socialization of the African American Child: Images of Marginality." *Journal of Comparative Family Studies* 29 (2): 233–42.

Bettie, Julie. 2014. *Women without Class: Girls, Race, and Identity.* Berkeley: University of California Press.

Blumer, Herbert. 1958. "Race Prejudice as a Sense of Group Position." *Pacific Sociological Review* 1 (1): 3–7.

Bobo, Lawrence, D., James Klugel, and Ryan Smith. 1997. "Laissez-Faire Racism: The Crystallization of a Kinder, Gentler, Antiblack Ideology." In *Racial Attitudes in the 1990s: Continuity and Change,* edited by Steven A. Tuch and Jack K. Martin, 15–44. Westport, CT: Praeger.

Bonilla-Silva, Eduardo. 1997. "Rethinking Racism: Toward a Structural Interpretation." *American Sociological Review* 62 (3): 465–80.

———. 2018. *Racism without Racists: Color-Blind Racism and the Persistence of Racial Inequality in America.* 5th ed. Lanham, MD: Rowman and Littlefield.

———. 2019a. "Feeling Race: Theorizing the Racial Economy of Emotions." *American Sociological Review* 84 (1): 1–25.

———. 2019b. "'Racists,' 'Class Anxieties,' Hegemonic Racism, and Democracy in Trump's America." *Social Currents* 6 (1): 14–31.

———. 2020. Foreword to *Protecting Whiteness: Whitelash and the Rejection of Racial Equality,* edited by Cameron D. Lippard, J. Scott Carter, and David G. Embrick, xi–xiv. Seattle: University of Washington Press.

Bonilla-Silva, Eduardo, and Tyrone A. Forman. 2000. "'I Am Not a Racist but . . .': Mapping White College Students' Racial Ideology in the USA." *Discourse & Society* 11 (1): 50–85.

Boskin, Joseph, ed. 1997. *The Humor Prism in 20th-Century America.* Detroit: Wayne State University Press.

Bracey, Glenn E. 2017. "Rescuing Whites: White Privileging Discourse in Race Critical Scholarship." Unpublished manuscript.

Briggs, Laura. 2020. *Taking Children: A History of American Terror*. Berkeley: University of California Press.

Brown, Tony N., Asia Bento, Quintin Gorman Jr., Lydia Koku, and Julian Culver. 2019. "'Who Cares?': Investigating Consistency in Expressions of Racial Apathy among Whites." *Socius: Sociological Research for a Dynamic World* 5:1–10.

Burton, Linda M., Eduardo Bonilla-Silva, Victor Ray, Rose Buckelew, and Elizabeth Hordge Freeman. 2010. "Critical Race Theories, Colorism, and the Decade's Research on Families of Color." *Journal of Marriage and Family* 72 (3): 440–59.

Byrd, W. Carson. 2017. *Poison in the Ivy: Race Relations and the Reproduction of Inequality on Elite College Campuses*. New Brunswick, NJ: Rutgers University Press.

Cabrera, Nolan L. 2014. "But We're Not Laughing: White Male College Students' Racial Joking and What This Says about 'Post-Racial' Discourse." *Journal of College Student Development* 55 (1): 1–15.

Cabrera, Nolan L., Jeffrey F. Milem, Ozan Jaquette, and Ronald W. Marx. 2014. "Missing the (Student Achievement) Forest for All the (Political) Trees: Empiricism and the Mexican American Studies Controversy in Tucson." *American Educational Research Journal* 51 (6): 1084–1118.

Cainkar, Louis A. 2011. *Homeland Insecurity: The Arab American and Muslim American Experience after 9/11*. New York: Russell Sage Foundation.

Calarco, Jessica McCrory. 2018. *Negotiating Opportunities: How the Middle Class Secures Advantages in School*. New York: Oxford University Press.

Campbell, David E., and Christina Wolbrecht. 2020. "The Resistance as Role Model: Disillusionment and Protest Among American Adolescents After 2016." *Political Behavior* 42 (4): 1143–68.

Carr, Leslie G. 1997. *"Color-Blind" Racism*. Thousand Oaks, CA: Sage.

Center for American Progress. 2020. "Release: 12 Million People Have Been Excluded From Emergency Increases in SNAP Benefits." July 29, 2020. www.americanprogress.org.

Cervantes, Wendy, Rebecca Ullrich, and Hannah Matthews. 2018. *Our Children's Fear: Immigration Policy's Effects on Young Children*. Washington, DC: Center for Law and Social Policy.

Chait, Jonathan. 2016. "Donald Trump Has Proven Liberals Right about the Tea Party." *New York*, December 7, 2016. www.nymag.com.

Chapman-Hilliard, Collette, and Valerie Adams-Bass. 2015. "A Conceptual Framework for Utilizing Black History Knowledge as a Path to Psychological Liberation for Black Youth." *Journal of Black Psychology* 42 (6): 479–507.

Cheah, Charissa S. L., Cixin Wang, Huiguang Ren, Xiaoli Zong, Hyun Su Cho, and Xiaofang Xue. 2020. "COVID-19 Racism and Mental Health in Chinese American Families." *Pediatrics* 146 (5): 1–10.

CNN Wire. 2019. "Crying Girl Who Begged for Dad's Release after Mississippi ICE Raids Still Not Reunited with Him." KTLA News, August 13, 2019. www.ktla.com.

Constantine, Madonna G., and Sha'Kema M. Blackmon. 2002. "Black Adolescents' Racial Socialization Experiences Their Relations to Home, School, and Peer Self-Esteem." *Journal of Black Studies* 32 (3): 322–35.

Corsaro, William. 2011. *The Sociology of Childhood*. 3rd ed. Los Angeles: Pine Forge.

Costello, Maureen B. 2016. *The Trump Effect: The Impact of the Presidential Campaign on Our Nation's Schools*. Montgomery, AL: Southern Poverty Law Center.

Cox, Joseph. 2018. "TikTok Has a Nazi Problem." *Vice*, December 18, 2018. www.vice.com.

Crenshaw, Kimberlé Williams. 1997. "Color-Blind Dreams and Racial Nightmares: Reconfiguring Racism in the Post–Civil Rights Era." In *Birth of a Nation'hood: Gaze, Script, and Spectacle in the O. J. Simpson Case*, edited by Toni Morrison and Claudia Brodsky Lacour, 97–168. New York: Pantheon.

Cypers, Miri. 2020. "ADL Finds White Supremacist Propaganda Up 225% in Washington State in 2019 and Reaches All Time High Nationwide." Anti-Defamation League, February 12, 2020. www.seattle.adl.org.

Daniels, Jessie. 2018. "The Algorithmic Rise of the 'Alt-Right.'" *Contexts* 17 (1): 60–65.

Darragh, Janine J., and Gina Mikel Petrie. 2019. "'I Feel like I'm Teaching in a Landmine': Teaching in the Context of Political Trauma." *Teaching and Teacher Education* 80 (1): 180–89.

Dawson, Michael C. 1995. *Behind the Mule: Race and Class in African-American Politics*. Princeton, NJ: Princeton University Press.

Desmond-Harris, Jenée. 2017. "'Crying Is an Everyday Thing': Life after Trump's 'Muslim Ban' at a Majority-Immigrant School." *Vox*, February 16, 2017. www.vox.com.

Diaz, Jaclyn, and Rachel Treisman. 2021. "Members of Right-Wing Militias, Extremist Groups Are Latest Charged in Capitol Siege." NPR, January 19, 2021. www.npr.org.

Doane, Ashley "Woody." 2020. "Post-Color Blindness? Trump and the Rise of the New White Nationalism." In *Protecting Whiteness: Whitelash and the Rejection of Racial Equality*, edited by Cameron D. Lippard, J. Scott Carter, and David G. Embrick, 27–42. Seattle: University of Washington Press.

Dow, Dawn. 2019. *Mothering While Black: Boundaries and Burdens of Middle-Class Parenthood*. Oakland: University of California Press.

Dreby, Joanna. 2015. *Everyday Illegal: When Policies Undermine Immigrant Families*. Oakland: University of California Press.

Du Bois, W. E. B. 1998. *Black Reconstruction in America, 1860–1880*. New York: Free Press.

Dubrofsky, Rachel E. 2013. "Jewishness, Whiteness, and Blackness on *Glee*: Singing to the Tune of Postracism." *Communication, Culture & Critique* 6 (1): 82–102.

Dunlap, David W. 2015. "Looking Back: 1973. Meet Donald Trump." *Times Insider*, July 30. www.archive.nytimes.com.

Emirbayer, Mustafa, and Chad Alan Goldberg. 2005. "Pragmatism, Bourdieu, and Collective Emotions in Contentious Politics." *Theory and Society* 34 (5–6): 469–518.

Evans, Carter. 2017. "Trump's Border Wall Faces Another Challenge with Indian Reservation." CBS News, April 24, 2017. www.cbsnews.com.

Ewing, Eve. 2018. *Ghosts in the Schoolyard*. Chicago: University of Chicago Press.

Feagin, Joe. 2009. *The White Racial Frame: Centuries of Racial Framing and Counter-Framing*. New York: Routledge.

———. 2013. *Systemic Racism: A Theory of Oppression*. New York: Routledge.

Ferguson, Ann Arnett. 2001. *Bad Boys: Public Schools in the Making of Black Masculinity*. Ann Arbor: University of Michigan Press.

Fine, Gary A. 1976. "Obscene Joking Across Culture." *Journal of Communication* 26 (3): 34–140.

Fine, Michelle. 1991. *Framing Dropouts: Notes on the Politics of an Urban Public High School*. Albany: State University of New York Press.

Finley, Laura, and Matthew Johnson. 2018. *Trumpism*. Newcastle upon Tyne, UK: Cambridge Scholars.

Flaccus, Gillian. 2017. "Tribes Bash Proposed Trump Budget Cuts to Native American Programs." *PBS NewsHour*, May 25, 2017. www.pbs.org.

Flores-González, Nilda. 2017. *Citizens but Not Americans: Race and Belonging among Latino Millennials*. New York: New York University Press.

Forman, Tyrone A. 2004. "Color-Blind Racism and Racial Indifference: The Role of Racial Apathy in Facilitating Enduring Inequalities." In *The Changing Terrain of Race and Ethnicity*, edited by Maria Krysan and Amanda E. Lewis, 43–66. New York: Russell Sage Foundation.

Forman, Tyrone A., and Amanda E. Lewis. 2006. "Racial Apathy and Hurricane Katrina: The Social Anatomy of Prejudice in the Post–Civil Rights Era." *Du Bois Review: Social Science Research on Race* 3 (1): 175–202.

———. 2015. "Beyond Prejudice? Young Whites' Racial Attitudes in Post–Civil Rights America, 1976 to 2000." *American Behavioral Scientist* 59 (11): 1394–1428.

Gaitán, Veronica. 2019. "How Housing Affects Children's Outcomes." Urban Institute, January 2, 2019. www.housingmatters.urban.org.

Gallagher, Charles A. 2003. "Color-Blind Privilege: The Social and Political Functions of Erasing the Color Line in Post Race America." *Race, Gender & Class* 10 (4): 22–37.

Garcia, Antero, and Elizabeth Dutro. 2018. "Electing to Heal: Trauma, Healing, and Politics in Classrooms." *English Education* 50 (4): 375–83.

Gartner, Meaghan, Lisa Kiang, and Andrew Supple. 2014. "Prospective Links between Ethnic Socialization, Ethnic and American Identity, and Well-Being among Asian-American Adolescents." *Journal of Youth and Adolescence* 43 (10): 1715–27.

Gershon, Livia. 2020. "A Century of Black Youth Activism." *JSTOR Daily*, September 12, 2020. www.daily.jstor.org.

Gershon, Sarah Allen, Celeste Montoya, Christina Bejarano, and Nadia Brown. 2019. "Intersectional Linked Fate and Political Representation." *Politics, Groups, and Identities* 7 (3): 642–53.

Gilliam, Walter S., and Golan Shahar. 2006. "Preschool and Child Care Expulsion and Suspension: Rates and Predictors in One State." *Infants & Young Children* 19 (3): 228–45.

Golash-Boza, Tanya. 2018. "President Obama's Legacy as 'Deporter in Chief.'" In *Immigration Policy in the Age of Punishment: Detention, Deportation, and Border Control*, edited by David C. Brotherton and Philip Kretsedemas, 37–56. New York: Columbia University Press.

Gonzales, Roberto G. 2015. *Lives in Limbo: Undocumented and Coming of Age in America*. Oakland, California: University of California Press.

Gould, Deborah B. 2009. *Moving Politics: Emotion and ACT UP's Fight against AIDS*. Chicago: Chicago University Press.

Goyal, Monika K., Nathan Kuppermann, Sean D. Cleary, Stephen J. Teach, and James M. Chamberlain. 2015. "Racial Disparities in Pain Management of Children with Appendicitis in Emergency Departments." *JAMA Pediatrics* 169 (11): 996–1002.

Grabar, Henry. 2019. "After ICE." *Slate*, August 18, 2019. www.slate.com.

Green, Donald, Bradley Palmquist, and Eric Schickler. 2004. *Partisan Hearts and Minds*. New Haven, CT: Yale University Press.

Green, Tristin K. 2013. "Racial Emotion in the Workplace." *USC Law Review* 86:959–1023.

Guardian, The. 2019. "Trump: 'I Am the Least Racist Person There Is Anywhere in the World.'" Video, July 30, 2019. www.theguardian.com.

Guidotti-Hernández, Nicole M. 2007. "Dora The Explorer, Constructing 'LATINIDADES' and The Politics of Global Citizenship." *Latino Studies* 5 (2): 209–32.

Hagerman, Margaret A. 2016. "Reproducing and Reworking Colorblind Racial Ideology Acknowledging Children's Agency in the White Habitus." *Sociology of Race and Ethnicity* 2 (1): 58–71.

———. 2017. "'The Celebrity Thing': Using Photographs of Celebrities in Child-Centered Ethnographic Interviews with White Kids about Race." In *Researching Children and Youth: Methodological Issues, Strategies, and Innovations*, Sociological Studies of Children and Youth 22, edited by Ingrid E. Castro, Melissa Swauger, and Brent Harger, 303–24. Bingley, UK: Emerald.

———. 2018a. "Those Who Care and Those Who Don't: Children and Racism in the Trump Era." *Los Angeles Review of Books*, December 14, 2018. www.lareviewofbooks.org.

———. 2018b. *White Kids: Growing Up with Privilege in a Racially Divided America.* New York: New York University Press.

———. 2020. "Racial Ideology and White Youth: From Middle Childhood to Adolescence." *Sociology of Race and Ethnicity* 6 (3): 319–32.

Halberstadt, Amy G., Alison N. Cooke, Pamela W. Garner, Sherick A. Hughes, Dejah Oertwig, and Shevaun D. Neupert. 2020. "Racialized Emotion Recognition Accuracy and Anger Bias of Children's Faces." *Emotion* (American Psychological Association), 1–15.

Halley, Jean, Amy Eshleman, and Ramya Mahadevan Vijaya. 2011. *Seeing White: An Introduction to White Privilege and Race.* Lanham, MD: Rowman and Littlefield.

Hattam, Robert, and Michalinos Zembylas. 2010. "What's Anger Got to Do with It? Towards a Post-Indignation Pedagogy for Communities in Conflict." *Social Identities* 16 (1): 23–40.

Healy, Patrick, and Jeremy W. Peters. 2016. "Donald Trump's Victory Is Met With Shock across a Wide Political Divide." *New York Times*, November 9, 2016. www. nytimes.com.

Heath, Chris. 2015. "This Donald Trump Interview Is the Best. You're Gonna Love It." *GQ*, November 23, 2015. www.gq.com.

hooks, bell. 1995. *Killing Rage: Ending Racism.* New York: Holt.

Huang, Francis L., and Dewey G. Cornell. 2019. "School Teasing and Bullying after the Presidential Election." *Educational Researcher* 48:69–83.

Hughes, Diane, and Lisa Chen. 1999. "The Nature of Parents' Race Related Communications to Children: A Developmental Perspective." In *Child Psychology: A Handbook of Contemporary Issues*, edited by Lawrence Balter and Catherine S. Tamis-LeMonda, 467–90. Philadelphia: Psychology Press.

Hughes, Diane, James Rodriguez, Emilie P. Smith, Deborah J. Johnson, Howard C. Stevenson, and Paul Spicer. 2006. "Parents' Ethnic-Racial Socialization Practices: A Review of Research and Directions for Future Study." *Developmental Psychology* 42 (5): 747–70.

Hughes, Laurel E. 2001. *Paving Pathways: Child and Adolescent Development.* Belmont, CA: Wadsworth.

Hughey, Matthew W. 2012. "Show Me Your Papers! Obama's Birth and the Whiteness of Belonging." *Qualitative Sociology* 35 (2): 163–81.

Jackman, Mary. 1996. *The Velvet Glove: Paternalism and Conflict in Gender, Class, and Race Relations.* Berkeley: University of California Press.

Jacobo, Julia. 2016. "Students Chant 'Build the Wall' at Middle School Cafeteria the Day after the Election." ABC News, November 10, 2016. www.abcnews. go.com.

Jacobson, Gary C. 2016. "The Obama Legacy and the Future of Partisan Conflict: Demographic Change and Generational Imprinting." *Annals of the American Academy of Political and Social Science* 667 (1): 72–91.

Jefferson, Hakeem, and Victor Ray. 2022. "White Backlash Is a Type of Racial Reckoning, Too." *FiveThirtyEight*, January 6, 2022. www.fivethirtyeight.com.

Jenkins, Aric. 2017. "Read President Trump's NFL Speech on National Anthem Protests." *Time*, September 23, 2017. www.time.com.

Jennings, M. Kent. 1987. "Residues of a Movement: The Aging of the American Protest Generation." *American Political Science Review* 81 (2): 367–82.

Jennings, M. Kent, and Richard G. Niemi. 1981. *Generations and Politics: A Panel Study of Young Adults and Their Parents*. Princeton, NJ: Princeton University Press.

Jensen, Robert. 2005. *The Heart of Whiteness: Confronting Race, Racism, and White Privilege*. San Francisco: City Lights.

Johnson, Heather Beth. 2014. *The American Dream and the Power of Wealth: Choosing Schools and Inheriting Inequality in the Land of Opportunity*. 2nd ed. New York: Routledge.

Johnson, Kevin. 2017. "Attorney General Jeff Sessions Enacts Harsher Charging, Sentencing Policy." *USA Today*, May 12, 2017. www.usatoday.com.

Jones, Shawn C. T., Riana Elyse Anderson, Ashly Louise Gaskin-Wasson, Broderick A. Sawyer, Kimberly Applewhite, and Isha W. Metzger. 2020. "From 'Crib to Coffin': Navigating Coping from Racism-Related Stress throughout the Lifespan of Black Americans." *American Journal of Orthopsychiatry* 90 (2): 267–82.

Jung, Moon-Kie. 2015. *Beneath the Surface of White Supremacy: Denaturalizing U.S. Racisms Past and Present*. Stanford, CA: Stanford University Press.

Justice, Benjamin, and Jason Stanley. 2016. "Teaching in the Time of Trump." *Social Education* 80 (1): 36–41.

Kessler, Thomas, and Susan Hollbach. 2005. "Group-Based Emotions as Determinants of Ingroup Identification." *Journal of Experimental Social Psychology* 41 (6): 677–85.

Khoo, Isabelle. 2017. "Five-Year-Old Boy Detained at Airport for Hours Due to Trump Ban." *Huffington Post*, January 30, 2017. www.huffingtonpost.ca.

Kim, Janine Young. 2016. "Racial Emotions and the Feeling of Equality." *University of Colorado Law Review* 87 (2): 437–500.

Kim, Nadia Y. 2021. *Refusing Death: Immigrant Women and the Fight for Environmental Justice in L.A.* Stanford, CA: Stanford University Press.

Kinder, Donald R., and Lynn M. Sanders. 1996. *Divided by Color: Racial Politics and Democratic Ideals*. Chicago: University of Chicago Press.

Kohli, Rita, Marcos Pizarro, and Arturo Nevárez. 2017. "The 'New Racism' of K–12 Schools: Centering Critical Research on Racism." *Review of Research in Education* 41 (1): 182–202.

Kovel, Joel. 1984. *White Racism: A Psychohistory*. New York: Columbia University Press.

Kozol, Jonathan. 2012. *Savage Inequalities: Children in America's Schools*. New York: Broadway Books.

Krysan, Maria, and Kyle Crowder. 2017. *Cycle of Segregation: Social Processes and Residential Stratification.* New York: Russell Sage Foundation.

Krysan, Maria, and Amanda E. Lewis, eds. 2006. *The Changing Terrain of Race and Ethnicity.* New York: Russell Sage Foundation.

Ladner, Trevor. 2020. "Blackness on the Whiteboard: Teaching Race and Racism in Mississippi Social Studies Education." Undergraduate thesis, Harvard University.

Lavoie, Denise. 2021. "Woman Recalls 'Complete Terror' of Charlottesville Car Attack." *PBS NewsHour*, November 8, 2021. www.pbs.org.

Levy, Rachael, and Erin Ailworth. 2021. "Who Are the Proud Boys? Canada Names Far-Right Group a Terrorist Organization." *Wall Street Journal*, February 5, 2021. www.wsj.com.

Lewis, Amanda E. 2001. "There Is No 'Race' in the Schoolyard: Color-Blind Ideology in an (Almost) All-White School." *American Educational Research Journal* 38 (4): 781–811.

———. 2003. *Race in the Schoolyard: Negotiating the Color Line in Classrooms and Communities.* New Brunswick, NJ: Rutgers University Press.

———. 2004. "'What Group?': Studying Whites and Whiteness in the Era of 'Color-Blindness.'" *Sociological Theory* 22 (4): 623–46.

Lewis, Amanda E., and John B. Diamond. 2015. *Despite the Best Intentions: How Racial Inequality Thrives in Good Schools.* New York: Oxford University Press.

Lewis, Amanda, and Margaret Hagerman. 2016. "Using Ethnography and Interviews to Study Color-Blind Racial Ideology." in *The Myth of Racial Color Blindness Manifestations, Dynamics, and Impact,* edited by Helen A. Neville, Miguel E. Gallardo, and Derald Wing Sue, 157–71. Washington, DC: American Psychological Association.

Lewis-McCoy, R. L'Heureux. 2014. *Inequality in the Promised Land: Race, Resources, and Suburban Schooling.* Stanford, CA: Stanford University Press.

Lippard, Cameron D., J. Scott Carter, and David G. Embrick. 2020. Introduction to *Protecting Whiteness: Whitelash and the Rejection of Racial Equality*, edited by Cameron D. Lippard, J. Scott Carter, and David G. Embrick, 3–23. Seattle: University of Washington Press.

Long, Clara. 2019. "Written Testimony: Kids in Cages: Inhumane Treatment at the Border." Human Rights Watch, July 11, 2019. www.hrw.org.

Lopez, German. 2020. "Donald Trump's Long History of Racism, from the 1970s to 2020." *Vox*, August 13, 2020. www.vox.com.

Lyman, Peter. 2004. "The Domestication of Anger: The Use and Abuse of Anger in Politics." *European Journal of Social Theory* 7 (2): 133–47.

Mannheim, Karl. (1928) 1972. "The Problem of Generations." In *The New Pilgrims,* edited by Philip G. Albach and Robert S. Laufer, 101–38. New York: David McKay.

Marable, Manning. 2000. "A Conversation with Ossie Davis." *Souls* 2 (3): 6–16.

Massey, Douglas S., and Nancy A. Denton. 1993. *American Apartheid: Segregation and the Making of the Underclass*. Cambridge, MA: Harvard University Press.

Mathis-Lilley, Ben. 2017. "How Trump Has Cultivated the White Supremacy Alt-Right for Years." *Slate*, August 14, 2017. www.slate.com.

Matias, Cheryl E., and Peter M. Newlove. 2017. "The Illusion of Freedom: Tyranny, Whiteness, and the State of US Society." *Equity & Excellence in Education* 50 (3): 316–30.

McDermott, Monica. 2020. *Whiteness in America*. Medford, MA: Polity.

McDevitt, Michael, and Steven Chaffee. 2002. "From Top-Down to Trickle-Up Influence Revisiting Assumptions about the Family in Political Socialization." *Political Communication* 19 (3): 281–301.

McIntosh, Peggy. 1989. "White Privilege: Unpacking the Invisible Knapsack." *Peace and Freedom Magazine*, July–August 1989, 10–12.

Meckler, Laura. 2018. "Trump Administration Revokes Effort to Reduce Racial Bias in School Discipline." *Washington Post*, December 21. www.washingtonpost.com.

Meece, Judith. 2002. *Child and Adolescent Development for Educators*. 3rd ed. New York: McGraw-Hill.

Mercer, Jonathan. 2014. "Feeling like a State: Social Emotion and Identity." *International Theory: A Journal of Politics, Law, and Philosophy* 6 (3): 515–35.

Merchant, Natasha Hakimali. 2016. "Responses to Islam in the Classroom: A Case of Muslim Girls from Minority Communities of Interpretation." *International Journal of Multicultural Education* 18 (1): 183–99.

Metzl, Jonathan A. 2019. *Dying of Whiteness: How the Politics of Resentment Is Killing America's Heartland*. New York: Basic Books.

Meyer, John C. 2000. "Humor as a Double-Edged Sword: Four Functions of Humor in Communication." *Communication Theory* 10 (3): 310–31.

Miller, Gabe H., Guadalupe Marquez-Velarde, Apryl A. Williams, and Verna M. Keith. 2021. "Discrimination and Black Social Media Use: Sites of Oppression and Expression." *Sociology of Race and Ethnicity* 7 (2): 247–63.

Miller-Idriss, Cynthia. 2020. *Hate in the Homeland: The New Global Far Right*. Princeton, NJ: Princeton University Press.

———. 2022. "America's Most Urgent Threat Now Comes from Within." *New York Times*, January 12, 2022. www.nytimes.com.

Mills, C. Wright. 2000. *The Sociological Imagination: 40th Anniversary Edition*. New York: Oxford University Press.

Mills, Charles W. 2003. *From Class to Race: Essays in White Marxism and Black Radicalism*. Lanham, MD: Rowman and Littlefield.

Moore, Valerie Ann. 2002. "The Collaborative Emergence of Race in Children's Play: A Case Study of Two Summer Camps." *Social Problems* 49 (1): 58–78.

Morales, Amanda, Elvira Abrica, and Socorro Herrera. 2019. "The Mañana Complex: A Revelatory Narrative of Teachers' White Innocence and Racial Disgust toward Mexican-American Children." *Urban Review* 51:1–24.

Morrison, Toni. 1992. *Playing in the Dark: Whiteness and the Literary Imagination*. Cambridge, MA: Harvard University Press.

Mueller, Jennifer C. 2017. "Producing Colorblindness: Everyday Mechanisms of White Ignorance." *Social Problems* 64:219–38.

Natanson, Jannah. 2021. "It Started with a Mock 'Slave Trade' and a School-Resolution against Racism. Now a War over Critical Race Theory Is Tearing This Small Town Apart." *Washington Post*, July 24, 2021. www.washingtonpost.com.

National Public Radio. 2021. "Pro-Trump Extremists Storm Capitol in Deadly Attack." January 9, 2021. www.npr.org.

New York Times. 2016. "Transcript: Donald Trump's Taped Comments about Women." October 8, 2016. www.nytimes.com.

Nguyen, Chi, and Maraki Kebede. 2017. "Immigrant Students in the Trump Era: What We Know and Do Not Know." *Educational Policy* 31 (6): 716–42.

Niemi, Richard G., and Mary A. Hepburn. 1995. "The Rebirth of Political Socialization." *Perspectives on Political Science* 24:7–16.

Nilsen, Sarah, and Sarah E. Turner. 2014. *The Colorblind Screen: Television in Post-Racial America*. New York: New York University Press.

Noble, Safiya Umoja. 2018. *Algorithms of Oppression: How Search Engines Reinforce Racism*. New York: New York University Press.

Oakes, Jeannie. 2005. *Keeping Track: How Schools Structure Inequality*. Rev ed. New Haven, CT: Yale University Press.

Ojeda, Christopher, and Peter K. Hatemi. 2015. "Accounting for the Child in the Transmission of Party Identification." *American Sociological Review* 80 (6): 1150–74.

Oliver, Melvin, and Thomas M. Shapiro, eds. 2006. *Black Wealth / White Wealth: A New Perspective on Racial Inequality*. 2nd ed. New York: Routledge.

Omi, Michael, and Howard Winant. 1994. *Racial Formation in the United States: From the 1960s to the 1990s*. 2nd ed. New York: Routledge.

Paris, Francesca. 2019. "Video of Kentucky Student Mocking Native American Man Draws Outcry." NPR, January 20, 2019. www.npr.org.

Pascoe, C. J. 2014. "Bullying as Social Inequality." *The Enemy*. www.theenemyreader.org.

Patel, Leigh. 2018. "Immigrant Populations and Sanctuary Schools." *Journal of Literacy Research* 50 (4): 524–29.

Patler, Caitlin, Erin Hamilton, Kelsey Meagher, and Robin Savinar. 2019. "Uncertainty about DACA May Undermine Its Positive Impact on Health for Recipients and Their Children." *Health Affairs* 38 (5): 738–45.

Pérez, Raúl. 2017. "Racism without Hatred? Racist Humor and the Myth of 'Colorblindness.'" *Sociological Perspectives* 60 (5): 956–74.

Perry, Pamela. 2002. *Shades of White: White Kids and Racial Identities in High School*. Durham, NC: Duke University Press Books.

Pettigrew, Thomas Fraser, and Roel W. Meertens. 1995. "Subtle and Blatant Prejudice in Western Europe." *European Journal of Social Psychology* 25 (1): 57–75.

Picca, Leslie, and Joe Feagin. 2007. *Two-Faced Racism: Whites in the Backstage and Frontstage*. New York: Routledge.

Pirtle, Whitney N. Laster. 2020. "Racial Capitalism: A Fundamental Cause of Novel Coronavirus (COVID-19) Pandemic Inequities in the United States." *Health Education & Behavior* 47 (4).

Posey-Maddox, Linn. 2013. "Professionalizing the PTO: Race, Class, and Shifting Norms of Parental Engagement in a City Public School." *American Journal of Education* 119 (2): 235–60.

Quadagno, Jill. 1996. *The Color of Welfare: How Racism Undermined the War on Poverty*. New York: Oxford University Press.

Rafanell, Irene, and Hugo Gorringe. 2010. "Consenting to Domination? Theorising Power, Agency and Embodiment with Reference to Caste." *Sociological Review* 58 (4): 604–22.

Ray, Ranita. 2017. *The Making of a Teenage Service Class: Poverty and Mobility in an American City*. Berkeley: University of California Press.

Ray, Victor. 2019. "A Theory of Racialized Organizations." *American Sociological Review* 84 (1): 26–53.

——— (@victorerikray). 2022. "Since January 6, 2021, the open insurrection has morphed into the institutionalized erosion of democracy. The attacks on critical race theory, the attacks on school boards, and the attacks on voting rights are one movement. Racism is at the center of American democratic erosion." Twitter, January 6, 2022. https://twitter.com/victorerikray/status/1479051365691318272.

Reid, Darren R. 2020. *Native American Racism in the Age of Donald Trump: Historical and Contemporary Perspectives*. Cham, Switzerland: Springer Nature.

Reilly, Katie. 2016. "Here Are All the Times Donald Trump Insulted Mexico." *Time*, August 31, 2016. www.time.com.

Reilly, Ryan J. 2017. "Donald Trump Endorses Police Brutality in Speech to Cops." *HuffPost*, July 28, 2017. www.huffpost.com.

Rice, Douglas, Stephanie Schmit, and Hannah Matthews. 2019. "Child Care and Housing: Big Expenses With Too Little Help Available." Center on Budget and Policy Priorities, April 26, 2019. www.cbpp.org.

Rivas-Drake, Deborah, Eleanor K. Seaton, Carol Markstrom, Stephen Quintana, Moin Syed, Richard M. Lee, Seth J. Schwartz, Adriana J. Umaña-Taylor, Sabine French, Tiffany Yip, and the Ethnic and Racial Identity in the 21st Century Working Group. 2014. "Ethnic and Racial Identity in Adolescence: Implications for Psychosocial, Academic, and Health Outcomes." *Child Development* 85 (1): 40–57.

Roberts, Dorothy. 2002. *Shattered Bonds: The Color Of Child Welfare*. New York: Basic Civitas Books.

———. 2011. *Fatal Invention: How Science, Politics, and Big Business Re-create Race in the Twenty-First Century*. New York: New Press.

Roberts, Ebony M. 2004. "Through the Eyes of a Child: Representations of Blackness in Children's Television Programming." *Race, Gender & Class* 11 (2): 130–39.

Robinson, Russell K. 2008. "Perceptual Segregation." *Columbia Law Review* 108:1093–1180.

Rockquemore, Kerry Ann, David L. Brunsma, and Daniel J. Delgado. 2009. "Racing to Theory or Retheorizing Race? Understanding the Struggle to Build a Multiracial Identity Theory." *Journal of Social Issues* 65 (1): 13–34.

Roda, Allison, and Amy Stuart Wells. 2013. "School Choice Policies and Racial Segregation: Where White Parents' Good Intentions, Anxiety, and Privilege Collide." *American Journal of Education* 119 (2): 261–93.

Rodriguez, Gabriel, and Monica González Ybarra. 2020. "'This Is What I Go Through': Latinx Youth Facultades in Suburban Schools in the Era of Trump." *Race Ethnicity and Education.* 25 (7): 922–938.

Roediger, David R. 2007. *The Wages of Whiteness: Race and the Making of the American Working Class.* New York: Verso.

Rogers, John, Megan Franke, Jung-Eun Ellie Yun, Michael Ishimoto, Claudia Diera, Rebecca Cooper Geller, Anthony Berryman, and Tizoc Brenes. 2017. *Teaching and Learning in the Age of Trump: Increasing Stress and Hostility in America's High Schools.* Los Angeles: UCLA's Institute for Democracy, Education, and Access.

Rogers, John, and Michael Ishimoto. 2021. "Not 'a Good Example for Children': Racist Speech in America's High Schools in the Age of Trump." In *Why They Hate Us: How Racist Rhetoric Impacts Education*, edited by Lindsay Pérez Huber and Susana M. Muñoz, 49–70. New York: Teachers College Press.

Rogers, John, and Joseph Kahne, with Michael Ishimoto, Alexander Kwako, Samuel C. Stern, Cicely Bingener, Leah Raphael, Samia Alkam, and Yvette Conde. 2022. *Educating for a Diverse Democracy: The Chilling Role of Political Conflict in Blue, Purple, and Red Communities.* Los Angeles: UCLA's Institute for Democracy, Education, and Access.

Rosenbaum, Dottie, and Zoë Neuberger. 2020. "Presidents' 2021 Budget Would Cut Food Assistance for Millions and Radically Restructure SNAP." Center for Budget and Policy Priorities, February 18, 2020. www.cbpp.org.

Rosino, Michael L. 2017. "Dramaturgical Domination: The Genesis and Evolution of the Racialized Interaction Order." *Humanity & Society* 41 (2): 158–81.

Saltman, Kenneth. 2018. *The Politics of Education: A Critical Introduction.* 2nd ed. New York: Routledge.

Schaub, Michael. 2022. "Missouri School District Bans Toni Morrison Book." *Kirkus*, January 25, 2022. www.kirkusreviews.com.

Schuman, Howard, Charlotte Steeh, Lawrence D. Bobo, and Maria Krysan. 1998. *Racial Attitudes in America: Trends and Interpretations.* Rev. ed. Cambridge, MA: Harvard University Press.

Seaton, Eleanor K., Rachel Upton, Adrianne Gilbert, and Vanessa Volpe. 2014. "A Moderated Mediation Model: Racial Discrimination, Coping Strategies, and Racial Identity among Black Adolescents." *Child Development* 85 (3): 882–90.

Sewell, William H. 1992. "A Theory of Structure: Duality, Agency, and Transformation." *American Journal of Sociology* 98 (1): 1–29.

Shapiro, Thomas M., and Heather Beth Johnson. 2005. "Family Assets and School Access: Race and Class in the Structuring of Educational Opportunity." In *Inclusion in the American Dream: Assets, Poverty, and Public Policy*, edited by Michael Sherraden, 112–27. New York: Oxford University Press.

Shedd, Carla. 2015. *Unequal City: Race, Schools, and Perceptions of Injustice*. New York: Russell Sage Foundation.

Shelton, Eric J. 2019. "Relatives, Communities Step Up to Care for Kids Left Behind in ICE Raids." Mississippi Today, September 18, 2019. www.mississippitoday.org.

Shonkoff, Jack P., and Andrew S. Garner. 2012. "The Lifelong Effects of Early Childhood Adversity and Toxic Stress." *Pediatrics* 129 (1e): e232–46.

Simmons, Dena. 2021. "Why SEL Alone Isn't Enough." ASCD, March 1, 2021. www.ascd.org.

Skiba, Russell J., Robert H. Horner, Choong-Geun Chung, M. Karega Rausch, Seth L. May, and Tary Tobin. 2011. "Race Is Not Neutral: A National Investigation of African American and Latino Disproportionality in School Discipline." *School Psychology Review* 40 (1): 85–107.

Smith, Anna V. 2020. "Trump's Impact on Indian Country Over Four Years." *High Country News*, December 16, 2020. www.hcn.org.

Smith, Eliot R., and Diane M. Mackie. 2015. "Dynamics of Group-Based Emotions: Insights from Intergroup Emotions Theory." *Emotion Review* 7 (4): 349–54.

Sondel, Beth, Hannah Carson Baggett, and Alyssa Hadley Dunn. 2018. "'For Millions of People, This Is Real Trauma': A Pedagogy of Political Trauma in the Wake of the 2016 U.S. Presidential Election." *Teaching and Teacher Education* 70:175–85.

Southern Poverty Law Center. 2016. "Update: Incidents of Hateful Harassment since Election Day." *SPLC Hatewatch*, December 19, 2016. www.splcenter.org.

Sue, Christina A., and Tanya Golash-Boza. 2013. "'It Was Only a Joke': How Racial Humour Fuels Colour-Blind Ideologies in Mexico and Peru." *Ethnic and Racial Studies* 36(10): 1582–98.

Takaki, Ronald. 1998. *Strangers from a Different Shore: A History of Asian Americans*. Rev. ed. Boston: Little, Brown.

———. 2008. *A Different Mirror: A History of Multicultural America*. Rev. ed. New York: Back Bay Books.

Tatum, Sophie, and Mark Osborne. 2019. "ICE Releases Hundreds Rounded Up in Mississippi as Children Left Behind." *ABC News*, August 8, 2019. www.abcnews.go.com.

Thoits, Peggy A. 1989. "The Sociology of Emotions." *Annual Review of Sociology* 15 (1): 317–42.

Thomas, Anita Jones, and Sha'Kema M. Blackmon. 2015. "The Influence of the Trayvon Martin Shooting on Racial Socialization Practices of African American Parents." *Journal of Black Psychology* 41 (1): 75–89.

Thomas, William I., and Dorothy S. Thomas. 1928. *The Child in America: Behavior Problems and Programs.* New York: Knopf.

Thompson, John B. 1984. *Studies in the Theory of Ideology.* Cambridge, UK: Polity.

Thrasher, Steven W. 2014. "The Whiteness Project Will Make You Wince. Because White People Can Be Rather Awful." *The Guardian,* October 15, 2014. www. theguardian.com.

Tilly, Charles. 1999. *Durable Inequality.* Rev. ed. Berkeley: University of California Press.

Turner, Cory. 2022. "School Principals Say Culture Wars Made Last Year 'Rough as Hell.'" *NPR,* December 1, 2022. www.npr.org.

Tyson, Karolyn. 2011. *Integration Interrupted: Tracking, Black Students, and Acting White after Brown.* New York: Oxford University Press.

Umaña-Taylor, Adriana J., and Nancy E. Hill. 2020. "Ethnic-Racial Socialization in the Family: A Decade's Advance on Precursors and Outcomes." *Journal of Marriage and Family* 82 (1): 244–71.

Umaña-Taylor, Adriana J., Stephen M. Quintana, Richard M. Lee, William E. Cross Jr., Deborah Rivas-Drake, Seth J. Schwartz, Moin Syed, Tiffany Yip, Eleanor Seaton, and Ethnic and Racial Identity in the 21st Century Study Group. 2014. "Ethnic and Racial Identity during Adolescence and into Young Adulthood: An Integrated Conceptualization." *Child Development* 85 (1): 21–39.

Underhill, Megan R. 2018. "Parenting during Ferguson: Making Sense of White Parents' Silence." *Ethnic and Racial Studies* 41 (11): 1934–51.

US Census Bureau. 2010. "State Area Measurements and Internal Point Coordinates." www.census.gov.

———. 2020. "Urban and Rural." www.census.gov.

———. 2021a. "American Community Survey. Financial Characteristics for Housing Units with a Mortgage." www.census.gov.

———. 2021b. "American Community Survey. Income in the Past Twelve Months." www.census.gov.

———. 2021c. "Massachusetts: 2020 Census." www.census.gov.

———. 2021d. "Mississippi: 2020 Census." www.census.gov.

US National Archives and Records Administration. 2020. "2020 Electoral College Results." www.archives.gov.

Van Ausdale, Debra, and Joe R. Feagin. 2001. *The First R: How Children Learn Race and Racism.* Lanham, MD: Rowman and Littlefield.

Vandello, Joseph A., Jennifer K. Bosson, Dov Cohen, Rochelle M. Burnaford, and Jonathan R. Weaver. 2008. "Precarious Manhood." *Journal of Personality and Social Psychology* 95 (6): 1325–39.

Vittrup, Brigitte. 2018. "Color Blind or Color Conscious? White American Mothers' Approaches to Racial Socialization." *Journal of Family Issues* 39 (3): 668–92.

Warikoo, Natasha K., and Janine de Novais. 2015. "Colour-Blindness and Diversity: Race Frames and Their Consequences for White Undergraduates at Elite US Universities." *Ethnic and Racial Studies* 38 (6): 860–76.

Waxman, Olivia B. 2021. "'Critical Race Theory Is Simply the Latest Bogeyman': Inside the Fight over What Kids Learn about America's History." *Time*, July 16, 2021. www.time.com.

Weaver, Simon. 2011. *The Rhetoric of Racist Humour: US, UK and Global Race Joking.* Farnham, UK: Ashgate.

Weimann, Gabriel, and Natalie Masri. 2020. "Research Note: Spreading Hate on TikTok." *Studies in Conflict & Terrorism.* OnlineFirst.

Wells, Karen. 2017. "What Does a Republican Government with Donald Trump as President of the USA Mean for Children, Youth, and Families?" *Children's Geographies* 15 (4): 491–97.

Williams, Raymond. 1978. *Marxism and Literature.* Oxford: Oxford University Press.

Wills, John S. 2019. "Silencing Racism: Remembering and Forgetting Race and Racism in 11th Grade U.S. History Classes." *Teachers College Record* 121 (6).

Winkler, Erin N. 2012. *Learning Race, Learning Place: Shaping Racial Identities and Ideas in African American Childhoods.* New Brunswick, NJ: Rutgers University Press.

Woodiwiss, Catherine. 2016. "The Era of White Anxiety Is Just Beginning." *Sojourners*, March 8, 2016. www.sojo.net.

Wray-Lake, Laura, Rachel Wells, Lauren Alvis, Sandra Delgado, Amy Y. Syvertsen, and Aaron Metzger. 2018. "Being a Latinx Adolescent under a Trump Presidency: Analysis of Latinx Youth's Reactions to Immigration." *Children and Youth Services Review* 87:192–204.

Yoder, Paul J. 2020. "'He Wants to Get Rid of All the Muslims': Mexican American and Muslim Students' Use of History Regarding Candidate Trump." *Theory and Research in Social Education* 48 (3): 346–74.

Zayas, Luis H., and Laurie Cook Heffron. 2016. "Disrupting Young Lives: How Detention and Deportation Affect US-Born Children of Immigrants." American Psychological Association, November 2016. www.apa.org.

Zraick, Karen. 2016. "USA Freedom Kids Are in Dispute with Trump." *New York Times*, July 27, 2016. www.nytimes.com.

INDEX

action: emotions and, 71–72; kids and, 66, 70–73; racism and, 69–73; solidarity and, 96–101. *See also* protests

administrators, in schools, 1–3, 18, 116, 169–70

adults: politics and, 2–3, 24–25, 35, 61–62, 115; responsibilities of, 152–54, 156–57, 159–60, 162, 167–68. *See also* parents

agency, 32–33, 145, 196n12; anger and, 77–78, 100

Ahmed, Sara, 96

Albertson, Bethany, 35

analysis, critical, 71, 162–65

Anderson, Carol, 142

anger, 30–31, 41, 51, 58–64; agency and, 77–78, 100; change and, 151–53; fear and, 133; as racialized emotions, 95–96; Trump and, 96–97, 125

anti-Asian rhetoric, 11–12, 97

anti-Latinx policies, 14–17, 67, 91, 110

anti-Trump white kids, 29–33, 68, 138–39

anxiety, 10–11, 33–36, 77, 135

apathy. *See* racial apathy

approval, of Trump, 32, 80

Arab American kids, 17–18, 192n46, 192n48. *See also* Muslim kids

assault, 18, 90–91, 99, 153; sexual, 11, 57–58, 80. *See also* violence

awareness: of income inequality, 60; of racism, 34, 55–56, 159–62

"back to normal," 66–69, 139, 161

Baldwin, James, 90

Bartky, Sandra Lee, 111–12

behavior, 51; of kids, 91–92; racism and, 22–23, 36–37, 53–54, 140–41, 159–61; responsibility for, 94–95; on social media, 116; of Trump, 62, 79–80, 139; of white kids, 107–8

Bell, Joyce, 194n6

Biden, Joe, 1–2, 149

biology, racism and, 49

Black communities, 13, 82–83, 196n12

Black history, 100–101

Black Lives Matter, 13, 87–88, 96–97; white kids and, 125–27

Black parents, 51–52, 195n36

Blumer, Herbert, 124–25

Bonilla-Silva, Eduardo, 24–25, 40, 75, 135; on anger, 96; on colorblind ideology, 5, 64–65; feeling race and, 37, 90; on racialized emotions, 7, 29, 37, 102, 116, 157

border wall, 21, 40, 85, 105, 120, 129; "Build the wal" and, 1–2, 11, 16, 91, 93–94, 109; jokes, 109–11, 118–19, 147; racist play and, 114

Bracey, Glenn, 111

Brown, Tony, 195n22, 199n2

Brunsma, David L., 194n17

bullying, 17, 51, 160; racism and, 90–94; violence and, 90–91

Bush, George W., 161

Cabrera, Nolan, 198n7

Capitol, storming of, 20, 146, 160–61, 167

change, 71–73, 99, 147–48; anger and, 151–53; fear of, 144

child care, 12, 169

childhood: political context of, 17, 83, 87–88, 132–34, 148; racial context of, 7, 46–47, 56, 83, 134, 151–52, 154–55

Citizens but Not Americans (Flores-Gonzáles), 89–90

Clinton, Bill, 161

Clinton, Hillary, 17, 38–39, 58, 109, 112–13

colorblind ideology, 3–4, 22–23, 148, 193n66, 195n22, 195n26; Bonilla-Silva on, 5, 64–65; cultural racism and, 48–49, 51, 53; feelings and, 139–40; jokes and, 141; Obama and, 44–45; people of color and, 195n35; racial apathy and, 140–41; rhetoric and, 67; in US, 137–41; white kids and, 32–33, 46–47, 50–54, 66–75, 137–41; white nationalism and, 145; white privilege and, 48–49, 200n24

colorblind logic, 44, 46, 66–72, 162; racialized emotions and, 73–75, 161

colorblind racism, 23, 44, 48–49, 56, 137–42, 161–63; emotions and, 64–66

communities, 71–72, 87–88, 113; Black, 13, 82–83, 196n12; grief in, 82, 196n12; Indigenous, 12; racism in, 2, 94–96, 107; US and, 132, 154–55

Confederate symbols, 11, 13, 19–20, 62, 106, 122–23, 149–50

consequences: kids and, 91–92, 140–41; of Trump era, 15–17, 21, 68, 77–78

context. *See* political context; racial context

Corsaro, William, 115

COVID-19 pandemic, 11–12, 150–51

criminal justice system, 55–56, 62, 125–26, 169. *See also* police violence

critical analysis, 71, 162–65

"critical race theory," 116, 118, 160, 163–64

cultural racism, colorblind ideology and, 48–49, 51, 53

cynicism, hope and, 35, 151–52

data, 5, 149, 194n1; patterns in, 6, 18, 28, 41–42, 77–78, 102–3

Davis, Ossie, 37

dehumanization, 13–15, 34–35, 49, 127, 144, 146–47

Delgado, Daniel J., 194n17

delight, 106–7, 109, 113–14, 116–17, 120, 135–36

democracy, 23–25, 65–66, 168; multira-cial, 152, 156–57, 163, 169–71

demographics, 4, 9–10, 77, 194n1; of schools, 50, 60

deportation, 14–16, 18, 84, 88–89, 161

discrimination, 11–12, 48–49, 192n46, 193n66. *See also* racism

disgust, 17, 32, 58–64, 74, 95

disillusionment, 65–66, 69–70, 152

division, in politics, 26–27, 61, 169–71
Doane, Woody, 144–46
domination, racial, 40, 106, 111–12
doom, 34–35
Dow, Dawn Marie, *Mothering While Black*, 81–82
Dreby, Joanna, 89
Du Bois, W. E. B., 49

elections: feelings and, 9–10, 29–30; 2016, 9–10, 26–28, 135
emotions, 5, 27–28; action and, 71–72; colorblind racism and, 64–66; group, 6, 24–25, 29, 36–37, 63–64, 102–3, 156–57; race and, 6–7, 127–28; of white people, 65–66; white supremacy and, 63. *See also* racialized emotions
empathy, 134, 157–58
empowerment, 97–98, 100, 113, 152–53
engagement, with politics, 35, 41, 118–20, 163–68
environment, social, 92, 154–57, 160–61, 169, 198n7
equality, 51, 125; progress and, 46, 59–60. *See also* inequality
Ewing, Eve, 82, 196n12
exceptionalism, US, 71–72, 119
existence, of racism, 95, 105–7, 139, 157–58, 162, 164

families, 2–3, 81–82; politics and, 26–27, 30–32; separation of, 14–16, 21; white, 137, 154–55
far-right ideologies, 19–21, 142, 146–47, 159–61
Feagin, Joe, 117, 143, 155
fear, 15, 17, 33; anger and, 133; of change, 144; group membership and, 143–44; as racialized emotion, 83–90, 120–32; of violence, 84–85; white kids and, 132–33

feeling race, 28–29, 38, 66, 102–3, 156, 170–71; Bonilla-Silva and, 37, 90; racial learning and, 41–42, 80–83; white kids and, 73–74, 134–36. *See also* racialized emotions
feelings, 121; colorblind ideology and, 139–40; elections and, 9–10, 29–30; kids of color and, 153; rhetoric and, 106; Trump and, 27–28; white people and, 81, 142. *See also* emotions
Flores-Gonzáles, Nilda, *Citizens but Not Americans*, 89–90
Forman, Tyrone, 47, 68, 107–8, 140
future: hope for, 43–44, 67–69, 71; racial ideologies and, 137–48

gender-based violence, 57–58, 80
Gonzales, Roberto, 89
Gould, Deborah, 66
grief, 82, 196n12
group emotions, 6, 24–25, 29, 36–37, 63–64, 102–3, 156–57; trauma and, 84
group membership, 80, 94; fear and, 143–44; history and, 163; identity and, 101, 134, 197n34, 198n24; ideology and, 114–15; race and, 34, 42; racist play and, 113–14, 198n7; solidarity and, 85, 196n12; violence and, 98; white kids and, 120–22, 124, 132–34
guilt, 65, 68–69, 139
gun violence, 98; police violence and, 86, 126; schools and, 126

happiness, 38–40, 109, 121–22, 130
"happy talk," 45, 194n6
Hartmann, Douglas, 194n6
health, 15–16; of kids of color, 77; mental, 11–12, 77, 81, 89
hierarchies: racial, 34, 49, 52, 127; social, 6, 72–73, 93, 115, 121

historical racism, 47–49, 157–58, 163–65

history: Black, 100–101; group membership and, 163

hooks, bell, 78

hope: cynicism and, 35, 151–52; doom and, 34–35; for future, 43–44, 67–69, 71

hopelessness, 34, 54, 72–73

housing, 12, 16, 45, 48, 169

ICE. See Immigration and Customs Enforcement

identity, 17–18, 192n48; group membership and, 101, 134, 197n34, 198n24; politics and, 158–59, 200nn16–17; race and, 28, 37, 194n17, 197n34; sensemaking and, 134; whiteness and, 121–22, 164

ideologies, 41, 49; far-right, 19–21, 142, 146–47, 159–61; group membership and, 114–15; mainstream, 19–21, 144, 146, 152, 161, 170; racial, 5, 47–48, 56. See also colorblind ideology

imagination: kids and, 114, 118, 198n24; sociological, 6, 159

immigrants, 63; kids as, 14–15, 30–31; Latinx, 14–17, 67, 82–83, 89, 91, 110; threats and, 128–29

Immigration and Customs Enforcement (ICE), 14

immigration policies, 17, 62, 105, 110–11, 128–29; deportation and, 14–16, 18, 84, 88–89, 161

income inequality, 60

Indigenous communities, 12

inequality: bullying and, 93; income, 60; racial, 46, 48–49, 64–65, 139–40, 163–64; in schools, 101–2

injustice, racial, 65–66, 84, 101, 157–58

innocence, of white kids, 117–20, 153–54, 164

interpretive reproduction, 115, 117

interventions, 61, 153–71

Ishimoto, Michael, 92

January 6, 2021. See storming of US Capitol

Jefferson, Hakeem, 164

jokes, 198n7; border wall and, 109–11, 118–19, 147; colorblind ideology and, 141; racial domination and, 141; racial learning and, 112–14; Trump and, 112–14

justice: racial, 78, 152, 158; social, 60

Kaepernick, Colin, 84, 87, 96, 105, 124, 126

Kaiser Family Foundation, 18

kids, 5; action and, 66, 70–73; agency of, 32–33, 145, 196n12; Arab American, 17–18, 192n46, 192n48; behavior of, 91–92; colorblind ideology and, 46–47, 137–41; consequences and, 91–92, 140–41; critical analysis and, 71, 162–65; emotions and, 7, 27–28; empowerment of, 97–98, 100, 113, 152–53; health of, 11–12, 15–16, 77; housing for, 12, 16; imagination and, 114, 118, 198n24; immigrant, 14–15, 30–31; LGBTQ+, 61–62; Muslim, 17–18, 192n46, 192n48; politics and, 23–24, 118–20, 165–68; power and, 31–32; racial learning and, 6–7, 22, 25, 37, 74–75, 154–55, 170–71; racism and, 3, 7, 26–27, 90–91; racist play and, 109–12; radicalized, 146–47, 199n22; self-identification of, 4, 196n12; storming of US Capitol and, 149–51; as Trump supporters, 104–7; white privilege and, 153–54, 200n14. See also students; white kids

kids of color, 21; fear and, 83–90; feelings and, 153; health of, 77; racism

and, 23; 2016 election and, 33–38;
white kids and, 34, 36–37, 41, 51–53,
90–94, 99–100, 116
Kim, Nadia Y., 66
Kozol, Jonathan, *Savage Inequalities*,
101–2
Kushner Gadarian, Shana, 35

landscape, political, 3, 6, 42, 170
language. *See* rhetoric
Latinx immigrants, 14–17, 67, 82–83, 89,
91, 110
learning: political, 158–59; SEL and,
157–58, 200n14. *See also* racial
learning
lesbian, gay, bisexual, transgender,
queer, and more. *See* LGBTQ+
Lewis, Amanda, 82–83
LGBTQ+ kids, 61–62
Lippard, Cameron, 144
logic, colorblind, 44, 46, 66–75, 161–
62

macro-level dynamics, 24, 28, 103;
politics and, 55–56, 74–75, 92–93,
171; racial learning and, 148
mainstream ideologies, 19–21, 144, 146,
152, 161, 170
Make America Great Again, 12, 109
Mannheim, Karl, 158–59, 200n16
mental health, 11–12, 77, 81, 89
Mercer, Jonathan, 24, 194n4
Metzl, Jonathan, 143, 157
Miller-Idriss, Cynthia, 20–21, 146–47,
155–56, 159
Morrison, Toni, *Playing in the Dark*,
198n24
Mothering While Black (Dow), 81–82
Mueller, Jennifer, 64–65, 69, 111, 195n37,
197n4
multiracial democracy, 152, 156–57, 163,
169–71

Muslim ban, 2, 17–19, 130–31
Muslim kids, 17–18, 192n46, 192n48

National Football League (NFL), 55,
84, 105
negativity, 67–68, 151–52
new white nationalism, 144–47
NFL. *See* National Football League
"normal," back to, 66–69, 139, 161
normalization: of racism, 20, 141, 144,
147; of violence, 20–21
North Korea, 87; Trump and, 84–85,
196n15

Obama, Barack, 2–3, 76, 142–43, 161;
colorblind ideology and, 44–45;
representation and, 53–54; Trump
compared to, 34, 43–44, 46, 52–55,
79, 85–87, 129; white kids and, 44–
45, 50, 52–54
older people, 59–60, 62, 143, 166,
200n16

pandemic. *See* COVID-19 pandemic
parents, 2–3, 61–62, 133, 154–56; Anita,
150–52; Black, 51–52, 195n36; kids
and, 24; politics and, 38–39, 170;
white, 45
Pascoe, C. J., 93
patterns, in data, 6, 18, 28, 41–42, 77–78,
102–3
people of color, colorblind ideology
and, 195n35
Pérez, Raúl, 117, 141
Picca, Leslie, 117
play. *See* racist play
Playing in the Dark (Morrison), 198n24
pleasure, 40, 110, 112–14, 116–17, 120,
135
police violence, 13, 56, 84–86; gun
violence and, 86, 126; race and, 88,
123–24

policies, 168–69; anti-Latinx, 14–17, 67, 91, 110; immigration, 17, 62, 105, 110–11, 128–29; Muslim ban, 2, 17–19, 130–31; rhetoric and, 14–17

political context, of childhood, 17, 83, 87–88, 132–34, 148

political landscape, 3, 6, 42, 170; racialized emotions and, 32, 77, 83, 97, 156–59; racism and, 23–24, 46–47, 55–56, 70–74, 103, 134–36

political learning, 158–59

politics, 7; adults and, 2–3, 24–25, 35, 61–62, 115; division in, 26–27, 61, 169–71; engagement with, 35, 41, 118–20, 163–68; families and, 26–27, 30–32; identity and, 158–59, 200n16–17; kids and, 23–24, 118–20, 165–68; macro-level dynamics and, 55–56, 74–75, 92–93, 171; parents and, 38–39, 170; schools and, 163–64

positive racialized emotions, 104, 110, 114, 116–17, 120, 135, 140–41

power, kids and, 31–32

privilege, white, 64, 139, 158

problems, social, 55, 73, 76, 166

progress: equality and, 46, 59–60; racial, 44–45, 52, 64, 101, 169

protection, Trump and, 121–26, 128–32, 135–36

protests, 86, 97–98, 106, 130; Kaepernick and, 84, 87, 96, 105, 124, 126; NFL, 55, 84, 105; racism and, 123–24; storming of US Capitol, 20, 146, 149–51, 160–61, 167

race: emotions and, 6–7, 127–28; feeling, 28–29, 38, 66, 102–3, 156, 170–71; group membership and, 34, 42; identity and, 28, 37, 194n17, 197n34; police violence and, 88, 123–24; in schools, 36–37, 82–83; in US, 53–54,

66, 73–74; violence and, 87–88, 128; wealth and, 65

racial apathy, 68, 199n2; colorblind ideology and, 140–41; empathy and, 134, 157–58; racialized emotions and, 108–9, 133–36; SEL and, 157–58; social issues and, 106–9, 121

racial context, of childhood, 7, 83, 151–52, 154–55; social environment and, 46–47, 56, 134

racial domination, 40, 106, 111–12; jokes and, 141; threats to, 132–33, 143–44

racial hierarchies, 34, 49, 52, 127

racial ideology, 5, 47–48, 56; future and, 137–48

racial inequality, 46, 48–49, 64–65, 139–40, 163–64

racial injustice, 65–66, 84, 101, 157–58

racialized emotions, 24–25, 28, 42, 80–82, 145–48, 196n39; anger, 95–96; anxiety, 10–11, 33–36, 77, 135; Bonilla-Silva on, 7, 29, 37, 102, 116, 157; colorblind logic and, 73–75, 161; delight, 106–7, 109, 113–14, 116–17, 120, 135–36; disgust, 17, 32, 58–64, 74, 95; disillusionment, 65–66, 69–70, 152; fear, 83–90, 120–32; guilt, 65, 68–69, 139; happiness, 38–40, 109, 121–22, 130; negativity and, 67–68, 151–52; pleasure, 40, 110, 112–14, 116–17, 120, 135; political engagement and, 35, 41, 118–20; political landscape and, 32, 77, 83, 97, 156–59; positive, 104, 110, 114, 116–17, 120, 135, 140–41; racial apathy and, 108–9, 133–36; racial learning and, 102–3, 135–36, 139, 156–58; relief, 38–39; resentment, 142–44; in schools, 102–3; shock, 32, 54–58, 65–66; solidarity and, 77–78; surprise, 54–58; white kids and, 32–33, 64–66, 106–7

racial justice, 78, 152, 158; white su-
    premacy and, 127
racial learning, 6–7, 22, 25, 37, 74–75,
    154–55, 170–71; feeling race and, 41–
    42, 80–83; jokes and, 112–14; macro-
    level dynamics and, 148; racialized
    emotions and, 102–3, 135–36, 139,
    156–58
racial progress, 44–45, 52, 64, 101, 169
racial socialization, 81–83
racism, 4, 125; action and, 69–73; anti-
    Black, 13–14, 77; awareness of, 34,
    55–56, 159–62; behavior and, 22–23,
    36–37, 53–54, 140–41, 159–61; biol-
    ogy and, 49; bullying and, 90–94;
    colorblind, 23, 44, 48–49, 56, 137–42,
    161–63; in communities, 2, 94–96,
    107; existence of, 95, 105–7, 139,
    157–58, 162, 164; feelings and, 121;
    historical, 47–49, 157–58, 163–65;
    kids and, 3, 7, 26–27, 90–91; kids of
    color and, 23; normalization of, 20,
    141, 144, 147; political landscape and,
    23–24, 46–47, 55–56, 70–74, 103, 134–
    36; protests and, 123–24; in schools,
    1–2, 50–52, 60–61; SEL and, 157–58,
    200n14; structural, 168–69; teachers
    and, 16–17, 60–61; trauma and, 13,
    85, 89–90; of Trump, 32, 39, 45–46,
    56, 63, 104–6, 108; Trump Effect and,
    13–19; in US, 56–57, 64, 83–84, 150;
    white kids and, 23, 55–63, 77–78;
    white people and, 97–98
racist play, 109–12; fear and, 120–21;
    group membership and, 113–14,
    198n7; in schools, 114–15; in virtual
    spaces, 115–18; white kids and, 134
racist rhetoric, 35, 159–60
radicalized kids, 146–47, 199n22
rallies: Trump, 22; "Unite the Right," 13,
    19, 88, 98; white supremacist, 19–20,
    87–88, 97–98. See also protests

Ray, Victor, 160, 164
relief, 38–39
religion, 31–32, 61, 121–22
representation, 70–71; Obama and,
    53–54
reproduction, interpretive, 115, 117
resentment, 142–44
responsibilities, 71, 75; of adults, 152–54,
    156–57, 159–60, 162, 167–68; for be-
    havior, 94–95; of white people, 111–12
rhetoric, 41, 88, 103; anti-Asian, 11–12,
    97; colorblind ideology and, 67; feel-
    ings and, 106; policies and, 14–17;
    racist, 35, 159–60; slurs and, 13–14,
    22, 91, 93; of Trump, 1–2, 11–12, 14–16,
    85, 89, 124–25, 192n19
Rivas-Drake, Deborah, 197n34
Rockquemore, Kerry Ann, 194n17
Rogers, John, 92

Savage Inequalities (Kozol), 101–2
schools: administrators of, 1–3, 18, 116,
    169–70; demographics of, 50, 60;
    gun violence and, 126; inequality in,
    101–2; politics and, 163–64; race in,
    36–37, 82–83; racialized emotions in,
    102–3; racism in, 1–2, 50–52, 60–61;
    racist play in, 114–15; social media
    and, 160–61; suspension from, 99–
    100; violence in, 10–11, 17–18, 27, 77,
    99, 126, 164
Seaton, Eleanor, 197n34
SEL. See social emotional learning
self-identification, of kids, 4, 196n12
sensemaking, 5, 7, 77; group member-
    ship and, 114–15; identity and, 134
separation, of families, 14–16, 21
September 11, 2001, attacks, 17–18,
    192n46
sexual assault, 11, 57–58, 80
shock, 32, 54–58, 65–66
Simmons, Dena, 157–58, 200n14

slurs, 13–14, 22, 91, 93

Snapchat, 116

social emotional learning (SEL), 157–58, 200n14

social environment, 92, 154–57, 160–61, 169, 198n7; racial context and, 46–47, 56, 134

social hierarchies, 6, 72–73, 93, 115, 121

social issues, 47; racial apathy and, 106–9, 121

socialization, racial, 81–83

social justice, 60

social media, 21, 35; behavior on, 116; schools and, 160–61

social movements, 78. *See also* protests; rallies

social problems, 55, 73, 76, 166

sociological imagination, 6, 159

sociological thinking, 28, 89, 93, 103, 125, 148, 158–71

sociology, 6–7, 23–24, 37, 82. *See also* racialized emotions

solidarity, 157; action and, 96–101; group membership and, 85, 196n12; racialized emotions and, 77–78

Southern Poverty Law Center (SPLC), 13, 15, 18, 22; *Trump Effect*, 10–11

SPLC. *See* Southern Poverty Law Center

storming of US Capitol, 20, 146, 160–61, 167; kids and, 149–51

structural racism, 168–69

supporters, of Trump, 62, 88, 138; kids as, 104–7

surprise, 54–58

suspension, school, 99–100

symbols, Confederate, 11, 13, 19–20, 62, 106, 122–23, 149–50

tautologies, 111, 197n4

teachers, 3, 43–44, 91; racism and, 16–17, 60–61

thinking sociologically, 28, 89, 93, 103, 125, 148, 158–71

threats: immigrants and, 128–29; to racial domination, 132–33, 143–44; white kids and, 142. *See also* protection

TikTok, 21

trauma, 2, 15–16, 19, 77; group emotions and, 84; racism and, 13, 84, 89–90; Trump Effect and, 11

Trump, Donald, 59, 76, 143; anger and, 96–97, 125; anti-Black racism of, 13–14, 77; approval of, 32, 80; behavior of, 62, 79–80, 139; feelings and, 27–28; jokes and, 112–14; North Korea, 84–85, 196n15; Obama compared to, 34, 43–44, 46, 52–55, 79, 85–87, 129; protection and, 121–26, 128–32, 135–36; racism of, 32, 39, 45–46, 56, 63, 104–6, 108; rallies for, 22; rhetoric of, 1–2, 11–12, 14–16, 85, 89, 124–25, 192n19; supporters of, 62, 88, 138; white kids and, 29–33, 38–40, 68, 104–7, 138–42, 145; white nationalism and, 10, 13

Trump effect, 10, 12, 25, 160–61; racism and, 13–19; trauma and, 11; white supremacy and, 19–21

Trump Effect (SLPC), 10–11

Trump era, 23, 61, 144; consequences of, 15–17, 21, 68, 77–78; white kids and, 134, 161–62

trust, 4–5, 99–100

2016 election, 9–10, 26–28, 135; kids of color and, 33–38; white kids and, 29–33, 38–40

Twitter, 35

Umaña-Taylor, Adriana J., 197n34

uncertainty, 2, 15, 19, 57, 64, 85

United States (US): colorblind ideology in, 137–41; communities and, 132, 154–55; exceptionalism in, 71–72,

119; race relations in, 53–54, 66, 73–74; racism in, 56–57, 64, 83–84, 150; storming of Capitol, 20, 146, 149–51, 160–61, 167; white kids and, 54–63; white supremacy, 21, 75
"Unite the Right" rally, 13, 19, 88, 98

violence, 86, 94–95, 192n46; bullying and, 90–91; fear of, 84–85; gender-based, 57–58, 80; group membership and, 98; normalized, 20–21; race and, 87–88, 128; in schools, 10–11, 17–18, 27, 77, 99, 126, 164; white kids and, 10–11, 36–37, 150. *See also* gun violence; police violence
virtual spaces, racist play in, 116–18. *See also* social media

"the wall." *See* border wall
war, 84–86, 131
wealth, race and, 65
white families, 137, 154–55
white kids, 22; anti-Trump, 29–33, 68, 138–39; behavior of, 107–8; Black Lives Matter and, 125–27; color-blind ideology and, 32–33, 46–47, 50–54, 66–75, 137–41; fear and, 132–33; feeling race and, 73–74, 134–36; group membership and, 120–22, 124, 132–34; innocence of, 117–20, 153–54, 164; kids of color and, 34, 36–37, 41,

51–53, 90–94, 99–100, 116; Obama and, 44–45, 50, 52–54; racialized emotions and, 32–33, 64–66, 106–7; racism and, 23, 55–63, 77–78; racist play and, 134; threats and, 142; Trump and, 29–33, 38–40, 68, 104–7, 138–42, 145; Trump era and, 134, 161–62; 2016 election and, 29–33, 38–40; US and, 54–63; violence and, 10–11, 36–37, 150
white nationalism: colorblind ideology and, 145; new, 144–47; Trump and, 10, 13
whiteness, 139, 158, 198n24; identity and, 121–22, 164
white parents, 45
white people, 161, 200n24; emotions of, 65–66; feelings and, 81, 142; racism and, 97–98; responsibility of, 111–12
white privilege, 64, 139, 158; colorblind ideology and, 48–49, 200n24; kids and, 153–54, 200n14
"white rage," 142–44
white supremacy, 75; emotions and, 63; racial justice and, 127; rallies for, 19–20, 87–88, 97–98; SEL and, 157; Trump Effect and, 19–21
Winkler, Erin, 155
Wray-Lake, Laura, 25

Yoder, Paul J., 25